To Aunt Carol,

Stan Dane
aka Randy Somew

enjoy!

Prayer Man:

Out of the Shadows and Into the Light

By Stan Dane

MARTIAN PUBLISHING

To Sue, Gordon, Elliot, and Louise.

Oswald's statement of being on the First Floor during the "excitement."

Through a process of elimination, Sean Murphy shows that Prayer Man—standing on the steps of the Texas School Book Depository during the assassination of President Kennedy—was none other than Lee Oswald. He was where he said he was: *"Out with Bill Shelley in front."*

Now when I saw the images of Prayer Man, I knew who he was, I knew this was game over for the Lone Nut crowd that includes the Federal Government and Main Stream Media. The bias shown in the face of contrary evidence is like a child refusing to let go of a toy.

Sean Murphy used a scientific method and had his work "peer" reviewed. Not one person could show Prayer Man is anyone but Lee Harvey Oswald.

I encourage all who read this book to speak out against this injustice of monstrous proportions. Ask yourself why are the media and government so dead set on keeping the fairy tale alive when it has just been nullified?

It is time to right this wrong, correct the media and history books, because *Justice Is Never Too Late*. It's time to Re-Open the Kennedy Case.

I thank Stan Dane for all his work documenting this monumental moment in history!

– Ed Le Doux, CEO, Maui Film Industries.

TABLE OF CONTENTS

FOREWORD

Wikipedia states that:

> A cold case is a crime or an accident that has not yet been
> fully solved and is not the subject of a recent criminal
> investigation, but for which new information could emerge
> from new witness testimony, re-examined archives, retained
> material evidence, as well as fresh activities of the suspect.
> New technical methods developed after the case can be used
> on the surviving evidence to re-analyze the causes, often with
> conclusive results.

It goes on to say:

> A case is considered unsolved until a suspect has been
> identified, charged, and tried for the crime. A case that goes
> to trial and does not result in a conviction can also be kept on
> the books pending new evidence.

The Wikipedia article concludes with two lengthy lists: the first
on notable cold cases that have been solved, and the second on
notable unsolved cold cases. The JFK assassination appears on
neither list, despite being "notable" and meeting all other criteria.
The fact is that the assassination has successfully been removed from
the table. It cohabits some surreal netherworld with UFOs, Elvis and
the Loch Ness Monster.

Blame the mystique of Camelot. Blame the media and a
tranquilized public. Blame the constraints of the President's
Commission and a small army of subsequent theorists with their own
agendas.

President's Commissions have been around since the time of
George Washington and the Whiskey Rebellion and have at times
been attacked for appearing to breach the separation of powers
mantra. The trouble with that argument is that the designers of the

Constitution never meant for powers to be separate; only the institutions holding them. The powers are in fact, *shared, overlapping and competitively sought.* Whereas this creates a tension which is meant to maintain balance, it also creates the wiggle room necessary for opportunities to exploit commissions for political purposes.

It is the greatest of ironies that it was Oswald's good fortune that sealed his death warrant. Few in Dallas received true justice. It is now known that Henry Wade and the Dallas Police Department had the Dallas Justice system on a string. No trick in the book was off limit in securing a conviction. Planted evidence, witness tampering, junk science and compromised judges and defense lawyers were all part and parcel of the game. Some of those tricks were being used against Oswald. His "good fortune" was that unlike any other trial in Dallas; his would have the eyes of the world watching. Since a trial, for the reasons outlined, was never an option, they had a choice to either cut him loose for lack of *real* evidence or have him killed.

We know how that went. Cue President's Commission.

Among the tasks of cold case investigators is to reexamine the identified suspect(s) and any alibis claimed. Therein is the architectural beauty, integrity, and clarity of the Prayer Man narrative. It is a painstakingly clinical examination of Oswald's alibi which in turn exposes not only that his alibi was rock solid, but also the steps taken to negate it and how that perforce affected the evolving official history of the most misunderstood and misrepresented lunch hour in the history of the industrialized world.

In this book, Stan Dane has identified and captured the essence of the remarkable journey on which Sean Murphy took his readers via his research on what was happening inside the building and on those steps. No sign pointing the way has been missed; no wrong turns or pit stops taken.

It is not merely an engaging read with Dane's trademark mordant humor present, but measured. It is an essential read. It is a book that should make you angry.

Resolving this is easy. It will just take enough pressure for better quality frames to be obtained from the relevant films showing the front steps. It is a cold case, despite Wikipedia's omission, and it deserves no less than a thorough and proper cold case examination.

Greg R. Parker
August 22, 2015

PREFACE

Information reduces uncertainty.

– Claude Shannon

I'm guessing you're reading this book because you have some level of interest in the assassination of President John F. Kennedy. Whether you know very little about this important event in our history or you're an expert researcher, I believe the material presented here will give you some new and interesting things to think about.

You may be familiar with this quote attributed to Daniel Patrick Moynihan: "Everyone is entitled to his own opinion, but not his own facts." There's certainly no shortage of opinions when it comes to the assassination of JFK, but what about the facts? As it turns out, there's a great deal of debate in the research community as to what the facts really are.

For example, there are many official records and documents—facts—that conflict with other official records and documents—facts. Which facts are right? How does one choose? There's a large layer of metadata—data that describe other data—which fills the void between facts and the opinions. It all becomes blurry and bewildering to anyone trying to understand what really happened.

How do you get to the bottom of it all? There are no easy answers, but if first you seek out facts and evidence that cannot be denied—evidence as unimpeachable as is $3 + 2 = 5$—then you can lay a solid foundation for sound reasoning.

This is what this book tries to do. It showcases the brilliant research of Sean Murphy from Ireland, how I came upon it, how I was persuaded by it, and how it shaped my thinking. I try to succinctly lay his research out as he originally posted in The Education Forum. It's not possible to capture all of the detail and nuance of his arguments spread out over thousands of posts in one small book, but I hope I did a good enough job such that the information presented here will help reduce at least some uncertainly you may have concerning the murder of the 35th President of the United States of America.

Stan Dane
August 20, 2015

ACKNOWLEDGEMENTS

I am indebted to Sean Murphy. Without his brilliant groundbreaking work, we're not even here. This is the book I wished *he* would have written.

I am deeply grateful to Greg Parker, Terry Martin, and Alan Dixon for their advice, support, and encouragement in helping me get this project started and completed. They were always there when I needed them. And much thanks to Ed Le Doux and Lee Farley for their reviews and helpful comments.

Special appreciation goes to my lovely wife, Sue. She played a crucial role in getting this book ready for publishing and was immensely valuable in helping improve the clarity and quality of the text.

INTRODUCTION – THEN TO NOW

Lately it occurs to me what a long, strange trip it's been.

– Garcia, Hunter, Lesh, and Weir

1963

As I sat in Mr. DeGood's fifth grade class that cold, wet Friday afternoon on November 22, 1963, something seemed strange. Mr. DeGood stepped out of the classroom for a few moments, then he stepped back in briefly, and then back out again. When he came back in, he solemnly announced that school was letting out early. Just like that, we were dismissed.

Most days I walked home from my school in Grand Rapids, Michigan, but that day my mother was parked outside waiting. My younger brother and sisters were already in the car. Nice, I wouldn't have to walk home in the drizzle.

I raced over and climbed in the front seat. Before I could say a word, my brother blurted out "President Kennedy got shot and he's dead!" Stunned and confused, I looked at my mom. Sadly nodding her head, she said "he got shot in the temple" while riding in his car in Dallas Texas.

The rest of the weekend was a gloomy blur as we watched news nonstop. My parents were hard core Democrats so naturally I was too. We adored President Kennedy, and to me he was like a superhero. Before too long we learned the main suspect was Lee Harvey Oswald, a loner (I heard the word "loner" a lot that weekend). "What a dirty thing to do," was the only thing my dad could say, slowly shaking his head with bitter disgust.

Then on Sunday, Lee Oswald got shot right in front of our eyes on TV by Jack Ruby. Although I hated Oswald for what he did, I didn't feel good about him getting killed this way either. Something was weirdly wrong about that. I was conflicted.

The funeral was Monday and there was no school. A pall of quiet numbness hung over our house as we watched the funeral of John F.

Kennedy. My parents were impressed with the poise of Jacqueline Kennedy and how well she held up through all of this. My mom was moved to tears when she saw little John-John (John F. Kennedy Jr.) salute the funeral procession.

In the weeks that followed, I learned more about the assassination from a special edition of Life magazine. The pictures—especially the few Zapruder pictures they showed—were fascinating and creepy. Everything pointed to Oswald. He was guilty as sin.

1964

The Warren Commission concluded that Lee Harvey Oswald, acting alone, killed President Kennedy. I read all about it in the new issue of Life magazine. I accepted the official story because I trusted authority. Why shouldn't I? They're the good guys, and I like good guys.

1965 - 1972

I didn't think too much more about the Kennedy assassination for a number of years. There were plenty of new distractions to keep me occupied: the expanding Viet Nam War and two older boys who lived close to me who were killed over there, the Beatles, Rock and Roll and the 1960s in general with sex and drugs and hippies, (oh my!), the assassinations of Martin Luther King and Robert Kennedy, man-on-the-moon, first love, graduation, getting a job—to name a few.

Those were wild, head spinning times!

1973

Because I drew a very low number in the 1972 Selective Service System Draft Lottery, I joined the US Navy in 1973 to avoid being drafted. I took a battery of tests and they told me I scored high enough to have any job I wanted. They convinced me to enroll in the US Naval Nuclear Power Program and operate nuclear reactors. Yay, I thought.

While I was in training, a picture of President Kennedy eating an ice cream cone on the cover of Esquire magazine caught my eye at a local newsstand. "Trying to remember J.F.K."[1] was the lead article. I bought a copy. This was the first time in years I thought about the assassination. It brought back a lot of memories.

1975

I saw a replay of the Zapruder film on a TV show while I was undergoing reactor qualification training in Idaho. It was shocking, to say the least. The third and final shot looked like President Kennedy was hit by a sledgehammer. I winced watching it. I'd heard about frontal shots from the Grassy Knoll before, but seeing this made that look like a certainty. How could Oswald have done what they say he did?

I began to seriously doubt the official story. Heck, after President Nixon resigned because of Watergate the year before, I began to doubt "official things" in general.

But I was busy with life and life goes on.

1993

I'd been out of the Navy for twelve years and had a great career in nuclear chemistry. I was now married with three kids and life was fine. I remember the day I got a special double issue of the *U.S. News and World Report* magazine I subscribed to. The lead story titled "CASE CLOSED: After 30 Years of Conspiracy Theories, A Brilliant New Book Finally Proves Who Killed Kennedy."

The article captivated me. I felt pretty knowledgeable about the Kennedy assassination, but I had never dug into details to prove, or disprove what I had learned. This article seemed to deal with all of the pesky conspiracy questions I had over the years. I later bought the book, *Case Closed*, by Gerald Posner.[2]

Posner had explanations for everything. Yes, it sure looked like Oswald did it after all. Maybe we make things too complicated, I thought. I guess we can finally put this all to bed now.

1997

I was at my brother's place enjoying a cookout when we started discussing firearms and ballistics. I told him I had read about the single bullet theory (also called the "Magic Bullet") and how I thought it was explained well in the book Case Closed.

A look of surprised scorn came across my brother's face. He hadn't read the book, but he said there was no way the single bullet theory was true. "The guy who wrote that book doesn't know what the hell he's talking about," he said. You see, my brother has been trained in gunsmithing so he understands what bullets will or will not do under various circumstances.

He asked me, "Did you watch *JFK*[3] a few years ago? That will make a believer out of you!" I wasn't a big movie-goer so I hadn't seen it, but I realized I needed to dig deeper to see if any of Posner's claims were true or not. They seemed reasonable on the surface, so I had just accepted them.

That really struck me as odd because when it came to my job, I always had a questioning attitude and went to great lengths to find answers and root causes of problems. I knew that things were often not what they seemed.

I searched the Internet to see if anything was written about *Case Closed* and I discovered the writings of Michael T. Griffith. He had written a paper "Hasty Judgment: A Reply to Gerald Posner—Why the JFK Case Is Not Closed."

Griffith asked great questions and after I finished reading his paper, I had to agree. The Kennedy case is not closed, not by a long shot! Reading his other papers on the assassination only confirmed this.

I need to find more good stuff like this to read, I thought.

1998 – 2011

I did read quite a bit during these years. I bought books by James Fetzer, Harrison Livingstone, Wim Dankbaar, Joan Mellen, James Douglass, Barry Ernest, and others. If somebody talked about anything conspiracy-related, I usually gave them a hearing. But I didn't have a deep knowledge of the case, so it wasn't easy to verify many of the claims made by the authors of these books and papers.

To me it's one thing to point out there are problems with the official Warren Commission findings. That's pretty easy when you take time to study the case. It's quite another thing to offer alternatives of what may have happened. This is where my instincts kicked in as I considered various explanations by conspiracists (those who don't believe Lee Oswald was the lone assassin).

These years were a process of elimination for me. I learned to smell outlandish claims and reject them. Common sense was a big help. A huge help, actually.

The best book I had read was Barry Ernest's, *The Girl on the Stairs*.[4] If true, Lee Oswald could not have come down the stairs to be seen in the Second Floor lunchroom, a central plank in the Warren Commission's case against him.

I was left believing Lee Oswald was not on the Sixth Floor of the Texas School Book Depository (TSBD) Building when the Presidential motorcade passed by, he did not fire any shots, and was indeed a patsy—just as he said he was. There *was* a conspiracy to kill President Kennedy, but then, it didn't include half the people in the Western Hemisphere either.

2012 – 2013

I discovered a great blog by William Kelly, "JFKcountercoup."[5] He's a researcher with a questioning attitude who's a strong advocate of having the remaining files, documents and records associated with the JFK assassination released to the public. His blog became a regular stop for me. Very informative and well referenced.

In July, 2013, Bill Kelly posted the article in JFKcountercoup: "The Doors of Perception - Why Oswald Is Not Guilty."[6] Using the layout of the Second Floor of the TSBD building and considering official accounts and testimony, Bill showed how it was impossible for Lee Oswald to have come down the stairs from the Sixth Floor when the Second Floor encounter allegedly occurred. This dovetailed nicely with Barry Ernest's research. Slam-dunk stuff, I thought.

Around the same time, I learned of a new book *Into the Nightmare* [7] by Joseph McBride that focused on the murder of police officer J. D. Tippit as a key to solving the murder of JFK. I bought the book and while I was reading it, I discovered a thread in the JFK Assassination Debate section of The Education Forum where McBride's book was being discussed. As I reviewed that, I saw where Bill Kelly had just started a new thread "Oswald Leaving TSBD?"

I quickly learned about "Prayer Man." From that point on, nothing was the same for me. Everything changed.

This book is about my discovery of Prayer Man and the brilliant work of Sean Murphy. You will see the development of Sean's arguments and how he slowly and systematically takes Prayer Man out of the shadows and into the light. You will get answers and gain new insights. At times, you'll be amazed. I think you'll find the entire process absorbing, captivating, and rewarding.

For those readers who are not familiar with the assassination of John F. Kennedy, I will start off with a brief review of some basic facts in the case in Chapter One. In addition, I have provided some background information on the people who are discussed or mentioned in this book in Appendix B.

Let's get started!

CHAPTER ONE – WHAT HAPPENED

Assassination is the extreme form of censorship.

– George Bernard Shaw

A full account of all the people and events involved, associated, or in some way connected to the assassination of President Kennedy would fill an entire volume or more. To provide context for the subsequent chapters, we'll limit our review here to a very brief outline of the main points as they pertain to the subject of this book and the official findings and conclusions. For a larger, more in-depth assessment, I recommend *Accessories After The Fact* by Sylvia Meagher[8] and *The Plot to Kill Lee Harvey Oswald* by C. Fenway Braxton[9] for starters.

Why Dallas?

Preparing for the 1964 presidential campaign, President John F. Kennedy visited several states in the fall of 1963 to showcase his accomplishments, raise money, and to establish themes for his reelection run the following year. Texas was considered one of the states crucial for victory in 1964 and Kennedy wanted to unify the party leadership there.

Right wing extremists in Texas created a climate of tension and hatred, especially in Dallas, when US Ambassador to the United Nations Adlai Stevenson was spit on and attacked by protestors in October 1963. Stevenson said the mood was "ugly and frightening," but Kennedy still went ahead with the five-city, two-day trip to The Lone Star State accompanied by his wife, Jacqueline. After stops in San Antonio and Houston on November 21, they flew to Fort Worth where Kennedy gave a speech the following morning on Friday, November 22, 1963. Then they made a short flight to Dallas, arriving at Love Field at about 11:40 a.m.

Ugly and Frightening

After mingling with enthusiastic well-wishers lining the airport fence, the motorcade left Love Field, embarking on a 10-mile trip that took them through downtown Dallas on the way to the Trade Mart where President Kennedy was to give a speech. Because the weather cleared up and had become sunny, the top was down on the presidential limousine. Kennedy sat in the right rear seat next to Jacqueline, with Governor Connally and his wife sitting in the middle jump seat.

The trip through Dallas went slower than planned due to large crowds that occasionally overflowed onto the streets. As the motorcade got toward the end of the planned route at 12:30 p.m., shots rang out after the limousine turned onto Elm Street and passed by the Texas School Book Depository building. Most witnesses say they heard three shots. The entire sequence along Elm was filmed by Abraham Zapruder who stood on a concrete abutment, part of the pergola on the Grassy Knoll, on the north side of Elm.

Killed and Wounded

Kennedy was hit in the back, possibly the throat (entrance or exit wound), and in the head, killing him. Connally was hit in the back, also experiencing a shattered wrist and a wound in his thigh. James Tague, a bystander standing over by the Triple Underpass, received a superficial wound on his the cheek from a stray bullet. The Xs on the aerial photo of Dealey Plaza below show the approximate location of the limousine when the shots hit:

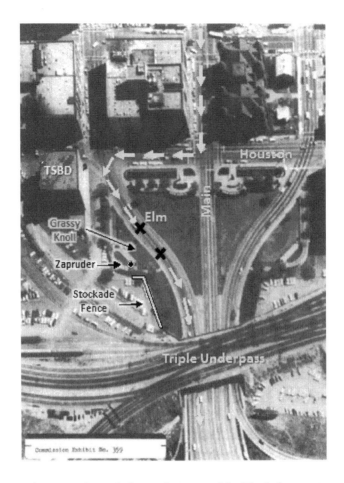

Commission Exhibit No. 359

Some witnesses heard shots above and behind the motorcade in the general vicinity of the TSBD building; many other witnesses heard shots come from the Grassy Knoll area. In fact, right after the shots, a large number of people were seen crossing Elm Street and running onto the Grassy Knoll. The general consensus on the number of shots was three.

Triage

After the final head shot, the limousine sped off to nearby Parkland hospital. Already mortally wounded, President Kennedy was pronounced dead at 1:00 p.m. local time. Seriously wounded, Governor Connally had surgery. He survived. Amidst all of the activity at the hospital, a pristine bullet was found on stretcher. Imagine that.

Meet the New Boss

Under heavy security, Lyndon Johnson was whisked away to Air Force One and sworn in as the 36th President of the United States. Kennedy's body was transported to Air Force One and the plane flew back to Washington D.C. Refusing to change clothes, Jaqueline Kennedy continued to wear her bloodstained pink suit for the rest of the day.

Back in Washington, President Johnson said these words to a stunned nation:

> *This is a sad time for all people. We have suffered a loss that cannot be weighed. For me, it is a deep, personal tragedy. I know the world shares the sorrow that Mrs. Kennedy and her family bear. I will do my best; that is all I can do. I ask for your help and God's.*

Dealey Afterglow

Immediately after the shots in Dallas, there was a flurry of activity in Dealey Plaza. Many people ran onto the Grassy Knoll. Policemen brandished shotguns. People lay on the grass. Photographers wandered around snapping pictures. There were reports of Secret Service agents flashing credentials to stop people from going to certain areas. A person was spotted running to a waiting car that drove off after he got in. Some people wept. Most all were shocked.

Patrolman Marrion Baker of the Dallas Police Department was riding his motorcycle toward the rear of the motorcade, and after hearing the shots, parked his motorcycle near the TSBD and rushed inside. Baker was said to have run into Lee Oswald in the Second Floor lunchroom, but Oswald's boss, Roy Truly, vouched for him, so they continued looking through the building. The police ultimately found a chintzy rifle on the Sixth Floor of the TSBD building. And right next to the southeast window on the Sixth Floor were three rifle cartridges all in a row.

Later, Truly told police Oswald was missing. Someone determined Oswald left the TSBD building at 12:33 p.m., got on a city bus, soon got off it, took a cab to a rooming house a few miles away where he stayed, changed clothes and then began walking.

Officer Down

A few minutes after 1 p.m., there were reports that Dallas Police Officer J. D. Tippit was shot. Some witnesses say the gunman looked like Oswald; others described an entirely different looking person. Oswald was next reportedly seen "ducking into" an entrance alcove of a shoe store. The shoe store manager then saw Oswald slip into the nearby Texas Theatre without paying. He informed the theatre ticket clerk who called police.

In no time at all, a ton of police officers converged at the Texas Theatre. They found Oswald in the theatre and claimed he resisted arrest, trying to draw his revolver before being forcibly subdued and taken into custody. He was later charged with the murders of President Kennedy and Officer Tippit. Oswald denied shooting anyone and claimed he was a patsy.

Extreme Censorship

Over the next two days, Oswald was paraded around like a circus animal before the press as the lone suspect. He underwent hours of interrogation, most of which was unrecorded. Captain Will Fritz of the Dallas Police Department declared the case was "cinched."[10] Oswald asked for legal representation but he never got the help he wanted because on Sunday, November 24, 1963, he was gunned down at Dallas Police Headquarters by Jack Ruby. Another lone nut.

Whodunit

With Oswald out of the way, the Dallas Police Department was never able to complete its investigation, but that really didn't matter seeing how the case was already cinched. The FBI wrapped up their investigation in less than three weeks. They concluded that Oswald did it all by his lonesome, firing three shots: the first hit Kennedy, the second hit Connally, and the third hit Kennedy in the head, killing him.

Warren Commission

In spite of the speedy work by the Dallas Police Department and the FBI to get to the bottom of it all—many might say hit the bottom—President Johnson decided to form a Presidential Commission to look into what was cinched. Why? Because the public had to be satisfied that Oswald did it and that he did not have confederates who were still at large, that's why.[11] Cinching things up even tighter probably couldn't hurt. So on November 29, 1963, Johnson established the President's Commission on the Assassination of President Kennedy, unofficially known as the Warren Commission because Chief Justice Earl Warren was the head honcho. Several commission members were not overly excited about participating. Some thought it might ultimately create more controversy than closure. Johnson had to twist Warren's arm to be chairman. Floating the threat of nuclear annihilation did the trick.[12]

Over the next year, the Warren Commission reviewed reports by the FBI, Secret Service, and lots of nifty stuff from Texas. Plus, they really dug into Oswald's personal history, his military record, and his political affiliations. The Commission heard testimony from hundreds of witnesses, and they went to Dallas several times to check things out firsthand. They conducted some re-creations of what they said happened so as to better understand what was already cinched up.

On September 24, 1964, the Commission presented its 888-page "Warren Report" to President Johnson. The conclusion? Oswald fired three shots from a rifle pointed out of a Sixth Floor window in the TSBD. These shots killed Kennedy and wounded Connally. The pristine bullet found on a stretcher at Parkland Hospital was said to have passed through Kennedy and into Connally. Because of the mid-air course corrections the bullet had to take to accomplish all of this, it was called the "Magic Bullet."

The Report said Oswald acted alone and went into much detail about his life, and they found that the Secret Service made poor preparations for Kennedy's visit and had failed to sufficiently protect him (mistakes were made). Oh, and they concluded that Ruby had acted alone in killing Oswald too.

Even though the Warren Report was clear on who did what, Earl Warren said "We may not know the whole story in our lifetime." Warren never indicated whether "the whole story" involved Oswald's guilt or innocence.

More Investigations

In 1976, the United States House Select Committee on Assassinations (HSCA) was created to take another look at the assassination of President Kennedy and Martin Luther King, Jr. They worked until 1978 and concluded in 1979 that President Kennedy was probably assassinated as a result of a conspiracy. No further action was taken. Because.

Through a Glass Darkly

In response to the public uproar following the movie *JFK,*[13] Congress passed the President John F. Kennedy Assassination Records Collection Act of 1992 (JFK Act). The goal was to collect and make publicly available all of the assassination-related records held by federal and state government agencies, private citizens and various other organizations. The JFK Act created the Assassination Records Review Board (ARRB). In the mid-1990s, the ARRB collected and released about 60,000 documents. However, government agencies requested many documents not be released for reasons of national security.

All remaining records are scheduled to be released by October 2017, unless the President decides that releasing documents would cause harm to the military, to intelligence operations, law enforcement, or conduct of foreign relations—*and* the identifiable harm is of such gravity that it outweighs the public interest to see them. In other words, they can pretty much keep the remaining documents sealed as long as they want.

We'll find out soon enough, but I wouldn't hold my breath.

CHAPTER TWO – THE MAN WHO WASN'T THERE

Believe your indications.

– Admiral Hyman G. Rickover

The first principle of nuclear safety taught to US Naval Nuclear Power Program candidates. In the absence of overwhelming evidence something is wrong, believe your indications when they tell you something isn't right. Because quite often, something isn't right. Investigate until you understand exactly what's going on.

August 14, 2013. It all began with two simple questions by Bill Kelly: "Is this a photo of Oswald leaving the TSBD?" and "Does anyone know who took this photo and when?" Thus began the greatest thread ever in The Education Forum or anywhere else: "Oswald Leaving TSBD?"[14]

Interesting, I thought. After reading Bill Kelly's analysis of the Baker-Oswald interaction on the Second Floor a few weeks earlier, I was 100 percent convinced Lee Oswald could not have done all of the things the Warren Commission said he did up on the Sixth Floor, *and then* run down to the Second Floor and be spotted by Officer Marrion Baker going into the Second Floor lunchroom 90 seconds later.

So yes, how did Oswald leave the TSBD that day and could this be a picture of him leaving?

Member Terry Adams said if he were to wager, he would lean heavily towards the man being Lee Harvey Oswald.

It wasn't long before forum member Sean Murphy responded. The photo was a frame from the James Darnell film[15] taken just moments after the shots were fired at JFK, he said. The man in the picture was in the very same spot as the shots were being fired because this same man was in the same location in the Wiegman film,[16] taken just seconds earlier. Sean said the man was not Billy Lovelady, William Shelley, or Buell Wesley Frazier, adding that his identity was still unknown.

It's obvious to me that Sean Murphy is already quite familiar with this mystery man in the photo. I guessed he'd been studying this issue for some time.

Another member, who runs his own forum and is regarded by some as an expert on photographic evidence, said that the frame was from the Malcolm Couch film, not the Darnell film. He said the man was not Oswald as Baker has not even reached the entrance at this point in the film. Sean corrected him, saying "It's not from Couch it's from Darnell. Robert Groden[17] spliced the two films together and labelled the result 'Couch'."

Sean was then asked if he had previously noticed this man and how he eliminated Shelley, Lovelady and Frazier. Sean said he nicknamed this guy "Prayer Man" a few years back (on account of the posture of his arms), and went on to say:

- Prayer Man is standing in this spot in the doorway.
- Prayer Man is standing in this spot in the doorway when Officer Marrion Baker reaches the front steps.
- Prayer Man can't be Billy Lovelady, whom he somewhat resembles, because Lovelady shows up beside him in the Wiegman film. Besides, Lovelady recalled looking back from the "island" on Elm Street and observing Baker and Roy Truly about to enter the building, so he couldn't have still been in the front entrance as Baker reached the steps.
- Prayer Man can't be Shelley who was with Lovelady out on the "island" at this time, and was identified in other photos that day wearing a dark suit and tie.
- Prayer Man can't be Buell Wesley Frazier who was wearing a dark blue jacket and looked nothing like him.

"Long story short: we still don't know who this man was," said Sean.

Member Richard Hocking proposed a process of elimination to narrow down the choices of who Prayer Man might be. Fourteen individuals identified themselves as being on the steps of the TSBD entrance and:

- Seven were women, so all can be eliminated.
- Shelley, Lovelady and Frazier can be eliminated.
- Two African-American males can be eliminated.
- This narrows it down to two men: Joe Molina and Otis Williams.

Hocking said that Joe Molina claimed to be the man in a suit standing next to Lovelady in the famous Altgens photo,[18] and since Prayer Man appears to be wearing a shirt, Molina should be eliminated.

ALTGENS 6

As far as Otis Williams is concerned, he was bookkeeping supervisor at the TSBD and it's unlikely he would be wearing an unbuttoned shirt at work. And after hearing the third shot and thinking it came from the triple underpass, Williams claims to have entered the building immediately and climbed the rear stairs to the Fourth Floor to be able to see the underpass.[19] Because of this, it's highly unlikely Prayer Man is Williams.

Furthermore, all of the employees testified that there were no strangers in the TSBD that day, indicating Prayer Man is an employee of the TSBD because he is not included in any testimony provided by the fourteen individuals, Hocking added.

Sean responded that Otis Williams also said that he had JFK's limousine in view until it "went behind a little wall going toward the underpass,"[20] a view not available to Prayer Man.

Bill Kelly said if Prayer Man was indeed Lee Oswald, "Then he isn't leaving the building, but is still standing there when Baker runs past him, and then he must have re-entered the building and ascended the front steps to the Second Floor and proceeded to the lunchroom to purchase his coke, walking past the closed lunchroom door when Baker saw him through the window. Just a correction as the title of this thread is then misleading."

I was soon to learn that the title was the *only* thing misleading about this thread. It was about Prayer Man and I found the discussion absorbing. Even though the Darnell image was fuzzy and grainy, Prayer Man did seem to resemble Lee Oswald. If not Lee, then who? Could we be onto something here?

Another member thought that this does put Oswald outside as Prayer Man because Oswald said he went outside to see what all the excitement was, not to watch the parade. This would mean that he just stepped outside to see why there was so much commotion and moving about, and then went back in the building and up to the Second Floor lunchroom to get a coke. He further recalled that Officer Baker wrote that Oswald had a coke in his hand and that part was later marked out.

Richard Hocking provided an excerpt from Will Fritz's interrogation notes:

> *claims 2nd floor Coke when*
> *off came in*
> *to 1st floor had lunch*
> *out with Bill Shelley in*
> *front*
> *lft wk opinion nothing be*
> *done that day etc.*

So Will Fritz was saying Lee Oswald claimed he was *out in front* with Bill Shelley? Was this during the motorcade?

Bill Kelly said that Oswald had not yet purchased the coke when he was confronted by Officer Baker. The statement Baker wrote in which he crossed out the coke was written days later and is not the first day statement. Bill believed Baker must have heard of the coke story from others and after mentioning it in his statement realized that he did not see Oswald with the coke in hand and crossed it out.

Kelly also said Gary Mack, curator of the Sixth Floor Museum in Dallas, says the frame that shows Prayer Man is indeed from the 16 mm Darnell film. When coordinated with other films, Mack says it took Baker forty seconds after the first shot to reach the front door of the TSBD. Mack also says that no one who worked at the TSBD saw, or said they saw, Oswald on the steps, and besides, the Prayer Man is too short to be the 5 ft. 9 in. Oswald.

Kelly added that even though no one claims to have seen Oswald on the steps or actually leaving the TSBD, the Warren Report concludes that he did leave through the front door at 12:33 p.m., three minutes after the last shot and just a minute and a half after encountering Baker and Truly.

I began to sense there was something a bit strange about the well-known Second Floor encounter, but I couldn't put my finger on it. And Gary Mack saying Prayer Man is too short to be Oswald? How could he tell that? And how could the Warren Commission conclude that Oswald left at 12:33 p.m. when he wasn't seen at all? Nobody saw Prayer Man either. And forty seconds for Marrion Baker to reach the front entrance to the TSBD? Seems to be a lot of wild guessing going on here.

Sean Murphy clarified that he wasn't claiming Prayer Man is Oswald, only that it's one possibility meriting serious consideration. Because *where* on the First Floor did Oswald tell Fritz he was at the time of the shooting? We don't know. Those early interrogation reports are weirdly vague on that score—which is odd given that this would surely be the *single most important question* the suspect in the assassination could have been asked.

Sean mentioned something Billy Lovelady told a reporter several years after the assassination that had always stuck with him: on the weekend of the assassination the FBI visited Lovelady to show him the Altgens photo.[21] When Lovelady said he was the man standing in the doorway, the FBI men expressed great relief that it was not Oswald. But if Oswald wasn't claiming to have been out front, why the relief? Why would Oswald being captured in an image of the front entrance during the assassination even be considered a possibility?

Sean made one thing clear. If Baker and Truly encountered Oswald by the Second Floor lunchroom when and how they said they did, then it's very unlikely that Prayer Man can be Oswald.

Bill Kelly said if that's Baker in the Darnell film running to the front door and past Prayer Man at 40 seconds after the last shot, Prayer Man (if Oswald) could have turned around, gone up the steps next to the front door, walked through the offices and into the Second Floor lunchroom vestibule where he was seen by Baker walking past the window in the door. After the encounter with Baker and Truly—where he was observed to be cool, calm, not out of breath or agitated as he would have been had he just killed someone—Oswald bought the coke and backtracked through the door he entered and into the office where the secretary was, having just arrived from being out front on the curb. She saw Oswald with the coke and said something about the president being shot, and Oswald mumbled something she didn't hear, and he went down the steps and out the front door.

If Prayer Man is Oswald, Sean replied, it may be physically possible for him to make it up to the Second Floor in time for an encounter with Baker, though he would have to be mighty fast about it. The problem with this scenario, he said, is that it doesn't make any sense:

- Oswald is out front, standing unnoticed in the shadows...
- He hears shots...
- He watches the ensuing pandemonium...
- He sees a cop and Mr. Truly rush into the building and...
- He hurries upstairs to *buy a coke*?

Sean said what distinguishes Prayer Man is how detached and impassive he appears. In neither the Wiegman film during the shooting…

…nor the Darnell seconds after the shooting…

…does he appear to show the slightest curiosity as to what's happening.

Frozen in shock? Possibly. Overtaken by a sudden thirst? Hardly.

Chapter Two Recap

So after four full days, where are we?

- We have an unidentified person standing in the shadowy corner of the entrance of the TSBD building in both the Darnell and the Wiegman films.
- This person appears to be a man in the Darnell image, and despite the poor quality of the image, he looks somewhat like Lee Oswald.
- All of the TSBD employees who testified they were on the steps when the motorcade passed by are accounted for. None can be Prayer Man.
- All of the employees testified that there were no strangers in the TSBD that day.
- Will Fritz's notes state Oswald said he was on the First Floor and went out in front with Bill Shelley.
- Billy Lovelady was the man peeking around the wall at the entrance of the TSBD building in the Altgens photo. The FBI was relieved that it was him and not Lee Oswald.
- If Prayer Man was Oswald, he apparently had time (if he hurried) to make it up to the Second Floor lunchroom for the encounter with Officer Marrion Baker.

Yes, we certainly have indications that there are things *wrong* with the official story. It would be wise to believe our indications.

CHAPTER THREE – BUILDING A THEORY

Don't worry about the key, just play.

– Django Reinhardt

Legendary gypsy jazz guitarist Django Reinhardt's response
to Duke Ellington when asked in what key he wanted to
rehearse a song. Reinhardt, who couldn't read music,
didn't know what "key" meant.

August 18, 2013. Just four days into this thread and I'm totally
hooked. I'm seeing the formation of a case that places Lee Oswald
near the TSBD entrance during the assassination. Will this
momentum continue? I sure hope so.

Member David Von Pein, a well-known "lone nutter," chimed in
today: "In this forum thread, once again, we're treated to people
using their vivid imaginations to stamp a specific identity on a fuzzy
and very indistinct human being seen in a low-quality film/photo.
How in the world can anyone positively say WHO 'prayer man' is
here? It's impossible."

Sean Murphy responded "But that's just the problem—no one
can say who this man is." He went on to point out it seemed
reasonable to assume Prayer Man was a TSBD employee, yet he's
none of the TSBD employees known to have been on the steps. "Any
ideas who he might be, David?"

Von Pein said he didn't know, but he wasn't quite sure why it
couldn't be Buell Wesley Frazier since Frazier stated in 1986 that he
was standing "back up in the shadows," a few steps behind
Lovelady.[22] Von Pein also pointed to the answer given by Oswald at
a press conference when asked if he was inside the building at the
time of the assassination: "Naturally, if I work in that building, yes,

sir."[23] If Prayer Man was Oswald, how could he be outside on the steps when he said he was inside?

Richard Hocking pointed out that there is a tall man with dark hair standing at the top of the steps in the center of the stairway where the rail is. This is exactly where Frazier claimed he stood in his Warren Commission testimony and he was just over 6 ft. tall. He was precise in describing his position at the center rail and locating both Shelley and Lovelady to his right, closer to the wall.

Frazier's own testimony rules him out as Prayer Man, replied Murphy.[24]

When asked if Oswald denied being on the front steps, David Von Pein replied "Pretty much, yes. He said he was INSIDE the building when President Kennedy was being shot. Do you think the front steps are INSIDE the building?" Sean Murphy responded that Oswald confirmed that his location at the time of the shooting was the Texas School Book Depository, his place of work.

Further confirmation, according to Sean, that Prayer Man cannot be Otis Williams was that Williams in his March 1964 FBI statement said he was "standing on the top step against the railing on the east side of the steps in front of the building." This also further confirms that Prayer Man cannot be Joe Molina either as Molina told the Warren Commission that Otis Williams was "right next left of me" on the steps.

Richard Hocking added that in addition to the testimony of their locations on the steps, Molina was a Credit Manager, and Williams was a Bookkeeping Supervisor. Both of these men would be expected to wear a coat and tie to work. Prayer Man is wearing an unbuttoned shirt and has the appearance of a manual laborer, so it's safe to dismiss Molina and Williams from consideration. Sean agreed, especially as both Williams and Molina can be fairly easily identified in the Altgens and Wiegman images standing just east of the center rail.

Referring to the Hughes film,[25] Hocking also observed that Lovelady appears to turn to his right as the Presidential limousine turns onto Elm Street. He speculated that Prayer Man and Lovelady begin to adjust their positions to the locations seen in Altgens and Wiegman, with Prayer Man making a late entrance to his spot. Due to all eyes being focused on the President and Jackie, no one is going to turn around and look behind them on the steps. After shots are fired and chaos erupts, it would be even less likely for witnesses to turn around and focus their attention to the back of the alcove.

Sean agreed. Prayer Man had the kind of lousy vantage point one would expect a late arrival to have. No witness seems to have noticed or recalled the presence of Prayer Man standing there. Yet the photographic evidence proves his presence. This is further indication that he arrived there when attention was focused elsewhere. How could he arrive unnoticed?

1. By appearing when attention is focused on the motorcade, and
2. By emerging onto the steps from inside the building rather than from the street.

"Prayer Man has surely got to be a TSBD man," said Sean.

Bill Kelly asked if the photos and still frames of Prayer Man could be further isolated and enhanced to see if he has anything specific in his hands, such as a bottle of coke which might help to identify him.

Murphy observed there does seem to be a "glint" in the Wiegman frame. "A bottle?" he wondered.

Hmm. What is that whitish spot, a reflection? Prayer Man might even be holding a camera. The position of his arms seems right for that. Another forum member, Robert Prudhomme, felt the same way. My, this is really getting interesting!

Sean then said that we have very good reason to believe that Lee Oswald visited the Second Floor lunchroom a few minutes before the assassination. That very good reason's name is Carolyn Arnold.

Terry Adams supplied information on the Warren Commission testimony of Harry D. Holmes, postal inspector, on what Lee Oswald said while in custody on Sunday, November 24, 1963.[26] When Oswald was asked where he encountered the policeman, Oswald said he was in the vestibule or approaching it, said Holmes. Holmes went on to clarify that Oswald was talking about the vestibule on the First Floor by the TSBD front entrance. When Officer Baker asked him who he was, Oswald began to reply when the superintendent, Roy Truly, came up and said "He is one of our men" and the officer asked him to step aside.

Richard Hocking wondered what Oswald meant by "vestibule." Did he mean the area between the inner and outer doors, or was he referring to the covered entryway steps and porch? If it's the latter, it would be strong evidence of Baker encountering Oswald at Prayer Man's location. Even if Oswald meant inside the door, it is still only a few feet away.

Along these lines, Hocking recalled that researcher Greg Parker presented a strong case that the Second Floor encounter between Oswald and Baker never happened on the Second Floor but rather somewhere else.

Robert Prudhomme agreed, adding he heard about a Fourth Floor encounter as well.

As this thread progresses, I'm getting the feeling there are some serious problems with the Second Floor encounter.

Bill Kelly mentioned the height of Prayer Man might be determined if the height of the front door of the TSBD is known. Because Oswald's height is known, this could either rule him out as Prayer Man or keep him in the running, though not positively confirming it. Hocking agreed, but pointed out there were important variables to keep in mind when attempting such a calculation, such as what step Prayer Man is standing on, is he standing erect, or slouching, the camera angles involved, etc.

Meanwhile, Sean Murphy provided an excerpt from a 1964 *New York Herald Tribune* article titled "The Picture with a Life of Its Own,"[27] emphasizing the second paragraph:

> Lovelady maintains it is he standing in the doorway at the moment of the assassination. "I was standing on the first step," he told me when I interviewed him two weeks ago in Dallas. "Several people in the picture saw me. That lady shading her eyes works here on the second floor."
> Lovelady said that the night following the assassination two FBI agents visited his home. "They said they had a blown-up

picture they wanted me to see. Right away I pointed to me and they seemed relieved. One had a big smile on his face because it wasn't Oswald. They said they had a big discussion down at the FBI and one guy said it just had to be Oswald."

"Why would the FBI be relieved?" mused Sean. How could Oswald showing up in a front entrance image have been considered even a remote possibility? It's not as if Oswald himself was claiming to have been out in front, was it?

From Fritz's vague notes we know Oswald made reference to being out front with Bill Shelley, added Richard Hocking. We also know Shelley was out on the steps several minutes before and during the assassination, but then left with Lovelady for the railroad yard within a few seconds of the last shot. How could Oswald have known Shelley's location if he had not seen him there? If Oswald had indeed been with Shelley, it had to occur during the time referenced above when Shelley was on the steps.

Hocking then came back to the Second Floor encounter. He recalled:

- The Oswald Second Floor lunchroom encounter with Marrion Baker was not in Baker's original report
- The same report listed an encounter on the Fourth Floor between Baker and a man that Roy Truly vouched for as being an employee.
- A few days after the original report, Baker issued a "revised" report that now contained the famous lunchroom encounter.
- Oswald's encounter with Mrs. Robert (Jeraldean) Reid and the coke was also discussed.

Bill Kelly chimed in here saying that he thought the mention of "vestibule" refers to what is known as the vestibule of the Second Floor Lunchroom, a small three door entrance way—one door leading west—that Oswald would have had to go through if he was the Sixth Floor sniper, another door leading south, which is the door that he left by with the coke in hand that leads to the offices and steps to the front door, and the east door that is always open and is the entrance to the lunchroom.

Bill added that the case against the Second Floor lunchroom encounter is based primarily on the fact that in his November 22 statement, Baker said that he encountered a man on the Fourth Floor, and makes no mention of the Second Floor encounter, though this would require both Baker and Truly to lie, with the motive to implicate Oswald. However, Bill feels the Second Floor lunchroom encounter actually exonerates Oswald,[28] saying this subject should be discussed elsewhere and not in this thread.

Kelly gave a definition of vestibule:

1. A small entrance hall or passage between the outer door and the interior of a house or building.
2. An enclosed area at the end of a passenger car on a railroad train.
3. *Anatomy* - A cavity, chamber, or channel that leads to or is an entrance to another cavity: the vestibule to the ear.

Bill said while the front entrance TSBD could refer to number 1, it also could refer to the little alcove—a rectangle shaped chamber sandwiched by three doors at the entrance to the Second Floor lunchroom—the small nine square foot space where Oswald was seen by Baker through the window of the closed west door to that vestibule. In this context however, David Belin asked Holmes what Oswald said about being stopped by an officer—in which Holmes used "vestibule" for the first time and apparently two sets of doors— and it appears he is talking about the Oswald encounter with Baker in the Second Floor lunchroom vestibule, but then he says First Floor and begins to describe Oswald directing a newsman to a telephone and then walking out the front door. It seems Holmes is confused here, thought Bill.

Sean replied that Holmes is not confused at all; there were indeed "two sets of doors" in the building's vestibule, or front lobby. Here's how Marrion Baker described the layout of outer doors and inner doors:

Mr. BAKER - As I entered this building, there was, it seems to me like there was outside doors and then there is a little lobby.

Mr. BELIN - All right.

Mr. BAKER - And then there are some inner doors and another door you have to go through, a swinging door type. As I entered this lobby there were people going in as I entered.

This matches Holmes' description of the vestibule perfectly, said Sean. Murphy then went on to say there's a very odd detail in Roy Truly's FBI interview report from the evening of the assassination:

He then noticed a Dallas City Police officer wearing a motorcycle helmet and boots running toward the entrance of the depository building and he accompanied the officer into the front of the building. *They saw no one there* and he accompanied the officer immediately up the stairs to the second floor of the building, where the officer....

They saw no one there, Sean emphasized. Where was "there?" Just inside *the front of the building.*

Ask yourself, said Sean:

- Why is Truly even having to disclaim having seen "someone" there?
- Doesn't it seem to you like he has been asked the question, *"Did you see 'anyone' there?"*
- Now what might have given the interviewing agents the very idea of asking Truly such a question?
- Why is the writer of the report making a point of including such a non-event in said report?
- Could it be that "**someone**"—some significant third party—has been talking noisily about having seen Truly and an officer "**there**," just inside the front of the building, just after the shooting?
- If so, then might that "**someone**" be none other than the person we have been calling Prayer Man—a young white, short-haired male, evidently a person employed in the

TSBD building, who was at the front entrance during the shooting yet went oddly unnoticed by everyone else congregated there?

Wow. Yes, I thought. It makes perfect sense. It seems like he's doing things on the fly, but I get a strong feeling Sean knows exactly where he's going here.

Richard Hocking provided a diagram of the First Floor of the TSBD building, showing the vestibule area and the entrance alcove:

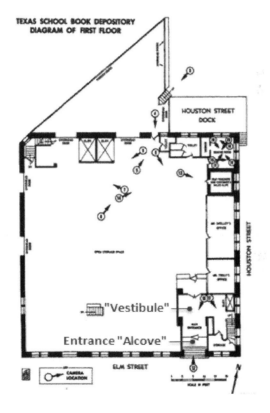

Member Jerry Dealey weighed in to say he has come to the conclusion the figure in the shadows, Prayer Man, is either Bill Shelley or Buell Wesley Frazier, mentioning that Frazier spoke recently stating that he had the "best seat" in Dealey Plaza, completely in the shade. Jerry confirmed that the glass door entrance was one of two. In between was a small lobby, with the passenger elevator, a cigarette machine, stairs that only went to the Second Floor, and a small storage closet under the stairs. This lobby could be called a vestibule. Inside the second glass doors was the "will call" counter. There are many photos of these areas. Jerry said neither he nor anyone else can put Oswald on the Sixth Floor with a rifle, but he also cannot put him anywhere else either.

Sean Murphy responded to Jerry saying Frazier and Shelley's own respective testimonies rule them out as Prayer Man. Frazier places himself by the center rail, with Lovelady and Shelley over closer to the side wall. Prayer Man in both the Wiegman and Darnell, by contrast, is right over by the side wall. Shelley recalls that immediately after the shots he and Lovelady went to the "island" on Elm Street from where they could look back towards the TSBD front entrance and notice Baker and Truly about to enter the building. Prayer Man in Darnell, by contrast, is standing still on the steps with Baker just a couple of seconds from those same steps.

Sean then furnished pictures of Buell Wesley Frazier to show what he looked like and what he was wearing on the day of the assassination:

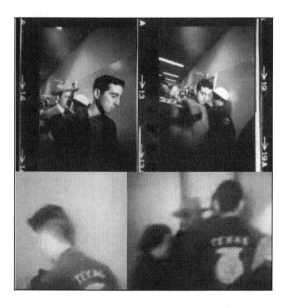

Doesn't look a bit like Prayer Man, he added.

Got that straight.

Sean said assuming we can safely say that Prayer Man is white (thereby ruling out Roy Lewis and Carl Jones), we have ourselves a genuine riddle here: a figure on the steps of the TSBD at the time of the shooting who appears to be…

- white
- male
- short-haired
- not wearing a suit
- employed in the Depository building

…and whose presence on the steps went

- unnoticed
- unremembered

Richard Hocking said he is nearly certain that the African-American man by the west column in the Altgens 6 photo is Roy Lewis. Carl Jones meanwhile claimed in his testimony that he was on the steps, but then he continued on to say he was with Truly, Campbell, and Reid, which places him out by Elm St. Jones also stated he saw JFK slump down; a view that was impossible from Prayer Man's position.

Sean Murphy said he is near-certain that this is Bill Shelley in these images:

Accordingly, he added, it seems safe to say that he is Person E in Altgens and Wiegman:

Bill Kelly furnished Warren Commission photos of the TSBD front stairs that go up to the Second Floor and another photo that includes the vestibule:

Sean Murphy finally returned to Carolyn Arnold. She insisted— to Anthony Summers,[29] Earl Golz,[30] Gary Mack and others—that she spotted Oswald in the Second Floor lunchroom several minutes *before* the assassination. Assuming that Arnold's claim is true, read the following section from the first interrogation report co-written by FBI Agents James Bookhout and James Hosty on November 22, 1963:

> (1) Oswald stated that he went to lunch at approximately noon and he claimed he ate his lunch on the first floor in the lunchroom; (2) however he went to the second floor where the Coca-Cola machine was located and obtained a bottle of Coca-Cola for his lunch. (3) Oswald claimed to be on the

first floor when President John F. Kennedy passed this building.

Sean said the startling possibility arises that Bookhout and Hosty are laying out Oswald's three claims in simple chronological sequence:

1. I went to lunch in the Domino Room
2. Then I went up to the Second Floor lunchroom and bought a coke
3. Then I went back down to the First Floor, which is where I was when the President passed the building

Claim 1 comes with a precise location—the Domino Room—and is supported by Oswald's noticing two black co-workers passing through (i.e. Norman and Jarman coming in the back entrance of the First Floor and proceeding across to the freight elevator).

Claim 2 comes with a precise location—the Second Floor lunchroom—and is supported by Carolyn Arnold's recollection.

Claim 3 comes without any precise location, a fact which just may be explained by the utterly calamitous location of the Prayer Man figure in Wiegman and Darnell.

Sean then popped this question: *"Did Lee Oswald offer Will Fritz a very precisely localized Claim 3 and were the details of this alibi-sealing claim suppressed?"*

Member Pat Speer cautioned others about trusting Holmes. He said his report was written weeks after the interview he witnessed and was not based on any notes. Speer said Holmes' memory was not very good and he'd added in stuff he'd heard from others.

Sean Murphy said not to be so quick to dismiss Holmes' recollection that Oswald spoke of an encounter in or around the First Floor vestibule. For one thing, *vestibule* is a distinctive word. It seems doubtful that Holmes would use it unless he had heard Oswald say it. Sean reiterated that the word vestibule means "front lobby of a building."

Furthermore, Holmes' version is corroborated by what Detective Ed Hicks was telling the press on the evening of the assassination.

From the *London Free Press* November 22, 1963 (and printed in multiple stateside newspapers that same day):

> Mothers threw their children to the ground, fearing the killer's bullets. As the presidential limousine sped to the hospital, the police dragnet went into action, Hicks said. Just about that time, Oswald apparently came out the front door of the red-bricked warehouse. A policeman asked him where he was going. He said he wanted to see what the excitement was all about.

Holmes: Oswald wanted to see what the "commotion" was. An officer challenged him at the front entrance.

Hicks: Oswald wanted to see what the "excitement" was. An officer challenged him at the front entrance.

(Note that Fritz also recalled—using the exact same word as Hicks—that Oswald claimed to have seen the "excitement.")

Sean added that unless Hicks was privy to Oswald's interrogation—which we have no reason to believe he was—how on earth was he able to tell the press on November 22 exactly what Harry Holmes would months later recall Oswald having said in custody? Hicks' statement stands as tantalizing *independent* corroboration of Holmes' account.

Sean said there is a simple alternative sequence of events to consider: Oswald goes to lunch in the First Floor Domino Room, he goes upstairs to the Second Floor lunchroom where he buys a coke, he takes the coke downstairs and makes his way to the front entrance to see the commotion/excitement, for some reason he is noticed and challenged by Officer Baker as the latter is running into the building, and Roy Truly vouches for him.

Chapter Three Recap

This thread is now seven days old but it almost feels like seven weeks! What have we learned in this chapter?

- Anticipating where the Prayer Man inquiry may be leading, objections are made that it's either impossible to say who Prayer Man might be, or it must be someone such as Buell Wesley Frazier.
- Buell Wesley Frazier's testimony rules him out as Prayer Man. His known appearance doesn't resemble Prayer Man either.
- Prayer Man appears to be dressed like a laborer, not like supervisory personnel or an office worker.
- The Hughes film may reveal signs that Prayer Man made a late entrance from inside the TSBD to the spot where he's seen in the Wiegman and Darnell films which might explain his being unnoticed.
- Prayer Man appears to be holding something.
- Harry Holmes testified that Lee Oswald said he was in or near the First Floor vestibule (front lobby between two sets of doors) by the TSBD front entrance when he encountered a police officer.
- The fact that the FBI was happily "relieved" that Lee Oswald was not one standing in the doorway in Altgens 6 indicates they may have known that Oswald claimed he was down in front.
- The Second Floor lunchroom encounter between Marrion Baker and Lee Oswald was not in Baker's original report. Instead it described an encounter on the Fourth Floor with a man that Roy Truly vouched for as being an employee. A few days later, Baker issued a revised report that referenced the Second Floor lunchroom encounter, while dropping any mention of an encounter higher up.
- Roy Truly's odd statement that "they saw no one there" as he and Baker entered the TSBD—"there" meaning just inside

the front of the building—suggests the possibility that someone (i.e., Lee Oswald) may have been talking noisily about having seen Truly and an officer just inside the front of the building, just after the shooting, something that had to be disclaimed.

- Carolyn Arnold told others that she spotted Oswald in the Second Floor lunchroom several minutes before the assassination.
- In their November 22, 1963 report, FBI Agents Bookhout and Hosty said Oswald claimed he (1) went to the First Floor Domino Room for lunch, and then (2) went to the Second Floor lunchroom to buy a Coke, and (3) went to the First Floor where he was at the time of the assassination.
- Oswald's claims in the Bookhout and Hosty report come with precise locations except for claim (3), suggesting the precise location for this alibi-sealing claim may have been suppressed.
- Holmes' recollection that Oswald spoke of an encounter in or around the First Floor is supported by his use of the word *vestibule*, a distinctive word.
- Holmes' version is corroborated by what Detective Ed Hicks told the press on November 22, 1963. Holmes said Oswald wanted to see what the "commotion" was, while Hicks used the word "excitement," which is the same word Fritz used as well. The words can be seen as pretty much interchangeable and as having the same meaning.

That's a lot of stuff to digest. A strong case that exonerates Lee Oswald is unfolding, seemingly with no plan, blueprint, or "sheet music." Whatever's happening, Sean Murphy shows no signs of being worried about anything. He just keeps playing. Beautifully.

CHAPTER FOUR – LAYING THE FOUNDATION

Standing in the shadows watching the world go by.

– Lynch, Dokken, and Pilson

August 21, 2013. Richard Hocking reiterated that one of the few items unanimously agreed upon by all witnesses in the TSBD was that they saw no strangers in the building that morning with the exception of Danny Arce who said he helped an old man in front of the TSBD use the men's room in the building and then see him out.[31]

Pertaining to Murphy's alternative scenario, Bill Kelly said Oswald couldn't have bought the coke and then be challenged by Baker at the front door if the Second Floor encounter with Baker and Truly is incorporated a minute and a half later. For the Second Floor encounter to have occurred, Baker and Truly had to go to the rear of the building and up the back stairs as Oswald, if he is Prayer Man, goes up the front stairs to the Second Floor and through the offices to the lunchroom vestibule—where he is seen by Baker, buys his coke, then goes back out the same way he came in and out the front door.

Richard Hocking said it's reasonable to suggest that Prayer Man was a TSBD employee and that his clothing indicates a manual labor type worker as opposed to a managerial type that would be wearing suit and tie. The available candidates that meet these criteria are limited and they include order fillers, janitor, clerks, and warehousemen. He provided a list of TSBD employees who meet that description with comments:

Danny Arce – floor laying crew at the TSBD. Watched Presidential Limo from north side of Elm Street in front of TSBD, (to the west of the entrance). Wrong location; not a candidate.
Jack Dougherty – Fifth Floor of TSBD, 10 feet from elevator. He is described by Roy Truly as being a "great big husky fellow."

Description and location disqualify him from consideration as Prayer Man.

Buell Wesley Frazier – top of front steps at the center rail. His precise description of his location, along with his tall thin physique rules him out.

Charles Givens – Mullendorf's Cafe or parking lot at Record Street. Being at least one block away means it could not have been Givens.

James Jarman – Fifth Floor window below sniper's lair. Photo evidence shows he was on the Fifth Floor.

Carl Edward Jones – sitting on the front steps, out by Elm Street with Truly, Campbell and Reid. Saw the President slump after being shot. He cannot be Prayer Man.

Roy Edward Lewis – standing with some ladies in the middle of the front steps. Roy Edwards is almost certainly the African-American watching from behind the West Column in Altgens 6. He is not Prayer Man.

Billy Lovelady – front steps. Seen next to Prayer Man in the Wiegman film. Gone from the Steps well before the Darnell shot was taken. Corroborated testimony and film show he is not Prayer Man.

Harold Norman – Fifth Floor window below sniper's lair. Photo evidence shows he was on the Fifth Floor.

Eddie Piper – sitting on a box watching through the second window from the corner on the First Floor. Location and other factors rule him out.

Troy Eugene West – making coffee on the First Floor. Did not know JFK had been shot until people rushed into building talking about it. He is not Prayer Man.

Bonnie Ray Williams – Fifth Floor window below sniper's lair. Photo evidence shows he was on the Fifth Floor.

Pat Speer said Jeraldean Reid saw Oswald coming out of the break room after the shooting. If Oswald is Prayer Man, and if the Baker/Truly run-in with Oswald happened on the First Floor, she would have to have been a liar. If she was lying, however, one would have to wonder why she said she thought Oswald was wearing a T-shirt at the time, and not the brown shirt he was wearing when arrested.

Sean expressed doubts about Jeraldean Reid's testimony. For one, it's contradicted by the testimony of Geneva Hine. Two, it's a whopping coincidence that of all the people to come forward on Saturday with compelling corroboration of Roy Truly's Second Floor lunchroom story, it should be the very lady who was standing with Roy Truly, her boss, at the time of the shooting. Further to the question as to why Jeraldean Reid would testify that Oswald was wearing a white T-shirt when she saw him is that it's worth noting that Roy Truly told the authorities that to the best of his recollection, Oswald had worn either a white T-shirt or a light colored shirt that day. Another coincidence is that the other person watching the motorcade with Truly and Reid was Ochus Campbell, who is quoted as having told reporters that *same day* that Oswald had been seen just after the shooting on the First Floor.

Sean thought it seemed suspiciously pat that Jeraldean should just so happen to spot Oswald at the very moment he was coming through the door into the office with—and she noticed this!—a full bottle of coke in his hand. What a marvelous ticking of boxes for her boss' story.

Why did Mrs. Reid say T-shirt only? Hard to say, said Sean, but it's possible she actually did see Oswald in a white T-shirt on the Second Floor, but several minutes before the motorcade. When might this have been? The following snippet in her Warren Commission testimony may provide a tantalizing clue:

Mr. BELIN. All right. When you left the lunchroom, did you leave with the other girls?
Mrs. REID. No; I didn't. The younger girls had gone and I left alone.
Mr. BELIN. Were you the last person in the lunchroom?
Mrs. REID. No; I could not say that because I don't remember that part of it because I was going out of the building by myself, I wasn't even, you know, connected with anyone at all.
Mr. BELIN. Were there any men in the lunchroom when you left there?
Mrs. REID. I can't, I don't, remember that.
Mr. BELIN. All right.
Mrs. REID. I can't remember the time they left.

Did Reid see Lee Oswald there? It's hardly a stretch to suspect so, given Carolyn Arnold's claim to have seen him there just a little after that, Sean concluded.

As for Holmes, Sean found it odd that one would trust him on Oswald's claim in custody *less* than one would trust Will "Case Cinched" Fritz, the man who threatened to beat the living daylights out of Buell Wesley Frazier if he didn't cooperate. Sean has no doubts that Holmes was a shady insider, but wondered why he would deliberately tell the Warren Commission something so disastrous to the official story. No, he thinks it's perfectly reasonable to suspect that Holmes *let the cat out of the bag* by saying he had heard Oswald say just what Bookhout and Hosty had heard him say: I went upstairs to the coke machine, bought a coke and came on downstairs, which is where I was at the time the President passed the building. And Holmes, by the way, doesn't just reproduce the information in those press reports quoting Ed Hicks. He adds significant detail of his own: vestibule plus the correct description of the TSBD front lobby.

Sean also notes that James Jarman told the House Select Committee on Assassinations (HSCA) that Billy Lovelady told him that Oswald was stopped by an officer at the front entrance and vouched for by Roy Truly.

Sean said if the Second Floor lunchroom incident happened as Baker and Truly testified before the Warren Commission, then it's a clear indication that Lee Oswald could not have been the Sixth Floor shooter. However, if Oswald is Prayer Man and if those earlier reports of a First Floor incident give the real, suppressed story, then it really is game over altogether, he said.

I totally agree here. Bill Kelly previously convinced me that the Second Floor lunchroom encounter exonerates Oswald,[32] but if these First Floor reports are correct, then there would be zero wiggle room for anyone still wishing to pin the blame on Oswald. It would be "game over" indeed. Is Prayer Man none other than Lee Oswald with a bottle of coke in his hand? Could it really be that simple? Sean Murphy answers "You bet your life it could."

Sean then offered a simple scenario that may tell the story of what really happened between Lee Oswald, Marrion Baker and Roy Truly.

1. Oswald comes downstairs to lunch in the First Floor Domino Room at some point after noon.
2. Several minutes before the assassination he visits the Second Floor lunchroom where he buys a coke for his lunch.
3. He brings the coke downstairs and, just as JFK is passing the building, steps out the glass door at the front entrance and takes up the Prayer Man position.
4. Within seconds of the last shot, Marrion Baker rushes up the front steps, revolver drawn.
5. He notices Oswald, who has perhaps stepped inside the door into the lobby area, and asks him "Do you work here?" The reason for Baker's question is not that he suspects Oswald in any way but that he is looking for someone who can point him the way to the stairs (rather as a credentials-waving man will a short time after this ask Oswald where he can find a phone).
6. Just as Baker is beginning to engage Oswald in this way, Roy Truly arrives and tells him, "Yes, Officer, he works here but I am the building manager. I will show you the way upstairs."
7. Baker and Truly run off to cross the shipping floor for the rear elevators.
8. This innocent incident—with its basic elements still intact (Oswald... coke... asking whether Oswald is an employee...Truly confirming)—will later that evening be transplanted up to the Second Floor lunchroom in a hastily contrived attempt to deprive Oswald of his clear alibi.

Sean then said "Shall we take a look at Marrion Baker's same-day corroboration?"

Twist my arm.

AFFIDAVIT IN ANY FACT

THE STATE OF TEXAS

COUNTY OF DALLAS

BEFORE ME＿＿＿＿＿＿＿＿＿＿＿Mary Rattan＿＿＿＿＿＿＿＿＿＿＿＿＿＿＿＿＿＿＿＿

a Notary Public in and for said County, State of Texas, on this day personally appeared＿＿＿＿＿＿＿＿＿＿

M. L. Baker, Patrolman Dallas Police Department＿＿＿＿＿＿＿＿＿＿＿＿＿＿＿＿

Who, after being by me duly sworn, on oath deposes and says: Friday November 22, 1963 I was riding
motorcycle escort for the President of the United States.   At approximately 12:30 pm
I was on Houston Street and the President's car had made a left turn from Houston onto
Elm Street.   Just as I approached Elm and Houston I heard three shots.   I realized
these shots were rifle shots and I began to try to figure out where they came from.
I decided the shots had come from the building on the northwest corner of Elm and
Houston.   This building is used by the Board of Education for book storage.   I
jumped off my motor and ran inside the building.   As I entered the door I saw several
people standing around.   I asked these people where the stairs were.   A man stepped
forward and stated he was the building manager and that he would show me where the
stairs were.   I followed the man to the rear of the building and he said, "Let's take
the elevator."   The elevator was hung several floors up so we used the stairs instead.
As we reached the third or fourth floor I saw a man walking away from the stairway.
I called to the man and he turned around and came back toward me.   The manager said,
"I know that man, he works here."   I then turned the man loose and went up to the
top floor.   The man I saw was a white man approximately 30 years old, 5'9", 165
pounds, dark hair and wearing a light brown jacket.

M L Baker

SUBSCRIBED AND SWORN TO BEFORE ME THIS＿22＿DAY OF＿＿＿November＿＿＿＿＿＿A.D. 1963

Mary Rattan   Mary Rattan

Notary Public, Dallas County, Texas

CPS-GP-413

Sean reviewed the theory he is advancing where Lee Oswald is indeed about to have an encounter with a revolver-toting police officer. The *location*, *timing* and *meaning* of that encounter, however, will be very different to the location, timing and meaning of the encounter that will be fed to the public in the Warren Report. It will take place *not* in the Second Floor lunchroom but just inside the front door in the First Floor lobby, *not* within the next minute but within the next ten seconds, and Baker will *not* challenge Oswald only for Truly to vouch for his employee—he will ask Oswald for help only to have Truly helpfully cut in and introduce himself as building manager.

After some posters expressed disbelief that both Baker and Truly could lie about the Second Floor lunchroom encounter for this theory to be true, Sean responded how the intense emotional and cognitive investment of generations of conspiracy-oriented researchers in the Second Floor lunchroom story is understandable but unfortunate.

Regarding Marrion Baker's same-day affidavit, Sean said it gives report of an encounter several floors up the building with a light-brown-jacket-wearing man seen walking away from the stairway. Baker's affidavit makes no connection between this man and the suspect currently in custody—this despite the fact that said suspect, Lee Harvey Oswald, has been brought into the Homicide Office in front of Baker's own eyes just as he is giving that same affidavit. Not only does Baker's affidavit fail to corroborate the lunchroom story told to the Warren Commission, it is glaringly at odds with it. It may even be telling us that Baker apprehended—only to let loose—a man other than Oswald several floors up the building.

Sean reiterated that we don't know that Oswald "said he was in the Second Floor lunchroom when the policeman came in" because we weren't there and the interrogations were not recorded. We do however know what the same-day evidence has to say on that score: Oswald stated that he went to lunch at approximately noon and he claimed he ate his lunch on the First Floor in the lunchroom; however he went to the Second Floor where the Coca-Cola machine was located and obtained a bottle of coke for his lunch. Oswald claimed to be on the First Floor when President John F. Kennedy passed this building.[33] No mention whatsoever of an incident involving an officer and Truly.

For those who believe Oswald was Prayer Man and was at the front entrance at the time of the actual shooting, and the Second Floor lunchroom incident really did happen, Sean asked what they believe happened between the last glimpse of Prayer Man in the Darnell film and Marrion Baker's first glimpse of Oswald through the door window on the Second Floor.

Bill Kelly then put forth a scenario that incorporates Prayer Man being a TSBD employee—possibly Oswald—while preserving the Second Floor lunchroom encounter with Oswald:

1. Prayer Man checks out the commotion on the street, standing back against the glass wall, watching Baker run past him through the door, Truly behind him.
2. They then proceed to the back elevator and take the stairs, while Oswald—whether Prayer Man or not—is on the First Floor, near the door, where Arnold last saw him
3. Oswald/Prayer Man takes the *front* steps to the Second Floor offices.
4. Oswald walks through the office, and into the Second Floor Lunchroom vestibule where he passes the window of the closed door that Baker sees him through. Since Truly had been ahead of Baker and didn't see Oswald go through the door, he continued around the corner and then began ascending the steps to the Third Floor. (Truly later testified that he didn't know that Baker had seen Oswald through the window of the door until a few days later, and didn't recognize the significance of that fact at the time.)
5. After this confrontation, the cool, calm, not-out-of-breath or hyper assassin who had bought a coke walks back the way he entered through the office where he passes Mrs. Reid who sees the full bottle of coke in his right hand. They exchange a few garbled words before Oswald proceeds down the steps to the front door, where he then directs a reporter to the telephone.
6. Having just seen the President killed and running a hundred yards to find a phone, this reporter is excited and out-of-breath. This begs the question of why Oswald wasn't similarly out-of-breath if he had killed the president and ran across the Sixth Floor and down four flights of steps to meet Baker and Truly with such a cool and calm attitude. Mrs. Reid also described Oswald as cool and calm—definitely not in a hurry.

Kelly said it seems there were some important interactions at the front door of the TSBD—Baker running past Prayer Man, Baker hooking up with Truly, Oswald giving the reporter directions and Oswald hearing Shelley say something about there not being any more work that day—or at least Oswald having some type of interaction with Shelley before taking off.

At this point, this scenario made a lot of sense to me. It makes Prayer Man fit in with the known pieces—or I should say the "official pieces"—very well. Bill firmly believes in the Second Floor lunchroom encounter and he's hedging on Prayer Man being Oswald. That's OK when you're not sure.

Sean Murphy said the two Bookhout-authored November 22 interrogation reports make for interesting comparative reading. From Interrogation Report #1 (jointly written by Bookhout and Hosty, typed 11/23/63, dated 11/22/63, "dictated" 11/23/63):[34]

> Oswald stated that he went to lunch at approximately noon and he claimed he ate his lunch on the first floor in the lunchroom; however he went to the second floor where the Coca-Cola machine was located and obtained a bottle of Coca-Cola for his lunch. Oswald claimed to be on the first floor when President John F. Kennedy passed this building.

Sean said this account contains two rather bizarre omissions:

1. The precise location on the first floor of Oswald's claimed whereabouts at the time JFK passed the building
2. Any mention of an incident involving himself, a police officer and Mr. Truly

Assuming that the Prayer Man theory he's been outlining is correct, Sean said the reason for the two omissions in the Bookhout-Hosty report becomes instantly intelligible: there is no way on earth that such a potentially explosive double claim by the suspect in custody (I was at the front entrance during the shooting and interacted with my boss and a police officer just seconds later) is going to make it into the official record.

What happens next is key—you might even say it's the giveaway, Sean said. Bookhout goes solo. He takes the curious step of putting together a second, "improved" report on the very same interrogation. From Interrogation Report #2 (written by Bookhout, typed 11/25/63, dated 11/22/63, "dictated" 11/24/63):[35]

> Oswald stated that on November 22, 1963, at the time of the search of the Texas School Book Depository building by Dallas police officers, he was on the second floor of said building, having just purchased a Coca-cola from the soft-drink machine, at which time a police officer came into the room with pistol drawn and asked him if he worked there. Mr. Truly was present and verified that he was an employee and the police officer thereafter left the room and continued through the building. Oswald stated that he took this Coke down to the first floor and stood around and had lunch in the employee's lunch room. He thereafter went outside and stood around for five or ten minutes with foreman Bill Shelly, and thereafter went home.

Sean asked if people could see what's happened. The key elements of what Oswald had really claimed (coke, standing outside, police officer, Truly) have been transposed into a different timeframe. Why? In order to deprive the now dead Oswald of his absolutely watertight alibi by having him "confirm" the bogus Second Floor lunchroom story.

Sean invited for serious consideration the hypothesis that Bookhout's solo report needs just a small tweak to give us, for the first time, a credible guide as to what Oswald really said to Fritz in that first interrogation session (plain = original Bookhout text; *italics* = Sean's changes; **bold** = repositioned Bookhout text):

- Oswald stated that on November 22, 1963, at the time of the *shooting,* he was on the *first* floor of said building, having just purchased a Coca-cola from the soft-drink machine *on the second floor.*

- **Oswald stated that he took this Coke down to the first floor and stood around at the front door,**
- at which time a police officer came into the *vestibule* with pistol drawn and asked him if he worked there.
- Mr. Truly was present and verified that he was an employee and the police officer thereafter left the *vestibule [with Mr. Truly]* and continued through the building.

Sean asked what the most valuable piece of text was in Bookhout's entire solo report. Surely, he said, it's the phrase in bold here: *at which time a police officer came into the room with pistol drawn and **asked him if he worked there.***

Bill Kelly responded that Baker in his first report saying that the encounter with Oswald happened on the Fourth Floor and that Mrs. Reid recalling Oswald in a white T-shirt are reflective of mistakes all witnesses make—especially after hearing others talk and media accounts. Additionally Kelly stated that they don't alter the other facts that most of what they said has been confirmed by others, including Oswald. Bill said he thinks something did happen at the front door, both when Baker ran in and when Oswald left, but transposing the entire Second Floor encounter to the First Floor isn't the answer or a piece of the puzzle that fits, in his opinion.

I disagree with Bill here. I think it fits nicely. After reading the last few posts, Sean's arguments are winning me over. More and more I'm thinking the Second Floor lunchroom encounter never happened.

Sean assessed the situation as of the late afternoon/early evening of the assassination:

- Lee Oswald in custody claiming to have been at the front entrance on the First Floor during the assassination and to have had a fleeting encounter with a police officer and Mr. Truly as they rushed into the building.

- Detective Ed Hicks telling the press about an incident involving Oswald and a cop at the front entrance of the building shortly after the shooting.
- Marrion L. Baker on the record as having encountered a man walking away from the rear stairway several floors up the building.

So far, not a single reference anywhere—in a single news media report—to a second-floor lunchroom incident, said Sean.

But it gets even worse for the Second Floor lunchroom story, he added, for now two startling newspaper reports written on the evening of the assassination have to be added into the mix, and both refer to an Oswald sighting on—you guessed it—the First Floor.

1. From *The Dallas Morning News*, written by Kent Biffle, November 22, 1963, published November 23, 1963:

6—Section 1   The Dallas Morning News   Saturday, November 23, 1963 ★★★★

Suspected Killer Defected

Lee Harvey Oswald, charged with murdering the President and a Dallas policeman, defected to Russia in 1939.

In 1962 he returned to the U.S.

In August this year he passed out pro-Castro leaflets on a New Orleans street.

On Sept. 23 President Kennedy announced plans for a trip to Dallas.

A few days later Oswald got a job in the Texas School Book Depository Building, overlooking the motorcade route.

On Oct. 14 he rented a room in Dallas.

Friday Oswald was seen by R. S. Truly and a Dallas policeman in the book firm building just after a barrage of shots from the sixth floor struck President John Kennedy and Gov. John Connally.

O. V. Campbell, vice-president of the firm, said he and Truly, standing in front of the building at 411 Elm when the shooting started.

Campbell said he ran toward a grassy knoll west of the building where he thought the sniper had hidden. He said Truly and an officer ran into the building.

In a storage room on the first floor, the officer, gun drawn, spotted Oswald. "Does this man work here?" the officer reportedly asked Truly.

Truly, who said he had later-viewed and hired Oswald a "couple of months earlier," reportedly told the policeman that Oswald was a worker.

The policeman and Truly continued their search. Oswald later failed to report at a 1:15 p.m. roll call of employes. Truly reported this to police.

Sean said the dissonant element here to his theory is not "First Floor," not "the officer, gun drawn," not the question as to Oswald's being an employee. No, the *dissonant element* is "*storage room*." How, according to his theory—would the Baker-Oswald encounter have happened in a First Floor storage room? Wasn't it supposed to have taken place in the front lobby, he asked?

There were in fact two designated "storage rooms" on the TSBD First Floor—one beside the Domino Room near the rear of the building and one just off the front lobby. Obviously the latter is going to arouse our interest in the current context, said Sean. But the close proximity of the "storage room" to the lobby area doesn't quite explain how it could have become confused in the reporter's mind with "front lobby/vestibule."

In order to grapple with this conundrum, Sean said we must move on to the other newspaper report:

2. From the *New York Herald Tribune*, written November 22, 1963, published November 23, 1963:
    Mr. [Ochus V.] Campbell [vice-president of the TSBD] said, "Shortly after the shooting we raced back into the building. We had been outside watching the parade. We saw him (Oswald) in a small storage room on the ground floor. Then we noticed he was gone." Mr. Campbell added: "Of course he and the others were on their lunch hour but he did not have permission to leave the building and we haven't seen him since."

There it is again, he said: storage room. Only this time with three differences:

a) This is a "small storage room."
b) We are being given a direct quote from Ochus Campbell, the man just seen featured so prominently in the Biffle report.
c) The talk is of "we" having simply seen Oswald—no mention of an officer being involved.

"What the Sam Hill is going on here?" Sean asked. How about we do the unthinkable and take at face value what the *New York Herald Tribune* is telling us—that is Ochus Campbell recalled that he and at least one other person saw Oswald in a small storage room on the First Floor?

Ochus Campbell had been outside watching the motorcade with two other people: Roy Truly and Jeraldean Reid. We know that Truly separated from them immediately after the shots and ran into the building after Marrion Baker, said Sean, so that leaves Campbell and Jeraldean Reid.

Sean put forth the case:

- Oswald/Prayer Man, at some point after the shooting, slipped into the small storage room just off the front lobby.
- Ochus Campbell reentered the building around this time accompanied by at least one other person—Jeraldean Reid.
- They made their way to the front stairs in order to go up to the Second Floor office area.
- In order to do so they had to pass the small storage room beside the stairway.

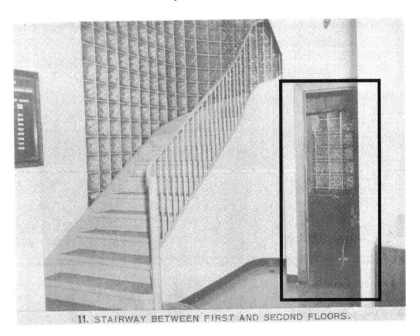

11. STAIRWAY BETWEEN FIRST AND SECOND FLOORS.

The door was open and they—or one of them—noticed and recognized Lee Oswald in there. Thinking nothing of it, they proceeded on up to the Second Floor office area.

Sean said "I'll let Geneva Hine tell us what happened next":[36]

> Mr. BALL. *When you came back in did you see Mrs. Reid?*
> Miss HINE. *No, sir; I don't believe there was a soul in the office when I came back in right then.*

Mr. BALL. Did you see anybody else go in through there?
Miss HINE. No, sir; after I answered the telephone then there was about four or five people that came in.

...

Mr. BALL. Do you have any definite recollection of Mrs. Reid coming in?
Miss HINE. No, sir; I only saw four or five people that came by and they all came and were all talking about how terrible it was.
Mr. BALL. Do you remember their names?
Miss HINE. Yes, sir.
Mr. BALL. Who were they?
Miss HINE. Mr. Williams, Mr. Molina (spelling), Miss Martha Reid [sic][37], **Mrs. Reid**, Mrs. Sarah Stanton, and **Mr. Campbell**; that's all I recall, sir.

Mrs. Reid...and Mr. Campbell. Sean said now to re-read that direct quote from Ochus Campbell in the *New York Herald Tribune*:

> Shortly after the shooting we [*I and the person with me*] raced back into the building. We [*I and the person with me*] had been outside watching the parade. We [*I and the person with me*] saw him [Oswald] in a small storage room on the ground floor.

Mrs. Reid accompanied Roy Truly to the Dallas Police Department headquarters the following day and gave a statement to the effect that she had seen Oswald—not loitering in a First Floor storage room—but entering the Second Floor office area.

Was she pressured by her two bosses—Ochus and Roy—to do so? Sean said he believes we have serious grounds for believing that the poor lady was. Now if only that pesky Geneva Hine hadn't been upstairs the whole time to ruin the marvelously efficient box-ticking story foisted upon her colleague, he added.

Sean said efforts to exonerate Oswald via the Second Floor lunchroom story have had a fatal flaw at their heart: they have Oswald, on the First Floor at the time of the shooting, responding to the shots and/or ensuing mayhem by going upstairs to buy a coke. This may account for Baker's first glimpse of Oswald off the Second

Floor landing, but only at the cost of casting Oswald as a sociopathic, dissociated man, he said.

If Oswald is Prayer Man, Sean thought it preposterous that his reaction to the firing of shots while JFK, the man he so deeply admires, is passing the building was along the lines of "Well, isn't that something. Time for that coke I promised to treat myself to." Quite preposterous, he said.

At this point, Sean Murphy sees only five serious scenarios:

1. *The Geneva Hine/Groden Scenario*: Oswald was on the Second Floor getting change for the coke machine when he and Hine heard loud bangs; not realizing what they were, Oswald went ahead and bought the coke. Second Floor lunchroom story true? Yes.

2. *The Prayer-Man-to-Second Floor Scenario*: Oswald is Prayer Man; after Baker and Truly rush off across the shipping floor for the rear stairs, Oswald for some reason decides to follow them by ascending the front stairs and making his way at speed to the northwest corner of the Second Floor; the purchase of a coke is the very furthest thing from his mind. Second Floor lunchroom story true? Yes.

3. *David Lifton's Baker-Taking-Out-Oswald Scenario*:[38] Oswald is instructed by his handler(s) to wait in the Second Floor lunchroom during the motorcade; Baker is tasked with running into the building and taking Oswald out there; only the unanticipated presence of Roy Truly stays Baker's hand. Second Floor lunchroom incident true? Yes.

4. *The Prayer Man Scenario*, as proposed in the current thread: Oswald is Prayer Man; after Baker and Truly rush off across the shipping floor for the rear stairs, he sticks around in the First Floor front lobby area. Second Floor lunchroom story true? No.

5. *The Non-Prayer Man Scenario*: Oswald is not Prayer Man; he is however near the front entrance of the building at the time of the shooting. Second Floor lunchroom story true? No.

Sean puts his money on #4, with #5 and #1 a not too distant second place.

Sean continued. If Oswald is Prayer Man, then he would have certainly heard at least part of the shooting. He would have certainly heard the screaming and panic out on the street. And he would have certainly seen a uniformed officer racing into the building. He would need to have been off-the-scale obtuse not to put two and two together, because it's not as if he could have thought the officer was bursting to go to the toilet.

What Sean finds really striking is precisely the fact that Prayer Man appears to be making absolutely no attempt to check out what's happening down the street. He's either frozen in shock (for reasons that are not hard to surmise as Oswald is suddenly realizing he's becoming a patsy) or he's not remotely surprised by or curious about the horror that's unfolding out on the street.

Recognizing the many instances of how witness testimony has converged around the official story when comparing first day statements with later testimony, member Larry Hancock cited research and studies on how memory becomes less dependable over time, making first-day statements much more reliable.

Sean argued that if Oswald is indeed Prayer Man, and if things went down as he has suggested, then the injustice inflicted upon him by the "investigating" authorities—with collusion from his bosses—was even more monstrous than we had imagined.

The first on-the-record reference to a Second Floor lunchroom incident (as opposed to an uneventful pre-assassination visit up to the lunchroom by Oswald to buy a coke) does not come until the evening of November 22 when Roy Truly is interviewed by the FBI. Sean said the interview takes place at some point after—*and as a result of*—Oswald's first interrogation which concluded around 4:15 p.m. We know this because Truly is asked to answer a disturbing allegation which Oswald has made:[39]

> Mr. TRULY advised that it is possible OSWALD did see him with a rifle in his hands within the past few days, as a Mr. WARREN CASTER, employed by Southwestern Publishing Co., which company has an office in the same

building, had come to his office with two rifles, one a .22 rifle which CASTER said he had purchased for his son and the other a larger more high powered rifle which CASTER said he had purchased with which to go deer hunting, if he got a chance. Mr. TRULY examined the high powered rifle and raised it to his shoulder and sited [sic] over it, then returned it to CASTER, and CASTER left with both rifles. Mr. TRULY stated he does not own a rifle and has had no other rifle in his hands or in his possession in a long period of time.

Sean said Truly's explanation was investigated and found to check out. But the rifle incident was not the only occasion for his name to come up in Oswald's interrogation. Oswald had also evidently mentioned an incident involving Truly and a police officer. He provided Truly's response to that claim:[40]

He then noticed a Dallas City Police officer wearing a motorcycle helmet and boots running toward the entrance of the depository building and he accompanied the officer into the front of the building. They saw no one there and he accompanied the officer immediately up the stairs to the second floor of the building, where the officer noticed a door and stepped through the door, gun in hand, and observed OSWALD in a snack bar there, apparently alone. This snack bar has no windows or doors facing the outside of the building, but is located almost in the center of the building. The officer pointed to OSWALD and asked if OSWALD was an employee of the company and he, TRULY, assured the officer that OSWALD was an employee. He and the officer then proceeded onto the roof of the building....

Sean said as far as he has been able to ascertain, the above text constitutes the very earliest reference anywhere to a Second Floor lunchroom incident. And it contains five words which, however seemingly innocuous, may well be of explosive significance:

...he accompanied the officer into the front of the building. They saw no one there and he accompanied the officer immediately up the stairs to the second floor of the building...

"*They saw no one there.*" The fact that Truly is even pointing out this gratuitous fact can only indicate one thing: that he has been confronted with Oswald's claim that it was precisely "there," inside the front of the building on the First Floor, that the officer and Truly met him. Truly's disclaimer draws ironic attention to what it is he is disclaiming, said Sean.

Whether Truly fed the FBI the Second Floor lunchroom version of events, or whether it was the FBI who helped him get it straight, the upshot is the same: the lunchroom story appears to be a fabrication, a fiction designed for the sole purpose of eliminating Oswald's all too real alibi for the President's murder.

Vigorously nodding my head in agreement.

Sean asked "But what of Marrion Baker?" He has gone on the record about having challenged a man walking away from the rear stairway several floors up the building. Like Ochus Campbell, with his loose words to the press about Oswald's being seen in a small storage room on the First Floor, Baker goes awfully quiet awfully fast after this.

Between the time of his November 22 affidavit and his participation in the Warren Commission's "reconstruction" in March 1964 of his and Truly's movements in the Depository, we hear astonishingly little from this crucial participant in the fateful day's events. All we have are two extremely brief FBI reports:

The first, dated November 26, 1963, is of almost nil evidentiary value:[41]

> Detective BAKER, Homicide and Robbery Bureau, Dallas Police Department, advised that the Dallas Police Department motorcycle patrolman, who first entered the Texas School Book Depository Building with Mr. ROY TRULY and who observed LEE HARVEY OSWALD in the

company snack bar on the second floor of that building immediately after the shooting of President KENNEDY was patrolman M. L. BAKER.

Sean reminded that these are Detective, *not* Patrolman, Baker's reported words. They do not, therefore, represent anything Marrion Baker might have told the FBI himself.

The second document, dated November 29, 1963 is more interesting:[42]

> M. L. BAKER, Patrolman, Dallas Police Department, Dallas, Texas, advised that he went into the building of the Texas School Book Depository shortly after President John F. Kennedy had been shot. He stated that he and Mr. ROY TRULY, the manager, observed LEE HARVEY OSWALD on the second floor of the building and he asked TRULY who that was and TRULY told him OSWALD was all right, that he worked in the building. He stated they proceeded on up the stairs and did not see OSWALD anymore until after his arrest by the Dallas Police Department.

At first glance, this appears to confirm Truly's story, Sean said. But it actually falls far short of a clear endorsement.

For one thing, Sean asks, why is Baker still saying absolutely zilch about the fact that he first spotted Oswald walking on the far side of a closed door? And why not a word that he himself went through this door to find Oswald in a room located near the middle of the building? Add to this complete lack of concrete context the fact that Baker gives the distinct impression that he and Truly only took to the stairs after having encountered Oswald—à la the First Floor encounter.

The incident in this November 29 document is placed explicitly on the "Second Floor" (as opposed to the "Third or Fourth Floor" of Baker's 11/22 affidavit). But there is not a single topographical reference within it that might reassure us that this really is the Second Floor Baker is talking about.

Indeed, assuming that the FBI didn't simply change Baker's "First" to "Second" when they wrote up this report (a very real possibility), there is a very elementary way they could have got him to put a First Floor incident on the "Second Floor": by telling him that the First Floor of the Depository was in reality known as the "Second" due to the fact that one had to go up a flight of steps at the front entrance to get onto it. Factor in such a minor sleight-of-hand on the part of the FBI, Sean said, and everything in the above statement bolsters the notion of a First Floor front entrance encounter.

In any case, there is not a single instance between the assassination and Baker's dealings with the Warren Commission in March 1964 of his actually describing in recognizable form the Second Floor incident which Roy Truly was happily narrating to anyone who asked. No door, no room, no machine, nothing. Apart from anything else, Sean said this suggests that it took quite some time to bring the perplexed Baker properly "on script."

Member Paul Rigby made the observation that a cover-up is a process, not an event, with many errors, early inadequacies, and/or improvisations, many of them subsequently abandoned.

Sean continued. According to Captain Will Fritz's interrogation report prepared for the Warren Commission, Lee Oswald claimed to have been on the First Floor at the time of the assassination but that *"he was on the second floor drinking a coca cola when the officer came in."* FBI Agent James Bookhout's solo second account of Oswald's first interrogation has Oswald making a near-identical claim:[43]

> …at the time of the search of the Texas School Book Depository building by Dallas police officers, *he was on the second floor of said building, having just purchased a Coca-cola from the soft-drink machine*, at which time a police officer came into the room with pistol drawn and asked him if he worked there.

If Oswald really made these claims, Sean said, then either he was lying or else Marrion Baker was lying about the circumstances under which he first glimpsed Oswald on the Second Floor. This is because Baker's story to the Warren Commission involves Oswald's being en route into the Second Floor lunchroom, not being already inside it at or near the Coke machine. The fact that **both Fritz and Bookhout's reports speak of Oswald not as having been on his way to buy a coke but as being already in possession of one** should give pause to any researcher thinking to cite those reports as compelling evidence that Oswald confirmed the story Baker would tell to the Warren Commission.

Wow. To say Sean Murphy is on a roll here is a gross understatement.

Sean submits that both Fritz and Bookhout really did hear Oswald say he was drinking a Coca-Cola, which he had just purchased from the machine in the Second Floor lunchroom, when an officer came in with pistol drawn and asked him if he worked there. But the officer was *not* coming into the lunchroom; he was coming into the building.

And Sean submits that Oswald—in saying these things—was telling the truth.

In March 1964, the managing editor of the *Dallas Morning News* gathered together the personal recollections of fifty-one press people relating to the Kennedy assassination and its aftermath. *Dallas Morning News* reporter Kent Biffle was one of these fifty-one. Included in his piece is the moment when Roy Truly alerted the police to the "missing" status of employee Lee Oswald. Biffle then adds the following fact:

> **The [TSBD] superintendent [Truly] would recall later that he and a policeman met Oswald as they charged into the building after the shots were fired.**

Sean clarified "*as they charged into the building.*" Not "as they charged up the building." Not: "as they charged through the building."

As they charged into it.

Sean submits once again that the posture of Prayer Man's arms in the Darnell film indicates clearly that he must be holding something—and that we have strong reasons for identifying this man as Lee Oswald holding the very bottle of Coca-Cola that will find itself transplanted in time and space by Fritz and Bookhout.

Sean then asked was there an encounter with a man by the rear stairway on the Third or Fourth Floor? That's the next question that needs to be explored, he said.

Chapter Four Recap

Twelve days into this thread and my head is spinning. I feel like I'm a part of something very special unfolding here, because if Prayer Man is Lee Oswald then it's back to square one with this case.

- No witness said they saw any strangers in the TSBD building the morning of November 22, 1963 and time leading up to the assassination.
- James Jarman told the HSCA that Billy Lovelady told him that Oswald was stopped by an officer at the front entrance and vouched for by Roy Truly.
- First-day evidence has Oswald claiming he went to lunch at approximately noon, he ate his lunch on the First Floor in the lunchroom, he went to the second floor where the Coca-Cola machine was located and obtained a bottle of coke for his lunch, then he claimed to be on the First Floor when President John F. Kennedy passed the TSBD building
- The location, timing and meaning of the encounter Oswald had with a police officer contained in the initial reports was changed to ultimately reflect what was in the Warren Commission report.
- This encounter did not take place on the Second Floor lunchroom, but the First Floor lobby.
- This encounter did not take place within the next minute, but the next ten seconds.
- This encounter was not about Baker challenging Oswald and Truly vouching for him. It involved Baker asking Oswald for help only to have Truly cut in and introduce himself as building manager.

- Jeraldean Reid watched the motorcade with her bosses, Roy Truly and Ochus Campbell. She reentered the TSBD with Campbell where Campbell was quoted as saying that he saw Oswald in a small storage room on the ground floor.
- Geneva Hine testified that she saw Reid and Campbell reenter the Second Floor right after they came up the front stairs.
- Jeraldean Reid said she saw Oswald entering the Second Floor office area, but her testimony is contradicted by the testimony of Geneva Hine.
- There are reasons to suspect that Jeraldean Reid may have been pressured by her two bosses to support the Second Floor lunchroom story.
- Scientific studies show that first day statements are more reliable than later recollections.
- Roy Truly's FBI statement where he describes entering the TSBD with a Dallas Police officer and upon entering, "They saw no one there," actually draws attention to what he is disclaiming: they did see Oswald there.
- Marrion Baker never described in any recognizable form the official version of the Second Floor encounter until his March 1964 Warren Commission testimony.

Prayer Man may have been standing in the shadows, but Sean Murphy is slowly bringing him out into the light.

CHAPTER FIVE – CONSTRUCTION CONTINUES

Talent hits a target no one else can hit. Genius hits a target no one else can see.

– Schopenhauer

August 26, 2013. Without missing a beat, Sean Murphy continues.

On September 23, 1964, Sean tells us that Roy Truly and Marrion Baker were asked to go back on the record to clarify an important point: was Oswald by himself in the Second Floor lunchroom when they saw him just after the assassination? There had been press reports—based in large part upon statements made by Jesse Curry on November 23—that Oswald was with others in the room when the officer came in.

Baker dictated a statement to FBI Special Agent Richard J. Burnett. It has become notorious because of a certain deletion evident in Burnett's handwritten sheet:

Dallas, Texas September 23, 1964

I, Marrion L. Baker, do hereby furnish this voluntary signed statement to Richard J. Burnett who has identified himself to me as a Special Agent of the Federal Bureau of Investigation.

...On the second floor ~~lunchroom~~ MLB, where the lunch room is located I saw a man standing in the lunch room. ~~drinking a~~ ~~MLB~~ He was alone in the lunch room at that time.

...and correct to the best of my knowledge. I have initialled each page and each correction.

Marrion L Baker

Witness
Richard J. Burnett, Special Agent, F.B.I., 9/23/64, Dallas
Bobby W. Hargis 1082 Dallas Police Dept.

Why did Baker originally say "drinking a coke," only to have it crossed out and the deletion initialed "MLB," Sean asked? Is not this little slip compelling evidence that—contrary to what Baker and Truly testified to the Warren Commission—Oswald *had already* bought the coke by the time of the incident? And does this not bear out Oswald's claim in custody (as reported by Fritz and Bookhout)? *And* doesn't it deprive him of *even more* time to get down from the Sixth Floor?

Not so fast, says Sean. He agrees that Baker's little slip is very telling indeed—devastating even—but what it is telling is *not* what people have generally suspected.

To understand the significance of "~~drinking a coke~~," we need to note two other little slips in the immediate vicinity. Though they have achieved far less attention, they are of no less importance he stressed. The first relates to the floor on which the lunchroom was located:

Second or third floor. This uncertain either-or formula echoes in an uncanny way Baker's original November 22, 1963 affidavit where he talks of having seen a man walking away from the rear stairway on "the third *or fourth* floor." At least on November 22 Baker might be said to have some excuse in that he was unfamiliar with the building, Sean said.

But this is different. Sean says here that we have Baker, on the far side of having taken part in multiple Warren Commission reconstructions of his movements inside the building—and on the far side of having testified in excruciating detail on the lunchroom incident to the Warren Commission—*still showing uncertainty* as to which floor the incident happened on!

The second interesting item is Baker's description of the circumstances of his first sighting of Oswald:

I saw a man standing in the lunch room. Even if we factor out the fact that this phrase originally closes with the words *drinking a coke*, it is still very troubling. It hardly needs to be pointed out that it's not consistent with Baker's November 22 affidavit words, which again use the very same phrase construction: *I saw a man walking away from the stairway.*

That's just the half of it, however, he said. This phrase is not even consistent with **the story that Baker had told to the Warren Commission**, the story of **a man spotted while walking towards and then into the lunchroom.**

Once again, Sean asked, what is going on here?

Good question!

To get a handle on Baker's very weird September 1964 statement, Sean said we need to bear in mind an important point made by Paul Rigby the other day: "The cover-up is a process, not an event, with many errors, early inadequacies, and/or improvisation, many of them subsequently abandoned."

Sean submits that the Second Floor lunchroom incident is not just a fiction, <u>it is a fiction contrived in haste and panic on the evening of the assassination</u>. The authorities knew that Oswald had an alibi and they knew that something, *anything*, had to be done fast to liquidate it. It didn't much matter what that something was, as long as it *got Oswald away from the damned front entrance at the time of the President's motorcade passed by*. The details, Sean said, could be worried about later.

So what did they do?

In order to maintain maximum consonance between the true story already circulating and being told by Oswald in custody, and in order to make things as easy as possible on Baker and Truly, Sean said they chose the simplest operation possible:

The Wholesale Switcheroo.

> *Fact*: Oswald was standing drinking a Coca-Cola when the armed officer burst into the front entrance became...
> *Fiction*: Oswald was standing drinking a Coca-Cola when the armed officer burst into the second-floor lunchroom.

The details could be refined later.

Sean said Marrion Baker's fellow motorcycle officer Stavis Ellis told Larry Sneed that Baker was known to be not "real bright." In fact, he was thought to be "slow" and was nicknamed "Momma Son."[44] Harold Weisberg,[45] years earlier, remarked that Baker was thought by his colleagues to be a "dope."

Put the case that this verdict, however unkind, had at least a grain of truth in it, said Sean. And put the case that Baker, at some point after the assassination, was fed the first draft of the lunchroom story as follows:

You saw a man standing in the second-floor lunchroom drinking a coke. Got that? A man. Standing in the lunchroom. Second Floor. Drinking a Coke.

Going in to give his September 1964 statement, Sean said Baker has not been heavily prepped in the way that he most assuredly was going into his Warren Commission session. The "finished" script is no longer fresh in his memory.

What happens? He gets successive drafts of the Oswald Encounter Story almost comically confused with one another. He talks like a man who is not drawing on primary memory to describe an actually experienced incident. That's because, Sean concludes, he is describing an event that *never happened.*

- When he writes (and crosses out) "drinking a coke", he is not betraying a real, empirical memory of having seen Oswald drinking a coke in the lunchroom, he is betraying a real memory of having at some point been **told to say** that he had seen Oswald drinking a coke in the lunchroom.
- When he writes of having seen the man "standing in the lunch room", he is not betraying a real, empirical memory of having seen Oswald standing in the lunchroom, he is betraying a real memory of having at some point been **told to say** that he had seen Oswald standing in the lunchroom.
- And when he writes (and crosses out part of) "second or third floor", he is not betraying uncertainty as to where the incident had really empirically taken place, he is...

Sean said we must hold that thought because it brings us to Baker's all-important November 22, 1963 affidavit story.

Richard Hocking posted Marrion Baker's original affidavit from November 22, 1963 (emphasis his):

Friday November 22, 1963 I was riding motorcycle escort for the President of the United States. At approximately 12:30

pm I was on Houston Street and the President's car had made a left turn from Houston onto Elm Street. Just as I approached Elm Street and Houston I heard three shots. I realized those shots were rifle shots and I began to try to figure out where they came from. I decided the shots had come from the building on the northwest corner of Elm and Houston. This building is used by the Board of Education for book storage. I jumped off my motor and ran inside the building. *As I entered the door I saw several people standing around. I asked these people where the stairs were. A man stepped forward and stated he was the building manager and that he would show me where the stairs were.* I followed the man to the rear of the building and he said, "Let's take the elevator." The elevator was hung several floors up so we used the stairs instead. *As we reached the third or fourth floor I saw a man walking away from the stairway.* I called to the man and he turned around and came back toward me. The manager said, "I know that man, he works here." I then turned the man loose and went up to the top floor. The man I saw was a white man approximately 30 years old, 5'9", 165 pounds, dark hair and wearing a light brown jacket.

Pat Speer, in reference to Fritz's notes, said "out with Bill Shelley in front," when taken in context, suggests Oswald told Fritz he saw Bill Shelley when leaving the building. Some have tried to twist it into being a claim by Oswald he was out front at the time of the shooting. But that doesn't make a lot of sense, seeing as none of those present recalled such a thing. Of course, one could say they all lied, Pat said.

Sean cautioned everyone to keep in mind that Oswald at this point is not someone whose presence will be especially noticed. He's still a couple of hours away from becoming one of the most infamous men on the planet. It's not as if anyone is going to be looking around going, "Gee, I wonder if Lee Harvey Oswald's here."

Richard Hocking agreed. Lee was not a real attention-grabber before 12:30 p.m. on November 22, 1963. Going through the TSBD witness testimonies, many of the employees had either never met him or never talked to him. Lee was a very low profile guy. Richard asked what do Joe Molina, Carl Edward Jones, Roy Edward Lewis, and Prayer Man all have in common? No one else standing in the entrance of the TSBD testified these individuals were on the steps.

Bill Kelly said the idea that the Second Floor lunchroom encounter was contrived is not a new theory, but one that has been previously proposed by Greg Parker, one of the best researchers who he has worked with on many areas of the assassination and who he has highest respect for.

Sean Murphy replied "Greg Parker is aces with me—always has been, always will be. My single favorite JFK researcher."

Whoa, what an endorsement! In twelve days following this thread, Sean Murphy has shown me he is something special. His reasoning and logic at times borders on genius. Anyone who's *his* favorite researcher is someone I need to learn more about.

Sean said let's forget Prayer Man for a moment. Let's forget First Floor encounters. Let's forget Third/Fourth Floor encounters. Instead let's consider Baker's supposed actions that day:

- Baker believed shots have been fired from the top of the building.
- Baker dashed into the building and, after a maddening delay at the elevators, began his ascent.
- Just one floor up in what he knows is going to be a high climb up a multi-story building he came out onto the Second Floor landing and, as he was turning to hit the next flight of stairs, noticed an indeterminate movement behind the glass pane of a closed door a good distance away…

- There is nothing intrinsically suspicious about this movement, and certainly no sign that the person behind it had just passed through the closed door.
- Yet Baker decided to interrupt his already delayed dash up the stairs and go after this person.

Sean asked, don't you find this decision of Baker's just a little...counterintuitive? And don't you find it just a little too fluky for comfort that Baker's decision should prove so inspired, bringing him face to face with—of all people—the very person who will later be arrested for the shooting of the President?

Now if Baker had gone after, say, a man caught walking away from the stairway several floors up the building, Sean continued, that would be a rather different matter...

A different matter indeed. The longer I follow this thread, the more I doubt the Second Floor encounter. It smells rather... manufactured.

Robert Prudhomme said if Prayer Man is holding a bottle of coke, it appears he is holding it with both hands, and wondered if that was normal. He added that Prayer Man's posture reminds him of the stance his father used to assume using his first 8 mm home movie camera in the early 1960s.

Sean replied that holding a coke with both hands is a little unusual but not unheard of. He added that it's possible Prayer Man is holding something other than a coke:

Mr. BALL. Did you ask him what he was doing in the lunchroom?
Mr. FRITZ. He said he was having his lunch. He had a cheese sandwich and a Coca-Cola.

A sandwich?

I lean toward Prayer Man holding a camera. The arm position seems right for it.

Richard Hocking said Joe Molina is a good example of someone nobody remembers being on the front steps. Joe gave his location as being on the top step of the entrance. He mentions Otis Williams standing next to him to his left, and Pauline Sanders being "close to there." He also mentioned seeing Roy Truly and Mr. Campbell standing together. But in Otis Williams March 19, 1964 FBI Statement, he cannot recall who was standing on either side of him that day. Campbell did vouch for Sanders being out near him.
As for Pauline Sanders, Richard said the only person she mentions being out on the steps with her is Sarah Stanton. Truly and Campbell likewise fail to mention Molina's name. Jones and Lewis also give specific information concerning their locations and who they were near. No one mentions either one of their names as being in the "Stair Group."

Richard asked, "So are we to believe, then, that Molina, Jones, Lewis, and Prayer Man were not on the steps?"

After it's been suggested numerous times that the failure of witnesses to include a certain individual in their testimony is proof that individual was not present, Richard said he was simply trying to illustrate the fault in that logic.

Impeccable reasoning trumps faulty logic. Richard Hocking has made some nice contributions to this thread so far.

Regarding the suggestion that the First Floor encounter between Baker and Oswald was in fact moved to the Second Floor, Richard Hocking said the motive would have been to get Lee Oswald away from a group that had been watching the motorcade at the time of the shots to a higher floor that could be designated as part of his escape route. The problem was that there were witnesses who had seen Oswald on the Second Floor during the timeframe in question. The Second Floor was the highest floor the encounter could be moved to that would not blatantly contradict the testimony of other witnesses. It would have been a simple adjustment to insert the Baker-Oswald encounter in prior to the encounter with Mrs. Reid. In other words, Reid does not have to be lying. Truly and Baker were the only witnesses who needed to alter their testimony in this scenario.

Sean said he thought the Second Floor lunchroom was in fact the only halfway feasible location for a transplanted Oswald encounter. He thought Richard's suggestion concerning Mrs. Reid was intriguing, and that Greg Parker had a similar thought in the past.

Imagine the following, said Sean:

1. Oswald is Prayer Man and has the brief and innocent Baker-Truly encounter at the front entrance within seconds of the last shot.
2. He does not go up for a coke immediately but hangs around a little bit on the First Floor before doing so (rather like Buell Wesley Frazier heading down to the basement for his lunch

not long after the shooting). There is no lunchroom *incident*, just an uneventful lunchroom *visit*.

3. Mrs. Reid sees him exactly as and where she claimed, only a little later.
4. The Second Floor lunchroom is chosen for the phony Baker-Truly story mainly because Oswald is known (by simple inference from Reid's information) to have been there shortly after the assassination.

Sean doesn't personally believe this could have happened, not least as Carolyn Arnold puts Oswald up on the Second Floor several minutes before the shooting—and the notion of two visits there is just odd. Sean said he also believes that Oswald would have come through a Second Floor office that was far from empty (but for Mrs. Reid) by that stage.

Sean said he must keep coming back to the crucial fact that Mrs. Reid was not just another person who worked in that building: she was the very person who had stood watching the motorcade with Truly and Campbell. Of all the three TSBD people who could have had an Oswald sighting in the building just after the shooting, it had to be these three. "What are the odds?" he asked.

Sean provided one variant scenario whereby Oswald could be Prayer Man and could still have a Second Floor lunchroom encounter with Baker and Truly:

- Oswald is at the front entrance at the time of the shooting.
- A few minutes after the shooting he goes up to buy a coke.
- As Baker and Truly make their way down from the roof, Baker does a quick sweep on each floor.
- On the Second Floor he pops his head into the lunchroom and sees Oswald standing there drinking a coke.
- He checks with Truly that Oswald is OK.

Not that he believes this happened, he said, but it is perhaps at least worth throwing out there for consideration. It certainly would give a new spin to the words in Bookhout's solo FBI report where the Second Floor lunchroom incident is being covered: *"...at the time*

*of the search of the Texas School Book Depository building by
Dallas police officers...."*

On December 23, 1963, Dallas Police Captain Will Fritz wrote a
letter to Police Chief Jesse Curry in which he outlined the case
against the late Lee Harvey Oswald. Amongst Fritz's points, Sean
says we find the following statement:[46]

> [T]his man [Oswald] had been stopped by Officer M. L.
> Baker while coming down the stairs. Mr. Baker says that he
> stopped this man on the third or fourth floor on the stairway,
> but as Mr. Truly identified him as one of the employees, he
> was released.

According to Sean, Fritz's source for this claim is clearly
Marrion Baker himself, or else the affidavit statement which Baker
gave at City Hall within a couple of hours of the assassination:[47]

> As we reached the third or fourth floor I saw a man walking
> away from the stairway. I called to the man and he turned
> around and came back toward me. The manager said, "I
> know that man, he works here." I then turned the man loose
> and went up to the top floor. The man I saw was a white man
> approximately 30 years old, 5'9", 165 pounds, dark hair and
> wearing a light brown jacket.

Sean thought Jesse Curry must have scratched his head when he
read Fritz's reference to a Third or Fourth Floor rear stairway
encounter. Was Fritz not aware that Oswald had actually been
stopped in a lunchroom on the Second Floor of the Depository?

If Curry was puzzled by this, Sean reasoned, then we must surely
be perplexed. Doesn't Fritz remember what Oswald himself told him
in their very first interrogation session?[48]

> Oswald stated that on November 22, 1963, at the time of the
> search of the Texas School Book Depository building by
> Dallas police officers, he was on the second floor of said
> building, having just purchased a Coca-cola from the soft-
> drink machine, at which time a police officer came into the

room with pistol drawn and asked him if he worked there. Mr. Truly was present and verified that he was an employee and the police officer thereafter left the room and continued through the building.

Has Fritz, for that matter, not even read his own interrogation notes?

claims 2nd floor Coke when
off came in

And how is it, Sean asked, by the time of his Warren Commission testimony in April 1964, Fritz will be mysteriously re-remembering what he has now apparently forgotten?[49]

> Mr. BALL. At that time didn't you know that one of your officers, Baker, had seen Oswald on the second floor?
> Mr. FRITZ. They told me about that down at the bookstore; I believe Mr. Truly or someone told me about it, told me they had met him—I think he told me, person who told me about, I believe told me that they met him on the stairway, but our investigation shows that he actually saw him in a lunchroom, a little lunchroom where they were eating, and he held his gun on this man and Mr. Truly told him that he worked there, and the officer let him go.
> Mr. BALL. Did you question Oswald about that?
> Mr. FRITZ. Yes, sir; I asked him about that and he knew that the officer stopped him all right.
> Mr. BALL. Did you ask him what he was doing in the lunchroom?
> Mr. FRITZ. He said he was having his lunch. He had a cheese sandwich and a Coca-Cola.
> Mr. BALL. Did he tell you he was up there to get a Coca-Cola?
> Mr. FRITZ. He said he had a Coca-Cola.

Sean asked, in sum, how can Fritz possibly believe, as of December 23, 1963, that Oswald had been stopped on the Third or Fourth Floor on or near the rear stairway?

Sean proposed Fritz's curious ignorance on this score may be explained by the simple, but disturbing, hypothesis we have been exploring in this thread: Oswald never said a word in custody about a post-assassination Second Floor lunchroom incident. He did however speak of a Second Floor lunchroom visit followed by a return downstairs to catch some of the motorcade. Fritz must have compared Oswald's claim with Baker's story about having stopped a man on or by the stairway several floors up the building, and concluded that Oswald was lying.

The lunchroom incident was, Sean suspects, invented by or for Roy Truly with the FBI on the evening or night of the assassination and Oswald's confirmation of it put in his mouth posthumously by James Bookhout of the FBI. It would not be until 1978, when Carolyn Arnold was contacted by Anthony Summers, that the truth which had been hidden in plain sight in Bookhout's first interrogation report (co-written with James Hosty) would be fully exposed: Oswald went to the Second Floor lunchroom several minutes before the assassination.

One need only give the gentlest of pulls on the tiny strand of Arnold's information to watch unravel the entire weave of lies put together around the question of Oswald's assassination-time whereabouts.

After several "take a breather" posts to reexamine images from the Darnell film, Sean resumed. For Oswald to be Prayer Man, and for the Second Floor lunchroom incident to have really happened as described by Baker and Truly to the Warren Commission, there's only one realistic scenario available, he said:

- Oswald stands in the front entrance, not showing the slightest curiosity about what's just happened on the street—that's because he's been expecting it.
- He is however taken by surprise by Baker's sudden and extraordinarily early dash into the building.
- He follows him and Truly upstairs by taking the front stairs and crossing the Second Floor.
- He looks through the door window at Truly crossing the landing.

- He also sees Baker come onto the landing, but is startled when Baker notices him back.
- Not wishing to draw attention to himself, he spins around and starts walking into the lunchroom.
- Etc.

Why would the Oswald of *this* scenario want to keep tabs on Baker and Truly's progress? The answer, Sean said, hardly needs spelling out.

Continuing, Sean said within a few short hours of the assassination, Marrion Baker gave an affidavit in the Homicide Office at Dallas Police Department Headquarters. Its central claim reads as follows:[50]

> As we reached the third or fourth floor I saw a man walking away from the stairway. I called to the man and he turned around and came back toward me. The manager said, "I know that man, he works here." I then turned the man loose and went up to the top floor. The man I saw was a white man approximately 30 years old, 5'9", 165 pounds, dark hair and wearing a light brown jacket.

According to Sean, there are three competing ways of accounting for these remarkable words:

1. Baker had encountered Oswald en route to the Second Floor lunchroom, as per his later Warren Commission testimony, and got badly confused afterwards as to the details.
2. Baker had encountered someone other than Oswald coming off the stairway several floors up the building.
3. Baker's words report not a real incident but a rushed first draft of what would soon become the lunchroom story.

For reasons previously outlined, Sean does not buy explanation #1. Both #2 and #3, however, do merit serious exploration on their own terms.

Citing Frazier's testimony,[51] member Robin Unger said his best guess was that Frazier was Prayer Man (emphasis Unger's):

> Mr. FRAZIER - Well, see, I was standing, like I say, one step down from the top, and Mr. Shelley was standing, you know, back from the top step and over toward the side of the wall there. See, he was standing right over there, and then *Billy was a couple of steps down from me over toward more the wall also.*

Sean replied that Frazier would be an obvious candidate but he honestly doesn't see how it can be him.

- Prayer Man's upper garment looks far too light to be Frazier's dark jacket.
- Frazier's comment that Billy "was a couple of steps down from me over toward more the wall also" makes it clear that Lovelady was closer to the wall than Frazier himself—whereas Prayer Man is right over by the wall and is making no attempt to improve his already lousy view.
- Frazier testified that his view of the Presidential limousine disappeared as it proceeded down Elm because of all the spectators lining the street. Prayer Man cannot see any of that. (Note that Lovelady, who is east of Prayer Man and thus has a better view, still has to move to his left and lean over just to follow the progress of the limousine, as seen in Altgens 6.)
- Prayer Man is clearly holding something; Frazier gives no indication that he was holding anything (Frazier said he went inside shortly afterwards to get his lunch).

Member Michael Griffin posted this testimony of Marrion Baker:[52]

> Representative BOGGS - Let me ask one other question. You later, when you recognized this man as Lee Oswald, is that right, saw pictures of him?

Mr. BAKER - Yes, sir. I had occasion to see him in the homicide office later that evening after we got through with Parkland Hospital and then Love Field and we went back to the City Hall and I went up there and made this affidavit.
Representative BOGGS - After he had been arrested?
Mr. BAKER - Yes, sir.
...
Mr. DULLES - I didn't get clearly in mind, I am trying to check up, as to whether you saw Oswald maybe in the same costume later in the day. Did you see Oswald later in the day of November 22d?
Mr. BAKER - Yes, sir; I did.
Mr. DULLES - Under what circumstances? Don't go into detail, I just want to tie up these two situations.
Mr. BAKER - As I was in the homicide office there writing this, giving this affidavit, I got hung in one of those little small offices back there, while the Secret Service took Mr. Oswald in there and questioned him and I couldn't get out by him while they were questioning him, and I did get to see him at that time.
Mr. DULLES - You saw him for a moment at that time?
Mr. BAKER - Yes, sir.

Michael went on to say that he's very intrigued as to whether Officer Baker laid eyes upon Lee Oswald at Dallas Police Department Headquarters before, during, or after giving his affidavit. When it comes to determining the timing of that, he finds Officer Baker's Warren Commission testimony to be very confusing. It seems as if Baker is saying that those questioning Oswald were physically blocking Baker's exit from a small office after he gave his affidavit, but did Officer Baker first spot the Oswald entourage before he had completed his affidavit?

Griffin suggests that this is a crucial question for the following reason: If Officer Baker had laid eyes upon the now suspect Oswald at police headquarters before or during the giving of his affidavit, then he finds it almost impossible to believe that Baker would not have mentioned the Second Floor lunchroom encounter in that affidavit if it had actually occurred.

Sean Murphy replied that, yes, Baker definitely did lay eyes on Oswald as he was giving his affidavit. We know this not only from his Warren Commission testimony, but also from Marvin Johnson's report which covers, among other things, Baker's giving of his affidavit: [53]

Officer Baker and the building manager then went to a stairway and started up the stairs to search the building. On about the 4th floor Officer Baker apprehended a man that was walking away from the stairway on that floor. Officer Baker started to search the man, but the building manager stated that the man was an employee of the company and was known to him. Officer Baker released the man and continued his search of the building. Officer Baker later identified Lee Harvey Oswald as the man he had seen on the 4th floor of the Texas Book Depository.

Note Johnson's recollection, said Sean, that Baker tended to place the encounter with the still unnamed "man" on the Fourth Floor. The word "later" in Johnson's report obviously caused some anxiety, because he added a curiously placed ending to his report:

Marvin Johnson-Page 3

that I would not have to report for duty Sunday. I was off Sunday and Monday. I returned to duty Tuesday November 26, 1963 at 8:00 am.

When Patrolman M. L. Baker identified Lee Harvey Oswald as the man that he stopped in the Texas School Book Depository Building, Patrolman Baker was in the Homicide Bureau giving an affidavit and Oswald was brought into the room to talk to some Secret Service men. When Baker saw Oswald he stated, "That is the man I stopped on the 4th floor of the School Book Depository."

If Baker really did say there and then, "That is the man I saw on the Fourth Floor," then it's strange that his affidavit fails to register the identification.

Sean said his money is still on Prayer Man taking a swig on a coke in Wiegman, returning to a two-hand clasp by Darnell. Or it could look something like this—minus the camera:

What was that Fritz said again,[54] asked Sean?

> Mr. FRITZ. He said he was having his lunch. He had a
> cheese sandwich and a Coca-Cola.

Sean recapitulated:

- Oswald comes down from the Fifth or Sixth Floor shortly
  after noon.
- He goes for lunch in the First Floor Domino Room and
  picks up his cheese sandwich and apple.
- Several minutes before the assassination, he goes upstairs
  to the Second Floor lunchroom and buys a coke.
- He brings the coke downstairs and, hearing the crescendo
  of applause and cheering for the motorcade, goes out onto
  the front steps.

- Everyone else's attention is naturally riveted on the motorcade and then the loud bangs; Oswald's presence goes unnoticed.
- Within seconds of the last shot, Marrion Baker has dismounted and is dashing to the front entrance of the TSBD.
- Oswald's hands are down from his mouth as he begins to take in what's going on:

- Baker reaches the front door and, needing directions for the stairs, notices Oswald and asks him if he works there.
- Before Oswald can answer, Roy Truly arrives at the front lobby and offers to escort Baker upstairs.
- Oswald at some point goes into the small storage room located just off the front lobby.
- He is noticed in there by Ochus Campbell and Jeraldean Reid as that pair are re-entering the building to take the front stairs to the Second Floor office.

How, Sean asked, do we get from all that to this?

AFFIDAVIT IN ANY FACT

THE STATE OF TEXAS
COUNTY OF DALLAS

BEFORE ME, _____ Mary Rattan _____

a Notary Public in and for said County, State of Texas, on this day personally appeared _____

M. L. Baker, Patrolman Dallas Police Department

Who, after being by me duly sworn, on oath deposes and says: Friday November 22, 1963 I was riding
motorcycle escort for the President of the United States. At approximately 12:30 pm
I was on Houston Street and the President's car had made a left turn from Houston onto
Elm Street.   Just as I approached Elm and Houston I heard three shots. I realized
these shots were rifle shots and I began to try to figure out where they came from.
I decided the shots had come from the building on the northwest corner of Elm and
Houston.   This building is used by the Board of Education for book storage.   I
jumped off my motor and ran inside the building.   As I entered the door I saw several
people standing around.   I asked these people where the stairs were.   A man stepped
forward and stated he was the building manager and that he would show me where the
stairs were.   I followed the man to the rear of the building and he said, "Let's take
the elevator."   The elevator was hung several floors up so we used the stairs instead.
As we reached the third or fourth floor I saw a man walking away from the stairway.
I called to the man and he turned around and came back toward me.   The manager said,
"I know that man, he works here."   I then turned the man loose and went up to the
top floor.   The man I saw was a white man approximately 30 years old, 5'9", 165
pounds, dark hair and wearing a light brown jacket.   *M. L. Baker*

SUBSCRIBED AND SWORN TO BEFORE ME THIS 22 DAY OF November A.D. 1963

Mary Rattan   Mary Rattan
Notary Public, Dallas County, Texas

CPS-GF-413

The first marked part is easy, he said: Baker is covering the time of his fleeting encounter with Oswald. But he has no reason to remember Oswald—or, even if he does remember him, to single either the man or the encounter out for special mention. He has, after all, got a much bigger fish to fry:

As we reached the third or fourth floor I saw a man walking away from the stairway. I called to the man and he turned around and came back toward me. The manager said, "I know that man, he works here." I then turned the man loose and went up to the top floor. The man I saw was a white man approximately 30 years old, 5'9", 165 pounds, dark hair and wearing a light brown jacket.

If there is one question as momentous as "Where was Oswald at the time of the assassination?" it is surely:

> **Did Baker encounter a man other than Oswald, a man fitting the above description, who was evidently coming down the rear stairway on (in the words of Marvin Johnson, who took Baker's affidavit) "about the fourth floor"?**

Sean stated there are strong arguments to be made both ways but on balance—and he's very much open to persuasion on this—he believes a close textual analysis of Baker's affidavit statement points to the answer: *no, he didn't.*

Continuing, Sean said Marrion Baker's November 22, 1963 affidavit describes the man caught walking away from the rear stairway on Third or Fourth Floor as follows:

> *...a white man approximately 30 years old, 5'9", 165 pounds, dark hair and wearing a light brown jacket.*

He said to now compare the description of the suspect which Herbert Sawyer had broadcast a quarter of an hour after the shooting:[55]

> *...about 30, 5'10", 165 pounds.*

The similarities are just too good to be true, said Sean. It stretches credulity to believe that Baker and Howard Brennan (the supposed source of Sawyer's description) should get the man's age and weight wrong in exactly the same way. And for their height estimates to be within a measly inch of one another given that

Brennan had no idea that the floor on the Sixth Floor was a very short distance below the window is improbably impressive also.

I now believe the Second Floor encounter was a fabrication to cover up what actually happened. Do you?

This is what Sean says he believes happened:

- Marrion Baker came back to Dallas Police Department Headquarters from Parkland Hospital and told of his movements in the TSBD. He had run into the building and, escorted by the building manager, gone upstairs. While in transit he had seen—no one at all.
- This sequence of non-events was very bad news indeed for Fritz and company who urgently needed evidence pointing to Oswald's having come down that escape route immediately after the shooting. "The solution kicked in with Dallas Texas '63 alacrity," Sean said.
- Baker was told to give an affidavit telling of his having encountered a man—an "employee"—fleeing down the rear stairway.
- He was fed the APB suspect description and told to add in "light brown jacket" for extra effect (reports were already coming in from Tippit witnesses that the man seen shooting Tippit and fleeing the scene had been wearing a light brown [or "tan"] jacket—a nice opportunity to seal the deal against this double murderer).
- Baker complied, hedging his bets as to location by offering "Third or Fourth Floor." (You never know who else might turn up claiming to have been near the rear of one of those floors at the time in question....)
- The man's height was chopped an inch for plausibility so as not to make the copy and paste from the APB description too blatant.

- And then, just as Baker is giving his affidavit, something dramatic happens: Lee Oswald is brought into the Homicide Office in front of his very eyes!
- Baker is stunned for he recognizes Oswald as the man he had seen and briefly spoken with at the front entrance.
- Up until this, he has genuinely believed he is just helping his boss nail a Presidential assassin and cop-killer. But now he realizes that he has just invented a story about man he knows to be innocent—*and who knows he knows!* If not for Oswald's sake then for his own, Baker is deeply disturbed. He has just risked exposure of having given a false report.
- His affidavit reflects this fact, for *it makes no mention* of the all-important fact that the man Baker has just described is the man currently in custody. If Baker is asked subsequently to identify Oswald in a lineup, then he refuses.

Officer after officer, even those with pretty tangential roles, will in the days and weeks ahead give detailed reports on their post-assassination movements inside the TSBD. **But not Baker**. He closes up. Not a word from him for months in clear confirmation of any story putting Oswald by the rear stairs. It will not be until he takes part in the Warren Commission "reconstructions" at the TSBD months later, in March 1964 that he will jump on board the final draft of the "Relocated Oswald Encounter."

Speaking of which, said Sean, by the evening of the assassination, a second alternative venue for the Relocated Oswald Encounter is being put together by or with the cooperation of Roy Truly: the Second Floor lunchroom. With judicious tweaks, it will become the story people stick to. Baker's affidavit story is buried as an unworkable first draft, he said.

Sean said we still haven't got an answer however to a powerful question that has been asked more than once in this thread: Why was the front entrance encounter relocated to the Second Floor lunchroom? Why not just stick with the far more incriminating rear stairway Third or Fourth Floor story? The shocking answer is given to us courtesy of three people who worked in the TSBD building:

Vicki Adams
Sandra Styles
Bonnie Ray Williams

Here's what they tell us: Baker and Truly never took the stairs up from the First Floor. They took one of the rear elevators, said Sean.

Richard Hocking said there was one other name that can be added to this list: Otis Williams:

> Fact is, as soon as the third shot happened, and everybody commenced milling around, I thought it came from the underpass. I entered the building immediately, climbed up the stairs where the warehouse elevator was which led to the 6th floor and went up to the 4th floor, which was the first one I could see from to see the underpass. After I got up there and saw that nothing was going on on the underpass, I turned around and came back down to the office, and called my wife. Soon, while we were talking, people came in, officers rushed in, and I had to get off the phone. I could have gone down the steps while Oswald came down, *but he came down on the elevator*. Anyway, I walked down the steps and didn't see him or anything.[56]

Williams, Adams, and Styles do not mention seeing anyone, including each other, said Richard.

Sean pointed to an interesting exchange towards the end of Roy Truly's first appearance before the Warren Commission:[57]

> Mr. McCLOY - From what you know of these young men who testified before you today, are they trustworthy?
> Mr. TRULY - Yes, sir; I think they are. They are good men. They have been with me, most of them, for some time. I have no reason to doubt their word. I do know that they have been rather, as the expression goes, shook up about this thing, ***especially this tall one, Bonnie Williams. He is pretty superstitious, I would say.***

Roy Truly has good reason to describe Bonnie Ray Williams (one of his "niggers," in *his* words) as superstitious. Bonnie has been going on the record with the silliest little story about having seen a ghost:[58]

> While we were standing at the west end of the building on the fifth floor, a police officer came up on the elevator and looked all around the fifth floor and left the floor. I did not see anyone come down from the fifth floor via the stairs.

And there we have it, in eight little nuclear words:

...a police officer came up on the elevator...

Note that these words are from Bonnie Ray's own first-person account. And what they do is expose the lie at the heart of the Baker-Truly story (or perhaps that should be *stories*). Baker and Truly will, as we know, tell the Warren Commission that they ran upstairs from the First Floor via the rear stairway and only found an available elevator on—*what a coincidence!*—the Fifth Floor.

Bonnie is telling us that something quite contrary to that happened: the Fifth Floor was where they—or at least one of them—got off the elevator. (How Baker and Truly continued on up after that is not stated in Williams's interview.) Joseph Ball rather foolishly draws attention to Williams's explosive FBI interview statement when questioning Williams for the Warren Commission:[59]

> Mr. BALL. Now, when you were questioned by the FBI agents, talking to Mr. Odum and Mr. Griffin, they reported in writing here that while you were standing at the west end of the building on the fifth floor, a police officer came up on the elevator and looked all around the fifth floor and left the floor. Did you see anything like that?

Bonnie Ray, no doubt having had word or two in his ear in recent weeks from his boss Mr. Truly, does the decent thing and "clarifies":[60]

Mr. WILLIAMS. Well, at the time I was up there I saw a motorcycle policeman. He came up. And the only thing I saw of him was his white helmet.

Mr. BALL. What did he

Mr. WILLIAMS. He just came around, and around to the elevator.

Mr. BALL. Which elevator?

Mr. WILLIAMS. I believe it was the east elevator.

Mr. BALL. Did you see anybody with him?

Mr. WILLIAMS. I did not.

Mr. BALL. You were only able to see the top of his helmet?

Mr. WILLIAMS. Yes, sir.

Mr. BALL. You could only see the top of his helmet

Mr. WILLIAMS. Yes, sir; that is the only thing I saw about it.

But it's too little too late, Sean said. The cat is already out of the bag. We must therefore refine our understanding of the circumstances behind Marrion Baker's November 22 affidavit.

Baker goes back to Dallas Police Department Headquarters on the afternoon of the shooting with a disastrously underachieving and under-dramatic story to tell his bosses: "I and the building manager took the rear elevator upstairs and...saw no-one."

Fritz and company find themselves saddled with a problem: they have a suspect who claims to have been at the front entrance having lunch at the time of the shooting, and they're having a damnably difficult time trying to establish an incriminating sighting anywhere near the assassin's escape route.

So Baker is coaxed into giving an affidavit which invents not merely an encounter with an (in hindsight, anyway) obviously fleeing employee by the rear stairway, but an entire climb up four flights of stairs.

It's an audacious gambit, said Sean, and it nearly comes off. If only Baker had not been both seen (by Bonnie Ray Williams) and not seen.

Enter Vicki Adams.

Martin Hinrichs said he thinks that Prayer Man is standing directly at the wall, but not on the top pedestal. Most likely he was one step lower. Richard Hocking agreed. I agree too.

Sean said Vicki Adams worked on the Fourth Floor of the TSBD and watched the assassination from a south-facing window on that floor in the company of several colleagues. She claimed to have run down the back stairs to the First Floor with her colleague Sandra Styles, and insisted that she and Sandra had left the Fourth Floor window within just seconds of the last shot being fired and had gone downstairs immediately.

For many years, conspiracy theorists have pointed to the eyebrow-raising fact that <u>she didn't see or hear Oswald coming down the stairs</u>. In more recent years however, and in particular since the appearance of Barry Ernest's provocative book *The Girl on the Stairs*,[61] Warren Commission defenders have pointed to a no less eyebrow-raising fact: <u>she didn't see or hear Mr. Truly and a police officer coming up the stairs</u>.

How, these Warren Commission defenders have asked—and not without good reason Sean said—could the two pairs of people have possibly missed each other entirely if Adams and Styles had really hit those rear stairs as quickly as Adams claimed? Does this not prove that Adams was mistaken and must have gone downstairs at some point after Baker and Truly had gone past the Fourth Floor?

This was Sean's own view at one time, for he had had a lengthy telephone conversation with Sandra Styles in 2008. Sandra told Sean that her recollection was that she and Vicki had gone downstairs significantly later than Vicki had claimed. That, Sean thought, was that. Oliver Stone would have to cut those memorable frames from his next edit of *JFK*, the movie.

Then Barry Ernest's book came out. In it he gave details of a telephone conversation he had had with Sandra several years earlier (and long before Sean's contact with her). Sandra, he reported, said that she and Vicki had left the front window just as the Presidential limousine was about to enter the triple underpass.

Sean said he immediately went on to a couple of JFK assassination research forums and, in so many words, accused Barry of being a liar, because Sandra had given him a very different timeline.

But Sean said something was bothering him. It was a certain document which Barry had discovered and reproduced in his book—a registered letter, dated June 2, 1964, sent by Martha Joe Stroud, Assistant U.S. Attorney for the Northern District of Texas, to J. Lee Rankin, Warren Commission General Counsel:

PLEASE ADDRESS ALL MAIL TO
UNITED STATES ATTORNEY
P. O. BOX 155

United States Department of Justice

UNITED STATES ATTORNEY
NORTHERN DISTRICT OF TEXAS
DALLAS 1, TEXAS

75221

June 2, 1964

AIR MAIL - REGISTERED - RETURN RECEIPT REQUESTED

Mr. J. Lee Rankin
General Counsel
President's Commission on the
Assassination of President Kennedy
200 Maryland Avenue N.E.
Washington, D. C. 20002

Dear Mr. Rankin:

I am enclosing the signed deposition of:

Victoria E. Adams

The following corrections were made: page 59 line 19 changed to "service"; page 59 line 20 add "and"; page 60 line 18 to "Martin"; page 64, line 14 to "there"; page 75 line 5 add "and"; page 79 line 4 to "officiously."

Mr. Belin was questioning Miss Adams about whether or not she saw anyone as she was running down the stairs. Miss Garner, Miss Adams' supervisor, stated this morning that after Miss Adams went downstairs she (Miss Garner) saw Mr. Truly and the policeman come up.

Sincerely yours

Barefoot Sanders
United States Attorney

Martha Joe Stroud, Assistant
United States Attorney

It was the words:

Miss Garner, Miss Adams' supervisor, stated this morning that after Miss Adams went downstairs she (Miss Garner) saw Mr. Truly and the policeman come up.

Sean asked, did not this sentence offer sensational vindication of Vicki Adams's unwavering claim to have gone downstairs at once?

Sean decided to re-contact Sandra Styles, this time by email, and put to her the information contained in the Stroud document. She seemed genuinely taken aback, if not nonplussed, by Garner's reported claim. She then restated several times something that she had said in their original conversation and in the follow-up emails, something that Sean had heard but not really processed, putting it down to her self-effacing modest personality: Sandra could not rule out the possibility that Vicki's recollection was the more accurate than hers. Memory, she said, plays funny tricks and all she could tell Sean at this point was that "logic tells me" that it was later than Vicki said.

Sandra also, for the first time, mentioned to Sean that the authorities who interviewed her had told her that the police had not started their search of the TSBD building until some 15-20 minutes(!) after the assassination. This had always bothered her, and seemed to have played a role in fixing her "memory" of having gone downstairs minutes rather than seconds after the shooting.

Sean said Vicki Adams's claim was suddenly back in contention, at least for him.

But the Stroud document, even as it supported her timeline, only undermined her story all over again, for, if Baker and Truly came up on to the Fourth Floor landing after Adams and Styles left it to take the stairs down, how in the world did they all manage to miss one another?

It's true, said Sean, there was a tiny window of time where this could conceivably have happened: Baker and Truly over at the Second Floor lunchroom entrance while Adams and Styles are running across the Second Floor landing. But it was not just a tiny window, it was also a rather ludicrous one—the sound of two women in high heels hurrying down the noisy wooden stairs from the Third Floor to the Second, across the landing and then down the stairs from Second to the First Floor—this would not have gone unnoticed.

In June 2011, Barry Ernest managed to track down Dorothy Garner, the Scott, Foresman and Co. office supervisor mentioned in the Stroud document. Sean said what she told Barry bears transcribing at length:[62]

Did Miss Adams and Miss Styles leave the window right away, I asked her.

"The girls did," she responded. "I remember them being there and the next thing I knew, they were gone."

They had left "very quickly…within a matter of moments," she added.

What did Mrs. Garner do after that?

"There was this warehouse or storage area behind our office, out by the freight elevators and the rear stairway, and I went out there."

Her move to that area clearly put her into a position where she could have observed activity on the back stairs as well as on the elevators. But how fast had she arrived there?

Mrs. Garner said she immediately went to this area, following "shortly after…right behind" Miss Adams and Miss Styles. She couldn't remember exactly why she went out there, other than to say, "probably to get something." Mrs. Garner said she did not actually see "the girls" enter the stairway, though, arriving on the fourth-floor landing seconds after. When I asked how she knew they had gone down, Mrs. Garner said, "I remember hearing them, after they started down. I remember the stairs were very noisy."

Were the freight elevators in operation during this time?

"I don't recall that," she answered. "They were very noisy too!"

Mrs. Garner said she remained at that spot and was alone for a moment before "several came out back from the office to look out those windows there."

Sean said anyone doubting that Barry is giving us a fair rendition of what Ms. Garner told him should consider very carefully what he says happened when he raised the crux question:

Did she remember seeing Roy Truly and a police officer come up the stairs together?

"I could have," she answered, "but there was so much confusion. It was, after all, a few years ago!"

117

It is, Sean submits, a testament to Barry's honesty as a researcher that he has given us faithfully what must have been for him a hugely anti-climactic answer from Dorothy Garner. After all, the Truly-Baker-coming-up-the-stairs issue was the chief *reason* for Barry's call to her.

Sean also submits that Garner's answer, when understood in proper context, is in fact *far* from anti-climactic. For had she told Barry that yes, she clearly remembered seeing Truly and Baker coming up the stairs together, then we would be back to square one. How did Adams and Styles not see Baker and Truly while descending, etc.? Garner's "failure" to confirm what the Stroud document says may be no failure at all. It may be inviting us to take another look at that document:

> Mr. Bellin was questioning Miss Adams about whether or not she saw anyone as she was running down the stairs. Miss Garner, Miss Adams' supervisor, stated this morning that after Miss Adams went downstairs she (Miss Garner) saw Mr. Truly and the policeman come up.

Sean said Dorothy Garner did indeed see Mr. Truly and the police officer come up. But, he asked, can someone please show us where it says she saw them come up *the stairs*?

Robert Prudhomme said he was impressed by the fact Sean was able to reexamine Barry Ernest's work and admit he may have been right all along. This brand of humility is sadly lacking in many researchers and prevents them, often, from seeing the truth. I wholeheartedly agree. Sean's a class act.

As shown earlier, Sean Murphy said Bonnie Ray Williams told the FBI in March 1964 that he had seen a police officer come up to the Fifth Floor on an elevator shortly after the assassination and take a look around the floor before leaving it again—an item of information that exposes the Baker-Truly stairs-climbing story as just that: a story. Lest anyone be tempted to write off Williams's March statement as unreliable due to confused memory after several months, here is the report of an FBI interview with Bonnie Ray Williams dated the day after the assassination:

Date _____ 11/23/63 _____

1

       BONNIE RAY WILLIAMS, residence 1502 Avenue B, Apartment B, employed at the Texas School Book Depository, furnished the following information:

       During the past three weeks he has been putting in new flooring in the Texas School Book Depository Building at the corner of Houston and Elm Streets. During that time, he became acquainted with a young man known to him as LEE.

       WILLIAMS stated on November 22, 1963, he worked installing flooring on the sixth floor of the building until about 11:30 a.m. At that time, he went down on an elevator from the sixth floor to the first floor. At the same time, CHARLES GIVENS was on the other elevator, descending at the same time. As they were going down, he saw LEE on the fifth floor. He had previously seen LEE at least once that morning at about 8 a.m. on the first floor, filling orders.

       At approximately 12 noon, WILLIAMS went back upstairs in the elevator to the sixth floor with his lunch. He stayed on that floor only about three minutes, and seeing no one there, descended to the fifth floor, using the stairs at the west end of the building. There he joined two other men known to him as HANK and JUNIOR. They were looking out window on the south side of the building approximately at the middle of the building and saw the car of President JOHN KENNEDY come north on Houston Street and then make a turn going west on Elm Street down into the triple underpass and passing directly in front of the Texas School Book Depository. While they were watching this car pass, WILLIAMS heard two shots which sounded like they came from right over his head. He stated he was not hanging out the window, but did glance up and saw no one. He stated he and the other two then ran to the west end of the building where they looked out and they did not realize that the President had been shot and WILLIAMS did not see him shot. While they were standing at the west end of the building on the fifth floor, a police officer came up on the elevator and looked all around the fifth floor and left the floor. WILLIAMS stated he and HANK and JUNIOR were standing where they would have seen anyone coming down from the sixth floor via the stairs and that they did not see anyone coming down. He

330

on __ 11/23/63 __ at Dallas, Texas _____ File # Dallas 89-43 _____

by Special Agents __ BARDWELL D. ODUM and __ WILL HAYDEN GRIFFIN/al __ Date dictated __ 11/23/63 __

Sean reminded us by the time of Williams's Warren Commission testimony, this straightforward sighting of Marrion Baker getting off an elevator onto the Fifth Floor will have been coached out of memory.

Richard Hocking provided an excerpt from one of Baker's Warren Commission sessions that fits into Sean's discussion of

Baker's movements on the elevator and stairs. There is some interesting interaction between Senator Cooper and Mr. Belin:[63]

> MR. BAKER - No; from the street in. As I ran in I was pushing them aside and running through them, and some way, Mr. Truly got from my back to my front. Now, he said he was right behind me. I never did see him until I got in and asked the question of where the stairs was, so evidently whenever I went in the door why he came on in. There were several people coming in as I, you know, came in, there were several in front of me and also around my sides and my back. And it seemed to me like a double door deal.
>
> SENATOR COOPER - As you went up on the elevator could you see out of the elevator onto floors?
>
> MR. BAKER - Yes, sir. The best that I could, that is the reason I wasn't paying too much attention to the elevator I was looking around all those floors.
>
> SENATOR COOPER - Did you see anyone?
>
> MR. BELIN - When you say up on the elevator, he didn't get on the elevator until he had got up on the stairs.
>
> SENATOR COOPER - I am aware of that.
>
> MR. BAKER - I was still looking.
>
> SENATOR COOPER - You went up on the second floor by stairs?
>
> MR. BAKER - Yes, sir.
>
> SENATOR COOPER - Then you got on the elevator.
>
> MR. BELIN - No, sir; he didn't get on the elevator until the fifth floor.
>
> SENATOR COOPER - Anyway, as you walked up the stairs could you see into each floor space as you passed from floor to floor?
>
> MR. BAKER - Partly. Now, this building has got pillars in it, you know, and then it has got books, cases of books stacked all in it. And the best that I could, you know, I would look through there and see if I could see anybody.
>
> SENATOR COOPER - Did you see anyone?
>
> MR. BAKER - No, sir.
>
> SENATOR COOPER - When you looked?
>
> MR. BAKER - Not from the second floor on up.

Sean enthusiastically told Richard this was a brilliant catch. And he noted how swiftly Belin corrects the "erroneous" impression being created by the startling turn in Cooper and Baker's little exchange.

Shifting gears, Sean said Roy Truly's troubles with the spooky elevator-related memories of the "superstitious" Bonnie Ray Williams did not begin on November 23, 1963. The problem was already evident—*doubly* evident in fact—in the affidavit given by Bonnie Ray on the very day of the assassination:

AFFIDAVIT IN ANY FACT

THE STATE OF TEXAS
COUNTY OF DALLAS

BEFORE ME, _____Patsy Collins_____

a Notary Public in and for said County, State of Texas, on this day personally appeared **Bonnie Ray Williams**

__1502 Avenue B. Apartment B, Bus. 411 Elm__

Who, after being by me duly sworn, on oath deposes and says: I went to work at 8 am this morning. I worked on the 6th floor today with Mr. Bill Danny, Charles and a Billy Lovelady. Charles was outside and couldn't get back in, so I guess he went home. We worked up until about 10 minutes to 12. Then we went downstairs. We rode the elevator to the 1st floor and got our lunches. I went back on the 5th floor with a fellow called Hank and Junior. I don't know his last name. Just after we got on the 5th floor we saw the President coming around the corner on Houston from Main Street. I heard 2 shots it sounded like they came from just above us. We ran to the west side of the building. We didn't see anybody. We looked down and saw people running and hollering. We stayed there and in a little while some officers came up. They left and then we took the elevator to the 4th floor. We stayed there awhile and then went on out. Lee Oswald was there when I got to work this morning at 8 am. He fills orders and goes all over the building. I didn't see Oswald anymore, that I remember, after I saw him at 8 am. I recognized him just a few minutes ago when the officers brought him in the office. Oswald has been working at the Texas School Book Depository for about 6 weeks.XXXXXXXXXXX

Bonnie Ray Williams

SUBSCRIBED AND SWORN TO BEFORE ME THIS 22 DAY OF *November* A.D. 196 63

Patsy Collins
Notary Public, Dallas County, Texas

CPS-GF-413

121

Sean pointed to three elements here:

1. Bonnie Ray noticed some officers come up to the Fifth Floor.
2. The officers then left the floor.
3. Bonnie Ray and his two co-workers then took the elevator down to the Fourth Floor.

Sean asks why Bonnie Ray says *some officers* and not one officer as he does in his statement the next day as well as his March 1964 statement. Simple: he had seen the elevator come up to the Fifth Floor and one officer get out and take a quick survey of the floor. That officer had then returned to the waiting elevator, shouting "OK, let's go," or words to that effect. Bonnie Ray correctly inferred that there must have been at least one other person inside the elevator, operating it. He incorrectly assumed that other person or persons to be another officer or officers. *What he had in fact seen was Marrion Baker and Roy Truly on their way up the building in an elevator.*

Bonnie Ray and the two black workers taking an elevator down from the Fifth to the Fourth Floor — is no less of a disaster for the Truly-Baker story. Truly and Baker told the Warren Commission that when they reached the Fifth Floor the *west* elevator had disappeared and the *east* elevator was available. So they took the east elevator. So what?

So this: how were Bonnie Ray and friends able to find an elevator to take them down to the Fourth Floor *given that Truly and Baker had just taken the one remaining elevator off the Fifth Floor*?

Sean said the usual explanation for the disappearance of the west elevator from the Fifth Floor between Truly's calling for it from the First Floor and reaching the Fifth Floor with Baker is that it was taken down by Jack Dougherty at some point during Truly and Baker's ascent of the building by stairs.

Well, Sean said, we need to talk about Jack.

Concerning Marrion Baker, Sean said there is an electrifying moment in the 1986 London TV Trial[64] when Gerry Spence shows Marrion Baker the Doorman figure in the Altgens 6 photograph. Baker looks at the figure and says:

"Resembles Oswald but I'm not... I don't know him."

Even Vincent Bugliosi[65] is taken aback, says Sean.

"Resembles Oswald but I'm not..." What is he about to say before he corrects himself? Surely this: *"I'm not sure."*

Since the fateful moment when a handcuffed Oswald was brought into the Dallas Police Department Homicide Office just as Baker was giving his affidavit, Sean said Baker has known Oswald was at the front entrance during the assassination. Although he did finally jump on board the "Lunchroom Express," at no point has he gone beyond that fairytale's minimal requirements of putting Oswald in the lunchroom some 90 seconds after the shooting.

And his insistence from day one that Oswald was not sweating or out of breath or agitated when he saw him in the lunchroom is perfectly consistent with his pointed refusal here to say in response to Spence what Bugliosi must be expecting him to say: *Resembles Oswald but it can't be him because I saw him in the lunchroom just after that.*

Sean tells us that whether from a principled refusal to add extra fuel to the Oswald-is-guilty myth or simply CYA insurance against the day that proof emerges—photographic or otherwise—that Oswald was out front, Baker at no point does anything to dilute the ambiguous significance of Oswald's presence in the lunchroom.

Sean paused for a quick recap of his counter-narrative so far:

1. Oswald/Prayer Man out front for the assassination,
2. The briefest of encounters with Baker as the latter was rushing into the First Floor,
3. Oswald remained around the front entrance/lobby area, and
4. Baker and Truly ran to the rear of the First Floor and took the west elevator upstairs.

There is nothing complicated in any of these real events, said Sean. All of Baker's and Truly's actions are innocent and intelligible. We might even say that Marrion Baker's actions are pretty heroic. All the complications and all the shenanigans come later, as the authorities scramble to put together a half-coherent cover story to bury the simple events they know to have taken place.

Later that afternoon, Baker is persuaded to give a phony affidavit report about challenging an "employee" by the Third or Fourth Floor rear stairway. Later that evening or night, a new improved version is put together.

It has become clear that the only halfway viable location for an Oswald encounter off the First Floor and anywhere near the rear stairway is the Second Floor lunchroom. It fits the bill.

On December 1, 1963 *The Washington Post* carried the following report:

A Backfire Noise

AT THE MOMENT the shots were fired, Roy S. Truly, director and superintendent of the Texas School Book Depository, was on his way to lunch with another company executive and they decided to look on as the President drove by.

"I heard what I thought was a backfire noise," Truly said. "Then I heard someone yell, 'Someone up there has a gun!'"

"That's my building!" Truly shouted back. "I work in there."

He was quickly joined by a policeman, and they ran up the steps together, the officer with gun drawn. The two men scrambled up the stairs to the second floor. As they made their way to a back stairway, the policeman saw Oswald standing beside a soft drink machine, sipping from a Coke bottle.

The officer ran toward Oswald and held the revolver at close range. "He's all right. He's one of my employes," assured Truly. The two men then continued on their way. Later, the employer described Oswald's demeanor in this incident as "cool as a cucumber —although he seemed a little bothered by the gun."

Over the years, researchers have been drawn to the last detail in the underlined sections: "sipping from a Coke bottle," and indeed, this was one version of the lunchroom story that Roy Truly had begun to give out on the evening or night of the assassination. However it's the details before that which are of most interest in the present context.

The story being told here is *not* of Truly and the officer running to the rear of the First Floor. Instead it has Truly and the officer *go up the front steps and then immediately go up the stairs to the Second Floor.*

The stairs in question are not the rear stairs but the front-of-house stairs (the small downward pointing arrow marks the "small storage room" where Campbell and Reid will soon see Oswald):

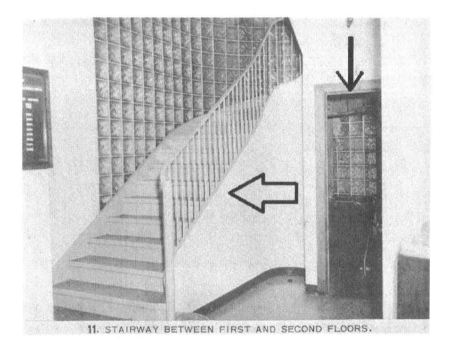

11. STAIRWAY BETWEEN FIRST AND SECOND FLOORS.

Now for the kick in the head, said Sean:

As they made their way to a back stairway...

These words are only puzzling if we forget the words just preceding them. Truly has led Baker up the front stairs so that they can go through the Second Floor (via either corridors or office area) and make their way to the back stairway which leads all the way up to the top of the building (the front stairs only went up as far as the Second Floor).

But why would the new lunchroom story need to delete the real-life dash to the rear of the First Floor? For the simple reason that *the officer needs to be given a route that will take him right by the Second Floor lunchroom*. It is impossible to go from the front stairs to the Second Floor rear stairs without passing the lunchroom.

Roy Truly's *very first* on-the-record mention of a Second Floor lunchroom incident, given late on November 22, is notable for the distinct impression it gives that he and the officer took the front stairs, not the back:

```
railroad yards adjoining the depository building. He then
noticed a Dallas City Police officer wearing a motorcycle helmet
and boots running toward the entrance of the depository building
and he accompanied the officer into the front of the building. They
saw no one there and he accompanied the officer immediately up
the stairs to the second floor of the building, where the officer
noticed a door and stepped through the door, gun in hand, and
observed OSWALD in a snack bar there, apparently alone. This
snack bar has no windows or doors, facing the outside of the building,
but is located almost in the center of the building. The officer
```

"They saw no one there": Truly's giveaway disclaimer as to Oswald's presence at the First Floor entrance. *"He accompanied the officer immediately up the stairs to the second floor of the building"* is talking about the front stairs here, for a route that will bring Oswald into Baker's path en route to the rear stairway.

Chapter Five Recap

Another week has gone by and the pace shows no signs of slacking off. There is so much information that I feel like I'm drinking from a firehose! How long can this continue?

- Marrion Baker's September 1964 clarification of his earlier Warren Commission testimony shows that he is uncertain on which floor the encounter with Lee Oswald occurred.

- Having started working at the TSBD only weeks prior to the assassination, Lee Oswald was not someone whose presence would especially be noticed.
- Greg Parker, Sean Murphy's favorite researcher, had years previously raised the suggestion that the Second Floor lunchroom encounter was contrived
- In addition to Prayer Man, Molina, Jones, and Lewis were also *not* identified by others as having been on the steps.
- Prayer Man appears to be holding something, perhaps a coke, a sandwich, or even a camera.
- Carolyn Arnold puts Oswald up on the Second Floor several minutes *before* the shooting. This makes a second trip there just minutes later for the Second Floor lunchroom encounter unlikely.
- In December 1963, a month after the assassination, Will Fritz was saying that Oswald was stopped on the Third or Fourth floor on the stairway by Baker. This was contrary to the early FBI interrogation reports and Fritz's own notes.
- By April 1964, Fritz again said that the Baker-Oswald encounter was on the Second Floor in the lunchroom.
- While in custody, Oswald didn't talk about a post-assassination Second Floor lunchroom incident. He did speak of a pre-assassination Second Floor lunchroom visit followed by a return downstairs.
- While Marrion Baker was giving his affidavit at Police Headquarters on November 22, he saw Lee Oswald.
- According to Marvin Johnson who took Baker's affidavit, Baker identified Lee Oswald as the man that he stopped on the Fourth Floor of the TSBD building.
- Unlike other officers, Baker is silent following the assassination on his post-assassination movements inside the TSBD. It's not until the Warren Commission "reconstructions" at the TSBD months later and his March 1964 testimony that he supports the final draft of the encounter relocated to the Second Floor lunchroom.
- Relocating the Baker-Oswald encounter to the Second Floor was the better choice over the far more incriminating Third

or Fourth Floor stairway because of Vicki Adams, Sandra Styles and Bonnie Ray Williams.

- Bonnie Ray said he saw a police officer come up on the elevator to the Fifth Floor, which means the officer didn't take the stairs.
- Vicki Adams and Sandra Styles did not see Baker and Truly coming up the stairs as they came down the stairs from the Fourth to the First Floor following the assassination.
- A December 1, 1963 *Washington Post* article has Truly and Baker scrambling up the stairs to the Second Floor, then—while on the Second Floor—they make their way to the back stairs, and in the process, encounter Lee Oswald. In other words, this early version has them climbing the *front* steps.

Sean Murphy's logic, intellectual curiosity, and exceptional research are proving the old adage: hard work transforms talent into genius.

CHAPTER SIX – THE STRUCTURE IS RAISED

*In a world that operates largely at random, coincidences are to be
expected, but any one of them must always be mistrusted.*

– Nero Wolfe, *Champagne for One*

September 1, 2013. This thread has been amazing so far. I have
no idea how long it will continue, but already Sean Murphy has
forever changed how I view the assassination of President Kennedy.

As we have seen, giving Baker and Truly a route up the front
stairs to the Second Floor and then through the Second Floor
towards the rear stairway in the northwest corner of the building
meant that Baker could have a realistic way of seeing into the
lunchroom and noticing Oswald. Just a few days after the
assassination, the Secret Service made a silent film reconstructing
Oswald's alleged route from the Sixth Floor sniper's nest down the
stairs and into the Second Floor lunchroom. Let's join the
reconstruction on the Second Floor, as the stand-in "Oswald" leaves
the landing area:

Where does "Oswald" end up after his travels? Not by the Coca-
Cola vending machine, but somewhere very different:

Now can anyone seriously believe, asked Sean, that this in situ reconstruction was undertaken by the Secret Service of the United States of America without either Roy Truly or Marrion Baker, the two protagonists in the Oswald sighting, being consulted first? Or that Roy Truly, the building manager and TSBD liaison man for investigators, was not present when this reconstruction was filmed? Or that there is no significance whatsoever in the fact that around the same time as this film was made the following appeared in the *New York Herald Tribune*?[66]

> R. S. Truly, head of the book depository, told the *Herald Tribune* in a telephone interview...
>
> ...
>
> "On the second floor he stuck his head into a snack bar we have and saw Oswald sitting at one of the tables."

Or that it is quite so easy to dismiss as a case of crossed wires the information that had been given to the press by Jesse Curry only the day after the assassination: "He was sitting in the lunchroom and one of my officers drew a weapon on him"?

Crossed wires, from first to last?

No—just a messily evolving fairytale.

Wow. It keeps getting worse for the Second Floor lunchroom encounter, or fiction.

Sean said on the night of November 22, 1963, Captain Fritz filed this Case Report on Oswald:

POLICE DEPARTMENT
CITY OF DALLAS
CASE REPORT

Disposition

Date_____

Court_____

Docket_____

Method_____ APPROVED FOR FILING

Disposition_____
SUPERVISOR

Filed

Date **November 22, 1963**

With **Alexander**

By **Capt. Fritz**

C. N. Dhority - C. W. Brown
Investigating Officers
Lt. L. E. Cunningham
H. N. McDonald
Arresting Officers

Deceased
Location of Defendant

Defendant **Lee Harvey OSWALD**

Race **White** Age **24** Sex **Male** Residence **1026 North Beckley**

Date of Arrest **November 22, 1963 - 2:00 PM** Identification No. **54018**

Place of Arrest **231 West Jefferson** Arrest No. **63-98155**

Date and Time of Offense **November 22, 1963, approximately 12:30 PM** Offense No. **F-85950**

Complainant **John F. Kennedy, w/m/47, Deceased**

Where and How Committed **On Elm West of Houston - Shot with rifle**

Charge **Murder**

Property Taken and Value_____

Evidence and Seizures **Attached**

Voluntary Statement **No**

Accomplices_____

List Witnesses and What Each Can Testify to on Reverse Side

Summary of Case **Deceased was riding in motorcade with his wife and Governor Connally and his wife. Witnesses heard gun shot and saw deceased slump forward. More shots were fired and deceased fell forward. Governor Connally was also shot. Officers determined where shots came from and covered the building and went into the building. Capt. Fritz had name of Defendant, but Defendant was not in the building. Capt. Fritz received information that Defendant had killed Officer Tippit in Oak Cliff. Arresting officers brought Defendant to City Hall.**

Any additional information may be placed on reverse side.

Page 2 of the report lists the roles played that day by key witnesses from law enforcement:

OFFICER WITNESSES:

M. L. Baker
Solo Motor Officer
Traffic Division

Saw Oswald in building after shooting. Identified him in line up. See affidavit.

Deputy S. Boone
Sheriff's Office

Found rifle used in offense, Northwest corner of sixth floor of Texas School Book Depository Building. Turned rifle over to Capt. Fritz.

Deputy Seymour Weitzman
2802 Oates Drive, DA 7-6624
Bus. Robie Love RI 1-1483

Same as above.

Capt. J. W. Fritz #9
CID

Made investigation of offense. Found empty and live shells used in offense.

Lt. J. C. Day
Crime Lab

Made investigation at Texas School Book Depository. Took charge of rifle used. Lifted prints on building and from rifle and paper rifle was wrapped in.

Det. R. L. Studebaker
Crime Lab

Made investigation where offense was committed.

Det. Johnny Hicks
Crime Lab

Made paraffin case of Defendant's hands and face.

Det. Pete Barnes
Crime Lab

Made paraffin cast of Defendant's hands and face.

Capt. G. M. Doughty
ID Bureau

Had charge of evidence which he turned over to F. B. I.

G.L. Hill, Sgt. 1180
Radio Patrol, Sta. 511

Arrested defendant.

M. N. McDonald 1178
City P. D., Sta. 511

Arrested defendant.

C. T. Walker 1529
City P. D., Sta. 501

Arrested defendant.

Ray Hawkins 887
City P. D., APB, Sta. 515

Arrested defendant.

T. A. Hutson 1146
City P. D., Sta. 501

Arrested Defendant.

B. K. Carroll 923
City P. D., Spl. Ser. Sta. 566

Arrested defendant.

Deputy Sheriff Luke E. Mooney
Dallas Co. Sheriff's Office

Found 3 empty 6.5 rifle shells on 6th floor Texas Book Depository Bldg. and notified Capt. Fritz.

On the top of this list:

M. L. Baker   Saw Oswald in building after shooting. Identified
Solo Motor Officer   ·   him in line up. See affidavit.
Traffic Division

The claim underlined is of course a brazen lie, said Sean: Baker hasn't identified Oswald in any lineup. If he *has* attended one, he must have refused to make an identification. All this lie does is draw attention to the weird failure of the affidavit (to which the reader is being pointed here) to offer any link between the "employee" confronted in the TSBD building and Oswald.

But the placing of Baker's name at the very top of this document indicates just how central a role Fritz already envisages for him in the mounting of a case against Oswald. If Baker, as we have reason to believe, is proving a less submissive witness than Fritz needs, that will be work for another day. For now, what counts is that Fritz has in the bank a damning affidavit supplemented by a lie compensating for what the affidavit so pointedly omits to mention: Baker's recognizing of Oswald as "Mr. Third or Fourth Floor Walking Away From The Stairway."

But "Mr. Third or Fourth Floor Walking Away From the Stairway" is himself a pure fiction, as are the circumstances of Baker's first sighting of him:

> *As we reached the third or fourth floor I saw a man walking away from the stairway. I called to the man and he turned around and came back toward me.*

To explain the relationship between the scene painted by the words above and the very different little scene enacted below…

133

...is to explain how the fix against Oswald was put in. It is, in a nutshell, A Tale of Two Fictions being mongrelized into a Third.

If you had a suspect for the shooting of President Kennedy in front of you, Sean reasoned, and you had just one question to ask him, that question would surely be:

Where exactly were you at the time of the shooting?

Yet, as we have already seen, the interrogation reports are remarkably silent when it comes to telling us how Oswald actually answered this question. All we are told is that he claimed to have been on the First Floor when the President passed the building. That's it. "On the First Floor". Could be anywhere on the First Floor.

Sean submits that this striking vagueness is indicative not of Oswald's refusal to give specifics but of the "investigating" authorities' wise refusal to allow his all-too specific answer be entered into the official record. For that answer was a disastrous one: *I was out front having my lunch at that time.*

There is, curiously, only one interrogation report that actually goes so far as to claim that Oswald explicitly admitted to not having watched the motorcade, said Sean. That report is titled "First Interview of Lee Harvey Oswald." It is written by Secret Service Inspector Thomas J. Kelley. Here's the sentence that's meant to break the hearts of anyone daring to claim that Oswald was indeed out front:

I asked him if he viewed the parade and he said he had not.

Game over for those longing to cry, *"Stop the lies, Oswald outside!"* Right?

Wrong, said Sean.

Here's that devastating sentence in context in Kelley's report:

> At this time Captain Fritz showed a Selective Service Card that was taken out of his wallet which bore the name of Alex Hidell. Oswald refused to discuss this after being asked for an explanation of it, both by Fritz and by James Bookhout, the FBI Agent. <u>I asked him if he viewed the parade and he said he had not.</u> *I then asked him if he had shot the President and he said he had not.* **I asked him if he has shot governor Connally and he said he had not.**

The content of the sentence in plain text is clearly reflected in rough notes jotted down during the interrogation.

The content of the sentence in *italics* is clearly reflected in rough notes jotted down during the interrogation.

The content of the sentence in **bold** is clearly reflected in rough notes jotted down during the interrogation.

The <u>underlined</u> sentence is <u>not</u> however reflected in any way in rough notes jotted down during the interrogation.

How do we know this, asked Sean? Kelley's notes have never seen the light of day, have they? Didn't he destroy them after using them to write up his report? Yes.

And yet, even though we don't have Kelley's notes anymore, **we do have access to the notes of someone else who was listening closely to Oswald's answers during the exact same moments of that interrogation session.**

Who was that someone else?

Does this look familiar to anyone?

That's right—it's Captain Fritz's handwriting. But these are <u>not</u>, contrary to myth, Captain Fritz's contemporaneous interrogation notes. **They are, like all five pages of the much-ballyhooed "Fritz notes," in reality a transcription of the contemporaneous interrogation notes of FBI Special Agent James W. Bookhout.**

Getting back to the elevator question, Sean said Truly and Baker never ran up the rear stairway. They ran to the rear of the First Floor, pressed the button for the west elevator and…it came down. It did this because, just minutes before, James Jarman and Harold Norman had taken the trouble to push the gate down on it after getting out on the Fifth Floor to watch the motorcade. There was no shouting up the shaft from Truly, no ringing of the bell, just a press of the button and the cables started moving immediately.

Sean says we can now understand why Truly and Baker would later claim not to have got on an elevator until the Fifth Floor: *the authorities badly needed an Oswald sighting on the escape route.* This meant switching the journey up to the stairway and concocting a cock and bull story of the west elevator being "stuck" up on the Fifth Floor.

But why did Truly testify that he and Baker then took the east elevator from the Fifth Floor to the Seventh, he asked? Why, if the story is a fabrication, don't they just say they came off the stairs onto the Fifth Floor landing and took the elevator they had in reality been on the whole time, i.e., the nearest elevator—the west elevator? Why say that this elevator was gone by the time they reached the Fifth Floor, leaving only the east elevator available? Why complicate the story in such an unnecessary fashion?

Actually, the switch over to the east elevator was *far from unnecessary* said Sean. It was, from the point of view of the "investigating" authorities, absolutely critical if they were to keep alive the notion of Oswald's sole guilt. For it was pretty apparent early on to those who were in the know about Baker and Truly's elevator ride up from the First Floor **that the assassin(s) had descended from the Sixth Floor using the east elevator.**

Again we have Bonnie Ray Williams to thank for this information, Sean points out. For the day after the assassination he finally brought himself to admit what he had held back in his previous day's affidavit: he had visited the Sixth Floor on his own shortly before the assassination and had joined his two friends on the Fifth Floor by coming down the stairs in the west rear corner of the building. And he makes a remark that tells us in plain English just how easy it was for the shooter(s) to escape using the east elevator which was still up on the Sixth Floor:[67]

> *He stated someone might have been coming down on the elevator and they would not have noticed that.*

But if Truly and Baker were responsible for the movements of the west elevator just after the assassination, where does that leave Jack Dougherty, the man who testified to having brought it down? And we still need to talk about Jack, Sean said.

Sean's like an expert plate twirler—he's keeping a lot of different parts of the story "twirling" simultaneously. He knows what he's doing and where he's going. It's been a great ride so far.

Taking up where he left off with the "First Interview of Lee Harvey Oswald" document, Sean shows that it contains another example of how Secret Service Inspector Thomas Kelley seems to have strategically distorted key statements made by Oswald in custody:

> *He said he ate his lunch with the colored boys who worked with him. He described one of them as "Junior," a colored boy, and the other was a little short negro boy. He said his lunch consisted of cheese, fruit, and apples, and was the only package he had with him when he went to work.*

This "claim," Sean said, was put to Jarman ("Junior") and Norman (the "little short negro") and of course they answered that no, they hadn't had lunch with Oswald. But did Oswald ever make such a claim in the first place? Here's Fritz's transcription of the

original note made by FBI Special Agent Bookhout as he was
listening to Oswald's actual words:

*Says 11-2[2]-63 sa[w] two negr[oes] come in
one Jr. - & short negro -. ask ? [what] for lunch says cheese
sandwiches & apple*

As you can see, the notes went from *"saw two negroes come in"*
to *"ate his lunch with the colored boys."* Sean said, what a way to
make a liar out of Oswald, Inspector. He notes that Bookhout
himself is not without sin in this regard. *His* report will also badly
muddle the sense of what Oswald said:

> *"saw two negroes come in"* gets turned into *"recalled
> possibly two Negro employees walking through the room."*

Sean says having the actual wording of Bookhout's original
rough notes—thanks to Fritz's copying of those notes—gives us the
precious ability to identify with some confidence what Oswald was
actually telling Fritz: *I saw Junior and the short negro come in [to
the First Floor via the back entrance].* Oswald, in other words, is
handing Fritz proof that he was indeed on the First Floor (probably
in or around the Domino Room) when Jarman and Norman reentered
the building and made their way up to the Fifth Floor.

Sean looked at what Marrion Baker told the Warren Commission
concerning his actions after coming down from the roof of the TSBD
with Roy Truly:[68]

> Mr. BAKER - We went to the, I believe it would be the first
> floor there.
> Mr. BELIN - All right. You got off the elevator then?
> Mr. BAKER - Yes, sir.

Mr. BELIN - Did you leave Mr. Truly or did you stay with him?

Mr. BAKER - I left Mr. Truly there.

Mr. BELIN - Then what did you do?

Mr. BAKER - I immediately went on out. I was with this motorcade and I went right on straight through the front door and got on my motorcycle and tried to find out what happened to the motorcade.

It's a little surprising, says Sean, in light of the above account, to find footage of Baker standing in conversation with Truly and several others on the First Floor:

Sean reminds us that Roy Truly's November 22, 1963 FBI interview says nothing about getting on a rear elevator on the Fifth Floor and using it to get to the Seventh Floor. Marrion Baker's November 22 affidavit says nothing about that either. However Truly's November 23 affidavit has this to say:

AFFIDAVIT IN ANY FACT

THE STATE OF TEXAS

COUNTY OF DALLAS

BEFORE ME, _____ Mary Rattan _____

a Notary Public in and for said County, State of Texas, on this day personally appeared _____ _ _ _ _

Roy S. Truly, 4932 Jade Dr., FR6 9893 _____

Who, after being by me duly sworn, on oath deposes and says: I am superintendent of the Texas School Book Depository, 411 Elm Street in Dallas, Texas. I was working in that capacity yesterday Friday November 22, 1963. I have 19 employees in the plant. Lee Harvey Oswald was one of these employees. We considered him a temporary employee. We work a lot of extra employees during the summer and fall. Mr. C. V. Campbell, one of the owners, and I started to lunch a few minutes after twelve o'clock. We saw that the parade was nearly down to us, so we stopped and watched the President go by. After the President passed, we heard what sounded like an explosion. I heard three such explosions. Then I realized that they must have been shots. I saw an officer break t through the crowd and go into our building. I realized he did not know anything about the building, so I ran in with him. The officer and I went through the shipping department to the freight elevator. We then started up the stairway. We hit the second floor landing, the officer stuck his head into the lunch room area where there are coke and candy machines. Lee Oswald was in there. The officer had his gun on Oswald and asked me if he was an employee. I answered yes. We then went up the stairs to the 5th floor where we found the elevator open. We took the elevator to the 7th floor and out on the roof. We searched the roof and a small room, also checked the landings. We could look out over the tracks and street below. We did not find anything. We started down on the elevator. The officer took a hurried look on a couple floors on the way down. We then met some other officers on the 4th floor searching the building. I overheard someone say that the shot came from the window of our building. By that time there was several people in the building. Some fifteen minutes later I was checking our employees, and I did not find Lee. I asked Mr. Shelley if he had seen Lee. He said no. I then contacted Chief Lumpkin and told him Lee was missing. Then both of us went up on the sixth floor where Captain Fritz was and I told Captain Fritz about Lee being missing and where he lived. I did not see Lee Oswald any more. We don't run a thorough check on our temporary employees. They fill out an application form. In Lee Oswald's case, a lady from Irving called and said a neighbor had a brother working for me, and he had said we could use some more help. This woman said she knew a nice young boy

R S Truly

SUBSCRIBED AND SWORN TO BEFORE ME THIS 23 DAY OF November A.D. 1963

Mary Rattan Mary Rattan

Notary Public, Dallas County, Texas

CPS-OF-413

JRL

…the 5th floor where we found the elevator open.

<u>Not</u>: *we saw an elevator*, <u>or</u>: *one of the elevators was there.*
<u>But</u>: *we found **the** elevator **open**.*
Sean said he can only be talking about the west elevator, the "freight elevator" to which he has just a few lines earlier told us, he and the officer had first gone down on the First Floor. The word

"open" is *only* meaningful when talking about that elevator, the elevator that shortly before had refused to come down: this is because that elevator, the west elevator, could be called remotely *as long as it was not open*.

Truly is giving the game away here said Sean: he is telling us that as he and the officer reached the Fifth Floor they discovered the reason why that elevator, the west "freight elevator," had not come down to them on the First Floor: *it was open*. Baker and Truly had in reality used the west elevator all the way up from the First Floor—it had <u>not</u> been open, the gate had been pulled down by Jarman and Norman, making it available for others to call.

Later that day, Sean tells us Truly's story will undergo yet another necessary change: they didn't find an *open west* elevator on the Fifth Floor; he noticed instead that the *east passenger-operated elevator* was still on the Fifth Floor and they ran over to that. In fact, the east elevator was the elevator used by the assassin(s) to come down the building shortly after the assassination. Truly and Baker <u>had</u> to be put upon after the event to hide this fact.

There's a lot more discussion on the details, nuances and permutations involving various people and the movement of the elevators in the "Oswald Leaving TSBD?" thread. I tried to capture the high points here without going off on a tangent. But the subject of the TSBD elevators relating to the assassination is very interesting and worth exploring further.

Sean reminded us that Captain Fritz's purported interrogation notes were released by the Assassination Records Review Board (ARRB) in November 1997. Although Fritz did indeed take these notes down, he did not do so during any of the interrogation sessions. They are in fact a copy he made in his own hand of the interrogation notes of FBI Special Agent James W. Bookhout. <u>Understanding this fact is essential</u> if we are to make sense of what is in these notes—and reconstruct how Oswald actually answered key questions under interrogation.

Here's page 2 of Fritz's copy of Bookhout's notes (Sean reminded us that the transcript below is not his and it contains a number of errors):

4 man left to right as #2   (2)

Time of filing 11:26 pm Johnson Pres 22nd   Precinct 2
                        F154
Received evidence 1st then filed

2nd Interview 23rd
Present 10:35-11:34
T.J. Kelly Robt Nash
Grant ??
B.O + myself
Boyd + Hall

Says 11-22-63 rode bus
got trans same out of pocket
says 1 p.o. box denied bringing
  package to wk. Denied telling Frazier
purpose of going to Irving - denied
curtain rods - got off bus after seeing
jam got cab etc .85 fare told you wrong before
at apt. Changed shirts + tr. Put in dirty clothes - long sleeve red sh
              + gray tr.

Here's the corresponding section of Agent Bookhout's Interrogation Report #4, reproduced in full by Sean except the preamble:

> Following his departure from the Texas School Book Depository, he boarded a city bus to his residence and obtained transfer upon departure from the bus. He stated that officers at the time of arresting him took his transfer out of his pocket.
>
> Oswald advised that he had only one post office box which was in Dallas, Texas. He denied bringing any package to work on the morning of November 22, 1963. He stated that he was not in the process of fixing up his apartment and he denied telling Wesley Frazier that the purpose of his visit to Irving, Texas, on the night of November 21, 1963, was to obtain some curtain rods from Mrs. Ruth Paine.
>
> Oswald stated that it was **not exactly true as recently stated by him that** he rode a bus from his place of employment to his residence on November 22, 1963. He stated actually he did board a city bus at his place of employment but that after a block or two, **due to traffic congestion, he left the bus and rode a city cab** to his apartment on North Beckley. He recalled that at the time of getting into the cab, some lady looked in and asked the driver to call her a cab. He stated that he might have made some remarks to the cab driver merely for the purpose of passing the time of day at that time. He recalled that his **fare was approximately 85 cents**. He stated that after arriving **at his apartment, he changed his shirt and trousers because they were dirty. He described his dirty clothes as being a reddish colored long sleeved, shirt** with a button-down collar and **gray colored trousers**. He indicated that he had placed these articles of clothing in the lower drawer of his dresser.

Continuing:

morning 23rd.   (3)
says 11-21-63   say two negr came in
one Jr. + short negro - ask ? for lunch says cheese
sandwiches + apple

says doesn't pay cash for wife staying with Mrs. Payne
denies owning rifle in garage or elsewhere admits other
things these
                    Came there 63 - N.O.
Says no visitors at apt. Claims never order
owns ???? for gun
denies belonging to Com party
says bgt gun 7 mo Ft W. didn't know what Place.
ams to grest ant questioning
Arv. July 62 from U.S.S.R. Int by F.B.I. Ft W
says Hard + Soft meth etc   Buddy
says on interview of Payne by F.B.I. He thought she was intimidated

The corresponding part of Bookhout's Interrogation Report #4:

Oswald stated that on **November 22, 1963,** he had eaten
lunch in the lunch room at the Texas School Book
Depository, alone, but recalled possibly **two Negro
employees walking through the room during this period.**

He stated possibly **one of these employees was called "Junior" and the other was short individual** whose name he could not recall but whom he would be able to recognize. He stated that his lunch had consisted of a **cheese sandwich and an apple** which he had obtained at Mrs. Ruth Paine's residence in Irving, Texas, upon his leaving for work that morning.

Oswald stated that **Mrs. Paine receives no pay for keeping his wife and children at her residence**. He stated that their presence in Mrs. Paine's residence is a good arrangement for her because of her language interest, indicating that his wife speaks Russian and Mrs. Paine is interested in the Russian language.

Oswald **denied having kept a rifle in Mrs. Paine's garage** at Irving, Texas, but stated that he **did have certain articles stored in her garage**, consisting of two sea bags, a couple of suitcases, and several boxes of kitchen articles and also kept his clothes at Mrs. Paine's residence. He stated that all of the articles in Mrs. Paine's garage had been brought there about **September, 1963, from New Orleans,** Louisiana.

Oswald stated that he **has had no visitors at his apartment** on North Beckley.

Oswald stated that he has no receipts for purchase of any guns and **has never ordered any guns and does not own a rifle** nor has he ever possessed a rifle.

Oswald **denied that he is a member of the Communist Party.**

Oswald stated that he **purchased a pistol**, which was taken off him by police officers November 22, 1963, **about six month ago**. He **declined to state where he had purchased it.**

Oswald stated that he **arrived about July, 1962, from USSR and was interviewed by the FBI at Fort Worth, Texas.** He stated that he felt they overstepped their bounds and had used **various tactics in interviewing him.**

He further complained that **on interview of Ruth Paine by the FBI** regarding his wife, that he **felt that his wife was intimidated.**

And finally:

(4)

Desires to talk to Mr. Abt. I ask who
says Smith act att.
Says did live N.O. 4706 Magazine St. From Apt.
Wked Wm B. Riley Co 640
says nothing against Pres does not want to
 talk further -   No Pahy at time in past had
refused
Oswald A.C.L.U. member he says says
Mrs. Payne was too. I ask abt organization
he says to pay lawyer fees when needed
B.O. asks about Heidel selective s. Card - adm having
would not admit signature - wouldn't say
why he had it. Says add. Book has names of Russian
Emigrants he visits - denies shooting Pres says didn't know
Gov. shot

The corresponding concluding section of Bookhout's Interrogation Report #4:

Oswald stated that he **desired to contact Attorney Abt,** New York City, indicating that Abt was the **attorney who had defended the Smith Act** case about 1949-1950. He stated that he does not know Attorney Abt personally. Captain Fritz advised Oswald that arrangement would be immediately made whereby he could call Attorney Abt.

Oswald stated that prior to coming to Dallas from New Orleans he had resided at a **furnished apartment at 4706 Magazine Street, New Orleans**, Louisiana. While in New Orleans, he had been employed by **William B. Reily Company**, 640 Magazine Street, New Orleans.

Oswald **stated that he has nothing against President John F. Kennedy personally**; however in view of the present charges against him, **he did not desire to discuss this phase further.**

Oswald stated that he **would not agree to take a polygraph** examination without the advice of counsel. He added that **in the past he has refused** to take polygraph examinations.

Oswald stated that he is a member of the American Civil Liberties Union and added that Mrs. Ruth Paine was also a member of same.

With regard to **Selective Service card** in the possession of Oswald bearing photograph of Oswald and the name of Alek James **Hidell, Oswald admitted that he carried this Selective Service card but declined to state that he wrote the signature of Alek J. Hidell** appearing on same. He further **declined to state the purpose of carrying same or any use he has made of same**.

Oswald stated that an **address book in his possession contains the names of various Russian immigrants residing in Dallas, Texas, whom he has visited with.**

Oswald **denied shooting President John F. Kennedy** on November 22, 1963, and added that he **did not know that Governor John Connally had been shot** and denied any knowledge concerning this incident.

Again, Sean reminds us, the "Fritz notes" are *not* contemporaneous notes taken by Fritz himself, but the copy he himself made of FBI Special Agent James W. Bookhout's contemporaneous notes. This fact is nicely brought home in the following little detail:

"Myself." Sean tells us if these notes were really being written by Fritz in real time during the interrogation session, the last thing he would need to be noting down for future reference would be the duh-level-obvious fact that he himself is one of the people present in the room! No, Fritz is copying from Bookhout's interrogation notes and, seeing the word "Fritz," naturally translating it as "myself."

Here is the fifth and final page of the "Fritz notes":

(5)

3rd 11-23 - 6:35

Shows photo of gun. Would not discuss photo
denies buying gun from Kleins.
Comp of wanting jacket for line up.
Says I made picture super imposed

arr 10-11:15
4th.   11-24   Insp Holmes - Sorrels - Kelley et al

Chief

From his own original of these notes, Sean says Bookhout wrote up his short and sweet Interrogation Report #5:

Date 11/25/63
Lee Harvey Oswald was interviewed at the Homicide and Robbery Bureau, Dallas Police Department, at **6:35 p.m**.... **Captain J. W. Fritz exhibited to Lee Harvey Oswald a photograph** which had been obtained by the Dallas Police Department in a search by search warrant, of the garage at the residence of Mrs. Ruth Paine, located at Irving, Texas, **which photograph reflects Oswald holding a rifle and wearing a holstered pistol**. Oswald was asked if this was a photograph of himself. **Oswald stated that he would not discuss the photograph** without advice of an attorney. He stated that the head of the individual in the photograph could be his but **that it was entirely possible that the Police Department had superimposed** this part of the photograph over the body of someone else. He pointed out that numerous news media had snapped his photograph during the day and the possibility existed that the police had doctored up this photograph.
Oswald denied that he had purchased any rifle from Klein's Store in Chicago, Illinois.
Oswald complained of a lineup wherein he had not been granted a request to put on a jacket similar to those worn by some of the other individuals in the lineup.
On 11/23/63 at Dallas, Texas. File#DL89-43 by Special Agent James W. Bookhout /wvm. Date dictated 11/24/63.

Sean says to track Police Chief Jesse Curry's evolving statements to reporters over that Friday and Saturday about the first post-assassination sighting of Oswald is to track the evolution of the story itself. On Friday evening Curry was admitting candidly that Oswald had been stopped leaving the building very shortly after the assassination:

Pro-Castro Fort Worth Marxist Charged in Kennedy's Assassination

From News Dispatches

DALLAS, Nov. 22 — Lee Harvey Oswald, 24, a pro-Castro Marxist, was charged tonight in the assassination of President Kennedy.

Police Chief Jesse Curry said the one-time U.S. Marine hid on the sixth floor of a textbook warehouse where he worked and snapped off the three quick shots that killed the President and wounded Gov. John B. Connally of Texas.

Earlier in the day, Oswald was charged with murdering Dallas policeman J. D. Tippitt, 38, who attempted to stop and question the man.

Oswald was arraigned on this charge before Justice of the Peace David Johnson and Curry said the case would be presented to the grand jury next week.

Curry told of the frenzied moments after the shooting when Oswald slipped through officers' hands as he fled the building.

Allowed to Leave Building

"He apparently got out of the building during the time we were surrounding it," Curry said. As an officer rushed into the building Oswald rushed out. The policeman permitted him to pass after the building manager told the policeman that Oswald was an employe.

"He apparently lost himself in the crowd, then," Curry added.

The building from which the gunman fired on the President is the headquarters of the Texas School Book Depository. Police said that Oswald had worked there for about six weeks as a laborer.

The firm does work for the public schools in relation to textbooks but is privately owned, police said.

Oswald, chairman of a local "Fair Play for Cuba Committee," has denied being involved in any way in the President's slaying.

"I did not kill the President. I did not kill anyone," Oswald said.

He admitted being an employe of the book firm, police reported. The suspect has been unable to account for his whereabouts at the time of the shooting, police said.

Policemen Shot

Shortly after the assassination, Patrolman Tippitt stopped Oswald on the strength of a lookout which had been flashed for the man. Authorities apparently became suspicious of Oswald after the first officer told them he had fled the building.

When Tippitt stopped Oswald a short distance from the scene of the shooting, the suspect drew a gun and shot the policeman, police said. Then he fled as witnesses notified police.

A short time later the cashier of a movie theater in the Oak Cliff section of Dallas, called police and told them that a man had run into the theater. The description matched that of Oswald.

The theater is located about five blocks from where Tippitt was killed.

Four policemen were dispatched to the theater. The movie was in progress, but only a dozen or so people were there. An usher led

See ARREST, A12, Col. 1

WASH. Post
11/23/63

151

Sean surmised that this very incident of Marrion Baker asking Oswald/Prayer Man if he worked there (i.e. could he point him to the stairs), could have clearly exonerated him as the Sixth Floor shooter. However, the Dallas Police Department's crucial spin of misprision made it appear that Oswald was clearly guilty. They described Oswald, *not* as a man who appeared on the front steps in time for the shooting, but as a man who had just that moment reached the front of the building and was leaving with suspicious haste. (Curry at this stage probably wasn't aware that Oswald was making this very claim in custody, so he wasn't even aware that he himself was blurting out the details of Oswald's alibi.):

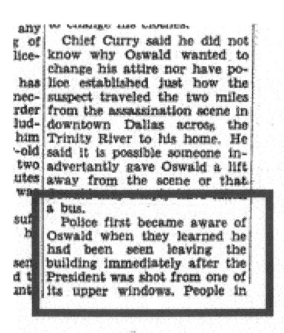

any | to change his attire.
g of | Chief Curry said he did not
lice- | know why Oswald wanted to
| change his attire nor have po-
has | lice established just how the
nec- | suspect traveled the two miles
rder | from the assassination scene in
lud- | downtown Dallas across the
him | Trinity River to his home. He
-old | said it is possible someone in-
two | advertantly gave Oswald a lift
utes | away from the scene or that
w: |
| a bus.
su: | Police first became aware of
h | Oswald when they learned he
| had been seen leaving the
se: | building immediately after the
d t | President was shot from one of
int | its upper windows. People in

President Kennedy slumps against his wife as the bullet from an assassin's rifle strikes him in the head. Gov. Connally, who was wounded in the attack begins to turn around just to the left of Mrs. Kennedy. This picture of Friday's assassination was made by Mrs. Mary Ann Moorman, wife of a Dallas plumber.—AP Wirephoto.

DALLAS

Captured Suspect Clings to Denial
That He Fired Shots Fatal to Kennedy

Continued From Page A-1

able discharge from the Marine Reserve. The request was denied.

Chief Curry was asked if police are considering the possibility that the sniper who killed President Kennedy may have been aiming at Texas Gov. Connally. He said he did not think so because the President was hit twice while the Texas Governor suffered only one wound.

Added to the case against the self-proclaimed Communist sympathizer and admirer of Fidel Castro was an FBI disclosure that it had made paraffin tests of Oswald's skin and found definite traces of nitrate (an ingredient of gunpowder) on both his hands. No traces of gunpowder were found on Oswald's face, the tests disclosed.

down the President and seriously wounded Gov. Connally.

The two bullets that mortally wounded the President in the head and neck are considered to be in relatively good condition for ballistics testing techniques. One of the bullets, as was learned, was found on the stretcher that bore President Kennedy from his car into the Dallas Hospital where he died. It apparently had fallen clear after penetrating the President's body.

Dallas police said they expect to receive reports on the laboratory tests late today or tomorrow but already are on record as saying they consider the evidence against Oswald to be "ample."

The rifle and three expended cartridge shells were found on the sixth floor of the Texas School Book Depository building overlooking the roadway

grand jury next Wednesday or on Monday, December 2.

If the grand jury returns indictments against Oswald, the Prosecutor said he expects he will be able to go to trial no later than January. Oswald will be tried for the murder of Kennedy first. District Attorney Wade declared.

He said Oswald, who now is being held without bond for the grand jury, is entitled to appear himself or present witnesses of his own to the secret panel. However, he said the suspect is not required to do this.

If indicted, Oswald is entitled to a habeas corpus hearing to determine if he can be held without bond, but Mr. Wade pointed out that Texas law provides that no bond be set in cases involving capital crimes.

Mr. Wade said he will de-

the building. Chief Curry said, thought nothing of it at the time because, to them, Oswald belonged there. Later, however, police decided to investigate him because of his quick departure, and a radio lookout was broadcast.

pitt, 39-year-old father of three, may have recognized Oswald on the street from the description and tried to question him.

Witnesses said Oswald fled one block on foot after shooting the policeman in the forehead and was trapped in the Texas Theater where he had taken refuge.

Meanwhile, Oswald's family rallied to his support. His blond, 22-year-old Russianborn wife, Marina, carrying their infant daughter in her arms, gave every indication she

Sean says this is not one of those early false rumors; it is one of those early true facts—and Curry is only too happy to tell the world about it:

Pro-Castro Marxist Held as Top Assassination Suspe

Patrolman M. N. MacDonald, to where Oswald was sitting. Oswald, according to police, jumped up and said, "This is it." He pulled a snub-nosed revolver and tried to shoot MacDonald, but the gun misfired, police said. The four officers jumped on the suspect. He fought wildly until they handcuffed him and dragged him to a car.

Asked what tended to confirm police suspicion that Oswald was connected with the slaying, Chief Curry responded that as a speculative matter his background of criticism of the President's Cuban policy might have proved a motive.

Secondly, the Chief said, there was "the opportunity he had. The fact that he worked there. He was placed there. He was seen to leave there immediately after it happened."

During the day, police brought to light the checkered career of Oswald which included an other than honorable discharge from the Marine Corps, defection to Russia in 1959 and his pro-Castro activities.

Police made several paraffin tests on Oswald, including one on his cheek. They said

this might prove whether he had fired a rifle recently. They did not announce the results of the test.

District Attorney Henry Wade declined to say whether fingerprints were found on the murder weapon.

After telling waiting reporters of the new charge against Oswald, police led the crew-cut Fort Worth man of 5 feet 9 inches into an assembly room so that photographers and newsreel cameramen might photograph the man charged with the murder of President Kennedy.

Police said FBI agents questioned both Oswald and his brother, Robert, of Denton. Oswald's Russian wife, who does not speak English, was brought to police headquarters and was questioned through interpreters. His wife lives in suburban Irving. Last Oct. 14 Oswald rented a box-like room for $8 per week from Mr. and Mrs. A. C. Johnson in Dallas.

Mrs. R. C. Roberts, who works for the Johnsons, said that about 12:45 p.m. (CST) today she had just learned that Mr. Kennedy had been shot when Oswald rushed into the house.

"He ran to his room, came running back with a gray zip-

per jacket, and out the door." Police found a leather pistol holster and some books on communism and political magazines in his 8-by-15-foot room.

As more details of Oswald's part became available police reported that they found a .765 German army Mauser rifle in the school book building where Oswald worked.

Beside it were three empty shells. One cartridge remained in the chamber of the rifle.

Oswald was born in New Orleans, Oct. 18, 1939. Twenty years later, on Oct. 30, 1959, he appeared at the American Embassy in Moscow, telling officials that he wanted to renounce his American citizenship. At the time, he was reported to have told officials that "I am a Marxist."

The FBI confirmed that Oswald did go to Russia and had asked for Soviet citizenship. He had then recently been discharged from the Marine Corps.

Oswald told the Embassy officials that he planned to tell Soviet officials everything he learned while he was a radar operator during his three-year enlistment in the Marines. Embassy officials said Russia never granted Oswald's request for citizenship.

In February, 1962, he apparently had a change of heart. He wrote the Embassy asking for a passport to the United States. In the meantime he

Secondly, the Chief said, there was "the opportunity he had. The fact that he worked there. He was placed there. He was seen to leave there immediately after it happened."

t Is Also Accused of Killing Policeman

ad married a Russian woman, Marina Nicholaevna, a hospital employe in the city of Minsk. They have one child. Embassy officials reviewed his case. Since he had not been given Soviet citizenship, it was decided to give him a passport to the United States. Government records show he left Moscow at the end of May, 1962. The Embassy advanced him $435 to defray the cost of his trip, a customary practice in the cases of Americans stranded in a foreign nation.

According to Carlos Brin ... of the Cuban Student Directory in New Orleans, Oswald was in the city two months ago as the chairman of

a pro-Castro "Fair Play for Cuba Committee." He was reported to have been arrested for allegedly distributing pro-Communist propaganda on a street corner. The House Committee on Un-American Activities said Oswald "appears to be" the same man who headed a Fair Play for Cuba committee in New Orleans.

This year Oswald applied for another passport. He told the State Department he wanted to visit England, France, Germany, Holland, Finland, Italy, Poland, and the Soviet Union.

The passport was issued at New Orleans June 23, 1963. It

is not clear, however, if Oswald ever repaid the money loaned for his passage back to the United States on his first trip.

Sean tells us Curry on Friday evening needs to stress the "immediate" nature of the Oswald-Officer incident, and hence the incriminatingly immediate nature of Oswald's departure from the building. But as soon as it becomes clear just how "immediate" the incident was and how soon after the last shot had been fired, Curry shuts the hell up. And so the next day we find him going out to bat with a very different story altogether:

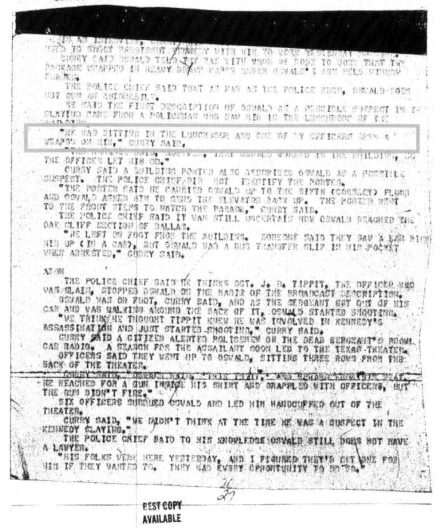

And again:

POLICE TELL STORY OF SWIFT CAPTURE

Big Force on Dallas Parade Route Able to Move Fast

By DONALD JANSON

DALLAS, Nov. 23—Police Chief Jesse E. Curry reconstructed today the swift steps that led to the apprehension of Lee H. Oswald.

Moments after the fatal shot was fired at President Kennedy at 12:30 P. M. yesterday, Chief Curry said, he radioed instructions that the Texas School Book Depository Building be surrounded and searched. Oswald, who worked in the building, has been charged with the assassination of the President.

The chief was riding in a car 40 feet ahead of the limousine carrying Mr. and Mrs. Kennedy and Gov. and Mrs. John B. Connally Jr. of Texas. The motorcade was on its way to the Trade Mart where the President was to have spoken at a lunch. Chief Curry said he could tell from the sound of the three shots that they had come from the book company building near downtown Dallas.

The department of 800 officers from his 1,100-man force along the route made fast action possible in the manhunt.

The first officer to reach the depository building, Lieut. Curry said, found Oswald among other persons in a lunchroom. But the building manager identified Oswald as an employe of the book-distribution concern that used the building. Oswald was questioned then.

When the main force of the investigating officers reached the building Oswald had left.

The police had found on the sixth floor the rifle they believed was the assassination weapon.

An elevator operator, the other said, revealed having taken Oswald to the top floor before the motorcade passed by.

Soon after a description had been broadcast, Patrolman J. D. Tippit saw a man who seemed to answer it. The man was on a sidewalk in suburban Oak Cliff, about two miles from the book depository building.

When Mr. Tippit got out of the car to question the suspect, he was shot and killed with a revolver, Mr. Curry said. A

citizen used the squad car radio to report this at 1:18 P.M., about 50 minutes after the President was shot. Policemen then converged on the area.

The killer of Patrolman Tippit fled on foot, witnesses said. A police search of surrounding buildings yielded nothing. Then a call from Julia Postal, cashier of the Texas Theater six blocks from the patrolman was slain, reported that an agitated man had entered the movie house.

Chief Curry and all officers searched the theater and found Oswald on the main floor in the third row from the back.

When Patrolman M. N. McDonald approached him, he sprang up, the police reported, and shouted:

"This is it!"

He reached for a revolver in his shirt, but was disarmed after a scuffle.

In the scuffle, Oswald received a black eye and a cut on his forehead.

He pulled the trigger before the gun was wrested from him, but the gun did not fire. The arrest came about 30 minutes after the assassination.

Accused of Murder

At police headquarters, Oswald was questioned for five hours, then arraigned for the murder of Patrolman Tippit at 7:15.

The interrogation, directed by Capt. Will Fritz, head of the Dallas Homicide Bureau, continued until midnight. At 1:30 A.M. today Oswald was arraigned on charges of murdering the President. He denied both charges. The questioning of Oswald was resumed this morning.

The police sent the confiscated revolver and the Italian-made military rifle found in the book depository building to the Federal Bureau of Investigation's crime laboratory in Washington.

Fingerprints and other evidence also were flown there late yesterday, Chief Curry said.

In the search of the book company's building, the police found the rifle hidden among stacks of books and boxes.

The police also found three spent shells and an unspent bullet, a soft-drink bottle, an empty cigarette package, a piece of chicken and a sack with chicken bones. Chief Curry said a palm print on a cardboard box at the window checked with prints of Oswald's palm taken later at police headquarters.

The manhunt and investigation were aided from the beginning, he said, by the F.B.I. and state highway patrolmen and Dallas County sheriff's officers.

Normal Use of DDT Is Found No Peril to Cutthroat Trout

JACKSON, Wyo. (Science News)—The concentration of DDT in brook water after normal insecticide use is not sufficient to kill the cutthroat trout (Salmo clarkii lewisi) and is not likely to interfere with a fishery, a team of Government scientists reported in Science, journal of the American Association for the Advancement of Science.

The statement was made here by Oliver B. Cope and Charles C. Van Valin of the Fish-Pesticide Research Laboratory, United States Bureau of Sport Fisheries and Wildlife, Denver, Colo.; Don Allison of the Fish - Pesticide Research Laboratory, Jackson, Wyo., and Burton J. Kallman of the Vedrans Administration Center, Los Angeles.

Students See-Saw 10 Hours

NOTTINGHAM, England (Canadian Press)—Two Nottingham University students say they have set a world see-saw record. They rocked for 10 hours as a charity stunt.

From Oswald being stopped as he walked out the front entrance, *to* Oswald being seen sitting in a Second Floor lunchroom: the fix was in. But, Sean says, we'll see it didn't work.

Sean said the theory he's been outlining does not require Roy Truly to be "in" on the conspiracy to assassinate President Kennedy. If Truly had really vouched for a non-employee by the Third or Fourth Floor rear stairway, then it would be hard to see how he could not have been in on the plot. But Sean's theory has him performing actions that are not suspicious. Nor are they even foolhardy, he said. Rather than take to the rear stairs ahead of an armed officer, as per the later lunchroom fiction, Truly simply gets on an elevator with him and (as per Bonnie Ray Williams' information) stays on the elevator while Baker gets off to check out upper floors.

But if Truly is innocent, why does he later shop Oswald to Captain Fritz as "missing" so very quickly? Does this not indicate a key role for him in the "patsification" of his employee?

Not necessarily, says Sean. It has always been deeply puzzling why Truly should tell Fritz about Oswald without mentioning in the same breath that he had seen this employee of his in the Second Floor lunchroom right after the shooting. Surely it would have been salient information?

Sean believes what may have actually happened is this:

- Truly ran into the First Floor after Baker and, just as Baker was engaging with Oswald/Prayer Man, introduced himself and offered to accompany the officer.
- After coming down from the roof with Baker, he noticed that Oswald was gone and incorrectly assumed that Oswald must have been on his way out of the building when Baker had passed him.
- This strikes him—understandably—as an odd and indecent kind of haste on his employee's part and so he conscientiously reports it to Fritz.

In alerting Fritz to Oswald, however, Sean tells us the very furthest thing from his mind is that Oswald could be an actual shooter. All he is worried about is that Oswald may have been in some way involved in the plot such that he needed to leave the scene very quickly. What must have been Truly's astonishment when he later learned that Oswald was being treated by police as—of all ridiculous things!—the Sixth Floor shooter? He must have felt much as Marrion Baker had when he saw Oswald being brought into the Homicide Office and was told this was the man the police had been after.

Page 5 of the "Fritz Notes," at the top of which Fritz notates the date and time of the interrogation session (11-23 - 6.35):

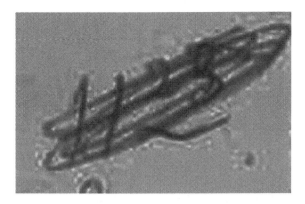

3rd. 11-23-6.35 -

Shows photo of gun - would not discuss Photo
denied buying gun from Kleins.
Comp of wanting jacket for time up.
says I made picture superimposed
4th. 11-24-   Insp Holmes - Sorrel- et al Kelley
          Chief

Except that's not quite what he does, says Sean. For the first
thing he writes is:

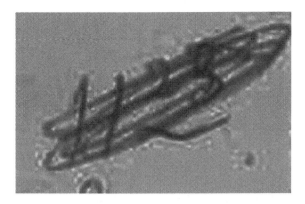

11 23: He's confused Bookhout's date notation with a time
notation. And then, coming to Bookhout's next entry—"6.35"—he
realizes his error and corrects it:

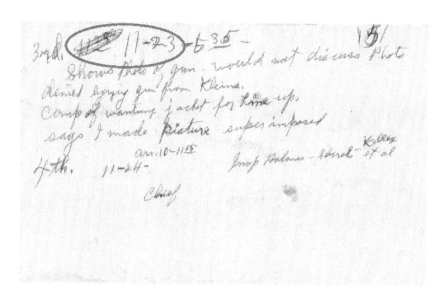

Date: 11-23. Time: 6.35.

Page 1 of "Fritz's Notes":

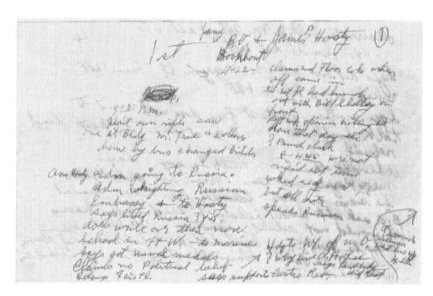

Another telling deletion:

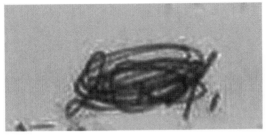

2nd to 1st: Fritz is hardly sitting in that first interrogation wondering to himself, "Now is this my first interrogation session with this suspect or my second?" asks Sean. No, he's jotting down a copy of Bookhout's notes and isn't sure at first which session it is covering. Once he gets clear on this he corrects 2nd to 1st, confirming the change with an arrow pointing to the date: 11/22.

Dougherty's Warren Commission testimony is a mess, says Sean, but his basic story does have one very important thing going for it: it was the story he told consistently from the very start.

Here's his November 22 affidavit, given within two hours of the assassination:

AFFIDAVIT IN ANY FACT

THE STATE OF TEXAS
COUNTY OF DALLAS

BEFORE ME, _____ Patsy Collins _____

a Notary Public in and for said County, State of Texas, on this day personally appeared ___ Jack E. Dougherty

___ w/m/40, 1827 So. Marsalis   WH-6-7170 _____

Who, after being by me duly sworn, on oath deposes and says: I am employed at the Texas School Book Depository at 411 Elm and have been since 1952. I was working on the sixth floor today. There was six of us working on the floor. The others were Bill Lovelady, William Shelby, Danny Arce, Bennie Williams, and Charles Givens. I worked until 12:00 noon, and went down on the first floor and ate my lunch and went back to work at 12:45 p.m. I had already gone back to work and I gone down on the fifth to get some stock when I heard a shot. It sounded like it was coming from inside the building, but I couldn't tell from where. I went down on the first floor, and asked a man named Eddie Piper if he had heard anything and he said yes, that he had heard three shots. I then went back on the sixth floor. I didn't see anyone on the floor except the people I named. There was another employee that is named Lee Oswald that I saw on the sixth floor. He works all over the building, but I saw him on the sixth floor shortly before noon. I didn't see Oswald in the building after lunch.XXXXXXXXXXXXXXXXXXXXXXXXXX

Jack E Dougherty

SUBSCRIBED AND SWORN TO BEFORE ME THIS 22 DAY OF November A.D. 1963

Patsy Collins
Notary Public, Dallas County, Texas

CPS-OF-413

And here's Dougherty's FBI interview from the same day:

FEDERAL BUREAU OF INVESTIGATION

1

Date 11/23/63

JACK EDWIN DOUGHERTY, 1827 South Marsalis, was contacted on November 22, 1963, and furnished the following signed statement:

"Dallas, Texas
11-22-63

"I, Jack Edwin Dougherty, make the following free and voluntary statement to Alfred C. Ellington and James W. Anderton who have identified themselves to me as Special Agents of the FBI.

"I am employed by the Texas School Book Depository, 411 Elm Street, Dallas as an order filler, and reside at 1827 S. Marsalis St., Dallas, Texas.

"I started to work today, 11/22/63, at about 7:00 AM o'clock.

"I recall vaguely, having seen Lee Oswald, (who started to work for the Texas School Book Depository about 3 weeks ago) when he came to work at about 8:00 AM today. I saw Oswald again about 11:00 AM today and do not recall seeing him at work after 11:00 AM.

"I was working on the 5th floor of the building at 411 Elm Street at about 12:45 PM or 1:00 PM, when I heard a loud explosion which sounded like a rifle shot coming from the next floor above me.

"I did not see anyone running from the building and did not see anyone fire the shot which I heard.

"I have read this Statement and this is true.

"/s/ JACK EDWIN DOUGHERTY

"Witnessed:
"/s/ ALFRED C. ELLINGTON, Special Agent, FBI, Dallas, 11/22/63.
"/s/ JAMES W. ANDERTON, Special Agent, FBI, Dallas, 11/22/63."

366

| 11/22/63 | | Dallas, Texas | | File # | DL 89-43 |

by Special Agent ALFRED C. ELLINGTON & JAMES W. ANDERTON/rab   Date dictated 11/23/63

This document contains neither recommendations nor conclusions of the FBI. It is the property of the FBI and is loaned to your agency; it and its contents are not to be distributed outside your agency.

Sean believes Jack Dougherty:

- is telling the truth in these first-day statements.
- is wholly innocent of any involvement in the assassination.

- has genuine cognitive problems, as evidenced not only in the statements which Roy Truly and Jack's own father will make on that score but also in his peculiar response pattern during his Warren Commission appearance.

Sean also believes his first-day statements above contain a vital clue that has been telling us all along how Jack really came down from the Fifth Floor just after the shooting: he ran down the stairs. Here's the clue:

```
f us working on the floor.  The othe
ny Arce, Bennie Williams, and C arle
went down on the first floor and ate
m.  I had already gone back to work
k when I heard a shot.  It sounded l
ng, but I couldn't tell from where.
  a man named Eddie Piper if he had h
heard three shots.  I then went back
n the floor except the people I name
```

```
"I was working on the 5th floor of the building at
411 Elm Street      about 12:45 PM or 1:00 PM  then I
he     a loud explosion    ich sounded lik  a rifle shot
coming from        ext floor above me.
```

Sean then tells us how he sees it. If Jack were inventing the trip up to the Fifth Floor, why on earth would he be telling us he heard just one shot—and then going on to point out the strangeness of this fact by telling us that Eddie Piper told him he had heard three shots? Surely if he were inventing he would make sure to harmonize the number of shots he heard with the number of shots he subsequently learned there had been? No, Sean's suggesting we take Dougherty's first-day affidavit at face value and see where its contents lead us.

Sean asked how a man could be at the rear of the Fifth Floor, some ten feet west of the west freight elevator, and hear only one shot. He covers the limited options:

1. There was only one shot fired from the Sixth Floor.
2. Due to adjustments in the position of the rifle at the window, only the first shot boomed loudly within the building.

3. Jack's reaction to the first shot was to stick his head deep inside a box full of cotton wool, plug his fingers in his ears or do something to make it possible for a man on the Fifth Floor to stop hearing loud noises.
4. Jack's reaction to the first shot was to make a terrified dash to the noisy, wooden-planked and enclosed rear stairway and run downstairs for his life.

Concerning the first point, Sean said he's aware this view has some adherents, but he's not one of them. Bonnie Ray Williams' earliest statements speak of two shots sounding as if they came from just over him.

On the second point, there may have been some variation in the inside-the-room boom levels, but Sean said he finds it very hard to believe that Jack could have remained standing there on the Fifth Floor after the first shot and heard nothing else by way of bang, pop, or what have you.

The third point is a nonstarter.

On the fourth point, Sean says Jack's description of his location some ten feet west of the west elevator is also a description of his location very near the down stairs.

If there was one place in his vicinity where the noise of a subsequent shot or shots might have failed to reach his ears, it was the very noisy stairwell down which a man (he himself) was stomping. But why would Jack react so quickly to that first shot?

Because he knew it was a rifle shot, Sean said. For, just prior to this, he had had the misfortune of wandering up to the Sixth Floor to get a bird's eye view of the motorcade only to see several strangers up there, including at least one man holding a rifle. That's why, the instant he heard the loud bang upstairs while down on the Fifth Floor, he knew exactly what it was. And he ran.

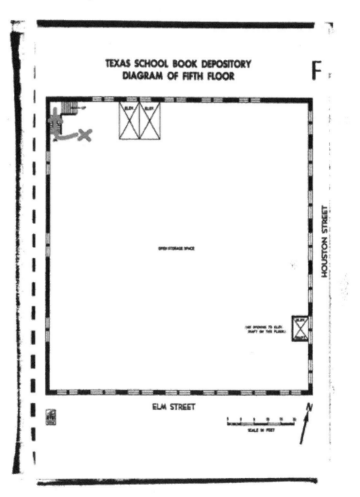

Robert Prudhomme said he sees exactly what Sean means now. Yes, it is possible Jack Dougherty returned to work on the Sixth Floor early enough to stumble upon the proceedings in the Sniper's Nest. And he may have just had time to descend to the Fifth Floor when the first shot went off. He certainly could not have spent much time on the Fifth Floor, or, no doubt, he would have been spotted by Williams, Norman and Jarman.

Yes, Robert said, when explained like this, it makes perfect sense. Jack hears the first shot, covers the ten feet to the stairwell and is heading downstairs, making a great deal of noise, before the second shot is fired, which, of course, he does not hear.

"Brilliant bit of deduction, Sean," said Robert.

Chapter Six Recap

Another intense week has passed with a ton of information to consider and digest. Where are we?

- A first-day Case Report filed by Captain Will Fritz states that M. L. Baker identified Lee Oswald in a police lineup. This is *not* true.
- There is no record of a specific answer to the most obvious question Lee Oswald should have been asked—"Where exactly were you at the time of the assassination?" Only a general answer—"On the First Floor."
- This vagueness is indicative not of Oswald's refusal to give specifics, but of the investigating authorities' refusal to allow his specific answer to be entered into the official record.
- That specific answer involved Oswald being out in front and eating his lunch.
- Truly and Baker never ran up the rear stairway. They ran to the rear of the First Floor and took the west elevator up.

- The story about Baker and Truly taking the stairway up to the Fifth Floor allowed for an Oswald sighting, which evolved into the Second Floor lunchroom encounter.
- There is evidence that key statements made by Oswald while in custody were distorted. Fritz's copying of FBI Special Agent James W. Bookhout's original rough notes ("Fritz notes") supplies much of this evidence.
- That the "Fritz notes" are not contemporaneous notes taken real time by Fritz himself, but the copy he himself made of Bookhout's contemporaneous interrogation notes is supported by the fact he refers to himself ("myself") as one of the people present in the room.
- Jesse Curry's evolving statements to reporters over the first few days mirrors the evolving nature of Oswald being on the First Floor to the Third or Fourth Floors to the final Second Floor lunchroom encounter story.
- Seeing strangers and a rifle on the Sixth Floor before the assassination, Jack Dougherty on the Fifth Floor heard one loud bang and, realizing it was a rifle shot, ran down the noisy stairs, not hearing anything else.

The official story of the assassination of President Kennedy is laden with unwarranted assumptions, conflicting evidence, and strange coincidences. Sean Murphy's work shows us why these should always be mistrusted and thoroughly examined.

CHAPTER SEVEN – FINISHING WORK

Every picture tells a story.

– Stewart and Wood

September 7, 2013. I'm running out of superlatives to describe the brilliant research and reasoning of Sean Murphy that's been on display here. And to think this whole thread got started over a question on the identity of an unknown person in a low-resolution frame from a film. Even without that image, Sean has made a strong and convincing case that Lee Oswald was down in front during the shots that killed President Kennedy.

During this past week I discovered Greg Parker's ReopenKennedyCase (ROKC) website and forum and I became a member. They are following the "Oswald Leaving TSBD?" thread with great interest. Greg and the ROKC members seem to be able to quickly recognize the important from the trivial. Right away I felt at home and welcome there.

Robin Unger told Sean he may have to rename Prayer Man *Prayer Woman*. He got some new Darnell frames from the Blu-ray version of the movie *JFK*[69] and thought the person standing there looked like a woman. Robin made the images available for downloading. He furnished a quick sample frame:

Sean thanked Robin, for uploading the higher-quality frames, but said he certainly will not be renaming Prayer Man "Prayer Woman" because the frame above puts the matter pretty much beyond doubt: **This is Lee Oswald.**

The womanly appearance is due to the fact that:

- His sleeves are rolled up.
- The back of a woman's head in front of part of Lee's torso makes it look distorted.

Here's the woman in question's lower leg and foot:

Sean said if you place your finger to the screen to cover where her head should be, the chief source of the "Prayer Woman" illusion becomes apparent.

This is Lee Oswald, he said. Just look at the hairline. And speaking of hairlines, this frame tells us something else: Buell Wesley Frazier knew—*knows*—Lee is innocent.

Someone urgently needs to show this image to him, said Sean.

Yowza, yowza, yowza! Is this a stunning find or what! I see Oswald here! Look at the hairline! And, yes, look at Buell Wesley Frazier! A strong case has already been made that Prayer Man is Lee Oswald. These images are icing on the cake!

Robert Prudhomme said he's studied the new frames and can find nothing that would indicate this person is a woman.

Robin Unger said his conclusion was reached before he was able to seriously examine the higher resolution images. He now thinks Prayer Man is probably a man, but as to him being Oswald, he'll defer judgment until a later time.

The single most important thing to note about these Darnell frames—and Sean says this after having carefully inspected several times every frame Robin uploaded—is that in one frame, *and one frame only*, does Prayer Man's head come into any kind of clear focus. The moment when that happens is a startling one…

…for it shows us not just that this is a man but that it is a man with Lee Oswald's hairline.

Sean said the lingering doubts he had when looking at previous images of Prayer Man related chiefly to his apparent baldness: where was the Oswald hair?

The clear frame above puts paid to that question, and definitively, he said:

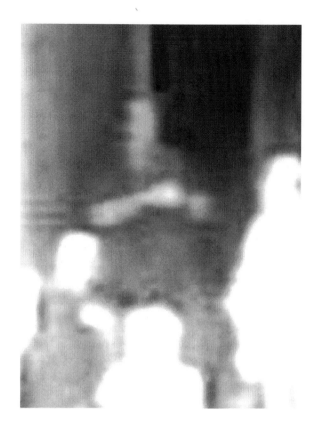

Now all things being equal, this man would be a toss-up between Billy Lovelady and Lee Oswald. But all things *are not* equal, Sean said. We know—for an absolute irrefutable fact, one backed up by the hard evidence of Wiegman movie frames—that Billy Lovelady was standing next to Prayer Man during the actual shooting. So this can *only* be Lee Oswald. And the man near him can *only* be Buell Wesley Frazier (who was put forward several times earlier as a candidate for Prayer Man)—his hairline and hairstyle are just too distinctive to allow any serious doubt on that score.

"Game over," said Sean.

Robin Unger said he doesn't recall ever seeing Lee Oswald in a shirt with the sleeves rolled up:

Sean replied that Oswald is reported as having told Fritz that he changed shirts at his N. Beckley apartment, which would make the arrest shirt irrelevant to Prayer Man images. The shirt he's wearing in the Prayer Man frames is either short sleeved or long sleeved with sleeves rolled up. Sean goes with the latter because Bookhout's contemporaneous interrogation notes (whose contents we know thanks to Fritz's handwritten copy) make mention of a long sleeve red/reddish shirt. It's hardly a stretch to imagine Oswald rolling up his sleeves while getting stock. And the reason we don't have any images of him with sleeves rolled up is that we don't have any images of him engaged in manual labor.

Sean said the improved Darnell frames show that Buell Wesley Frazier must have noticed Lee Oswald there. No wonder they gave him such a hard time down at Dallas Police Department Headquarters that night. He thinks it's perfectly possible that not a single other employee noticed Lee slipping out on to the steps just in time for the motorcade or standing by the front-entrance vestibule door just after the shooting.

Sean uses the word "employee" advisedly: Roy Truly did notice Lee there just after the shooting, for that's where and when the Baker encounter really happened.

There's no way that Buell Wesley Frazier didn't see Prayer Man. He's only a few feet away and looking toward him. Why has he been silent on this?

Member Ian Kingsbury asked Sean if this frame should be shown to the public so they can decide, adding that Buell Wesley Frazier will speak through others from now on or suffer a nasty "accident."

Sean said many pages back in the thread it was established beyond doubt that the only TSBD employee Prayer Man could conceivably be is Lee Oswald. All other candidates—Frazier, Lovelady, Molina, Otis Williams, Bill Shelley—were definitively ruled out. He said we all remember how quickly poor David Von Pein (an avid and very busy defender of the Warren Commission) found other things to do once he realized his wiggle room on this issue was precisely zilch. Each improvement in Darnell image quality has only made the case for this being Oswald more and more compelling.

Now let's not kid ourselves here as to the magnitude of what has just happened, said Sean. If a bona fide image even a quarter as clear as this one had emerged in recent days of a man at the Sniper's Nest window at assassination time, this would have been hailed by Warren Commission defenders as the final nail in the critics' ("kooks" to people such as Von Pein) collective coffin.

Well, Sean asked, things have not turned out quite that way, have they? It seems the Warren Commission defenders are left with one pitiful option if they are to avoid the checkmate reality that faces them: resort for dear life to the argument from incredulity and insist that Prayer Man just *has* to be someone other than Oswald. The argument from incredulity will run as follows:

*It's just plum **ridiculous** to claim that Oswald could have been on those steps for the motorcade and the aftermath without being noticed by any of his co-workers. Sheesh.*

This argument, being silly, is easily disposed of said Sean.

- Prayer Man is a fact.
- He was there.
- His presence there is not however recalled by a single witness in on-the-record statements or sworn testimony.
- And yet—was this mentioned?—he is a fact.
- He was there.
- The lack of attestation as to his presence puts not a dent, not even a scratch, in the integrity of that fact.
- Prayer Man was there.

Sean said to claim that Prayer Man is not Oswald is to claim that the presence of Oswald—a quiet and unexceptional worker in the building—would have been more liable to be notice up there at the entrance amongst the other TSBD folk than the presence of a total stranger—someone who didn't work in that building, had no business being there amongst the TSBD folk, would have had to walk up those steps from the street in order to end up in the Prayer Man position. And to claim that is to take terminal recourse to kook logic.

This, of course, is what the kook Warren Commission defenders will now do.

Sean is a prophet here. This is exactly what the defenders of the Lone Nut theory have done. Even many who call themselves conspiracy theorists ignore or disregard Sean's work today. Amazing when you think about it.

Robert Prudhomme and Richard Hocking praised Sean. Hocking said physical evidence most definitely trumps witness testimony on this one. Not only does the Oswald likeness improve with the latest Darnell improvement furnished by Robin Unger, the Frazier image just about jumps off the page.

Regarding Buell Wesley Frazier, Richard said he's not sure if we'll ever hear from him directly on this. He would not be surprised to hear from a "spokesman" in his stead.

As noted earlier, Richard said it may have been possible for a late-arriving Prayer Man to go unnoticed by employees on the lower steps and out in front of the TSBD. But there would be a small group on the top/back step near the door that may have noticed, including Buell Wesley Frazier, Joe Molina, Bill Shelley, and a couple others.

Richard said his opinion is that the mainstream media (MSM) will ignore this issue as long as humanly possible.

Sean said those who have been following this thread will know that there is nothing wildly surprising at our finding visual confirmation of Oswald's presence at the front entrance. That this would happen is predicted by (1) Jesse Curry's reckless description to the press on the evening of the assassination of the essentials of the brief Baker-Oswald encounter at the front entrance:

Pro-Castro Fort Worth Marxist
Charged in Kennedy's Assassination

DALLAS, Nov. 22 — Lee Harvey Oswald, 24, a pro-Castro Marxist, was charged tonight in the assassination of President Kennedy.

Police Chief Jesse Curry said the one-time U.S. Marine hid on the sixth floor of a textbook warehouse where he worked and snapped off the three quick shots that killed the President and wounded Gov. John B. Connally of Texas.

Earlier in the day, Oswald was charged with murdering Dallas policeman J. D. Tippitt, 38, who attempted to stop and question the man.

Oswald was arraigned on this charge before Justice of the Peace David Johnson and Curry said the case would be presented to the grand jury next week.

Curry told of the frenzied moments after the shooting when Oswald slipped through officers' hands as he fled the building.

Allowed to Leave Building

"He apparently got out of the building during the time we were surrounding it," Curry said. As an officer rushed into the building Oswald rushed out. The policeman permitted him to pass after the building manager told the policeman that Oswald was an employe.

"He apparently lost himself in the crowd, then," Curry added.

The building from which the gunman fired on the President is the headquarters of the Texas School Book Depository. Police said that Oswald had worked there for about six weeks as a laborer.

The firm does work for the public schools in relation to textbooks but is privately owned, police said.

Oswald, chairman of a local "Fair Play for Cuba Committee," has denied being involved in any way in the President's slaying.

"I did not kill the Presi-dent. I did not kill anyone," Oswald said.

He admitted being an employe of the book firm, police reported. The suspect has been unable to account for his whereabouts at the time of the shooting, police said.

Policemen Shot

Shortly after the assassination, Patrolman Tippitt stopped Oswald on the strength of a lookout which had been flashed for the man. Authorities apparently became suspicious of Oswald after the first officer told them he had fled the building.

When Tippitt stopped Oswald a short distance from the scene of the shooting, the suspect drew a gun and shot the policeman, police said. Then he fled as witnesses notified police.

A short time later the cashier of a movie theater in the Oak Cliff section of Dallas, called police and told them that a man had run into the theater. The description matched that of Oswald.

The theater is located about five blocks from where Tripitt was killed.

Four policemen were dispatched to the theater. The movie was in progress, but only a dozen or so people were there. An usher led

See ARREST, A12, Col. 1

Wash. Post
11/23/63

Had Darnell kept filming the front entrance for just a few seconds more, we would have actual footage of this encounter, Sean explained.

It is predicted by (2) the giveaway anxiety of the FBI over the weekend of the assassination that Oswald's claim to have been out front had found photographic corroboration in a certain photo that had gone out on the newswires shortly after the shooting:

> Lovelady maintains it is he standing in the door-
> way at the moment of the assassination. "I was stand-
> ing on the first step," he told me when I interviewed
> him two weeks ago in Dallas. "Several people in the
> picture saw me. That lady shading her eyes works here
> on the second floor."
>
> Lovelady said that the night following the assas-
> sination two FBI agents visited his home. "They said
> they had a blown-up picture they wanted me to see.
> Right away I pointed to me and they seemed relieved.
> One had a big smile on his face because it wasn't Os-
> wald. They said they had a big discussion down at
> the FBI and one guy said it just had to be Oswald."

It is predicted by (3) the clunky protest-too-much disclaimer contained in Roy Truly's first on-the-record account of his actions immediately following the assassination:

```
railroad yards adjoining the depository building. He then
noticed a Dallas City Police officer wearing a motorcycle helmet
and boots running toward the entrance of the depository building
and he accompanied the officer into the front of the building. They
saw no one there and he accompanied the officer immediately up
the stairs to the second floor of the building, where the officer
```

It is predicted by (4) Postal Inspector Harry D. Holmes' off-script moment during his Warren Commission testimony, where he has the bad taste to use the word "vestibule" in its correct sense (front lobby of a building):

> Mr. BELIN. By the way, where did this policeman stop him
> when he was coming down the stairs at the Book Depository
> on the day of the shooting?
> …
> Mr. HOLMES. He said it was in the vestibule.
> Mr. BELIN. He said he was in the vestibule?
> Mr. HOLMES. Or approaching the door to the vestibule. He
> was just coming, apparently, and I have never been in there
> myself. Apparently there is two sets of doors, and he had
> come out to this front part.

181

Mr. BELIN. Did he state it was on what floor?
Mr. HOLMES. First floor. The front entrance to the first floor.

Holmes got the basics right said Sean: Oswald had indeed not long before come out to "this front part," as shown in the relevant Wiegman frames.

It is predicted by (5) the telltale reticence in the various interrogation reports on where exactly Oswald claimed to have been during the assassination. The farthest anyone will go is: "on the First Floor."

It is predicted (6) in what—on the basis of a close comparison with the contemporaneous Bookhout interrogation notes (which we have access to thanks to the handwritten copy that Captain Fritz made and kept)—we established to be an almost certain interpolation by Secret Service Inspector Thomas Kelley in his first interrogation report of the first sentence below:

> *I asked him if he viewed the parade and he said he had not.* I then asked him if he had shot the President and he said he had not. I asked him if he has shot governor Connally and he said he had not.

And it is predicted (7) in the first page of Bookhout's contemporaneous interrogation notes.

Member Martin Hinrichs said he thought that the ***increase*** in the number of images from Robin Unger would help to ***exclude*** the presence of Oswald idea, but ***the opposite is the case***. The new Darnell frames show somebody in the doorway who really can be Oswald. Without the frames, Martin said he would be silent. But now…the more he looks at it, the more he sees Oswald.

Sean told Martin "It's him alright."

Sean said it's important to zoom out again and reiterate that the shape of Oswald's torso is distorted here because of the blocking presence of a woman on the steps in front of him. If you start with this woman's foot and lower leg, you can work your way up to where her head is and see how that makes Oswald's frame appear wider:

    With a note of sarcasm, Sean said what's going to happen next is that the Warren Commission defenders will attempt to stave off a collective nervous breakdown by channeling the spirit of kooky conspiracy theorists and denying that this is the man he so very obviously looks like. "The lapel is wrong!" "The hands are too big!!" "He has breasts!!!" Maybe they'll even go with the Two Oswalds theory by claiming one was on the steps while the other was upstairs taking potshots at JFK!

Two TSBD men remained standing stock still on the front entrance steps after the shots were fired, said Sean. Two TSBD men were threatened with a conspiracy-with-Oswald—himself charged within 24 hours of the shooting. Two TSBD men did not remember seeing Marrion Baker run into the building. Who were these two men? *Buell Wesley Frazier and Joe Molina.*

Sean again focused on Will Fritz's personal handwritten copy of FBI Special Agent James W. Bookhout's contemporaneous interrogation notes:

Did Oswald say: "I don't own a rifle saw"? Of course not, said Sean. There is a slight elevation in the position of the word "saw" with respect to the previous word:

This is indicative of the beginning of a new thought:

Oswald said:

- I don't own a rifle.
- However I did see one in the building…

Distinct thoughts, but run-on lines, said Sean.

Has Bookhout or Fritz erroneously written the word "says" twice? Of course not, said Sean. There is a slight elevation in the position of the second instance of the word "says" with respect to the previous word:

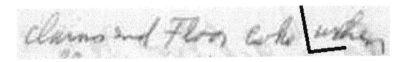

This is indicative of the beginning of a new thought:

Oswald:

- I am a member of ACLU
- Mrs. Pa[i]ne is too…

Distinct thoughts, but run-on lines, said Sean.

Did Oswald say: "I bought a coke on the second floor when..."? No, says Sean. There is a slight elevation in the position of the word "when" with respect to the previous word:

This is indicative of the beginning of a new thought:

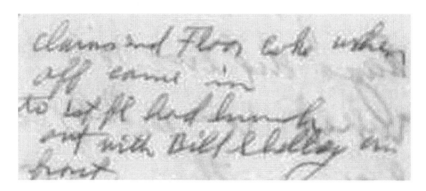

Again, distinct thoughts, but run-on lines, said Sean.

Oswald:
- *Claims 2nd Floor coke*
- *When off[icer] came in to 1st fl[oor] [was having]
lunch out with Bill Shelley [and others] in front*

Oswald is making special mention of Shelley simply because he was the most senior TSBD man standing on the steps. Shelley however probably never even noticed that Oswald was there. Fritz, as we have already seen, let this very big moggy out of the bag during his Warren Commission testimony:

> Mr. FRITZ. Well he told me that he was eating lunch with some of the employees when this happened, and that he saw all the excitement...

Sean says we know now that *Lee was telling the truth...*

In their joint interrogation report written while Oswald was still
alive, Sean said Bookhout and Hosty mentioned Oswald's non-toxic
trip upstairs for the coke but completely fudged the issue of his
claimed whereabouts at the time of the shooting and the officer's
dash up the front steps and into the First Floor:[70]

> Oswald stated that he went to lunch at approximately noon
> and he claimed he ate his lunch on the first floor in the
> lunchroom; however he went to the second floor where the
> Coca-Cola machine was located and obtained a bottle of
> Coca-Cola for his lunch. Oswald claimed to be on the first
> floor when President John F. Kennedy passed this building.

As this report was being put together by the two agents, Bookhout was looking at his notes which contained (we now know, thanks to Fritz's copy) explicit mention of an officer coming in. Yet that massively important detail is not even mentioned in the account of the lunchroom visit, says Sean. Why? Because the officer coming in had nothing to do with the lunchroom visit. It had however everything to do with Oswald's alibi. And there was simply no way *any* of that was ever going into an official interrogation report.

James Hosty in the months and years ahead would never offer any corroboration for Bookhout's solo report claim that Oswald talked about such an incident in the lunchroom. It is not in Hosty's own contemporaneous interrogation notes. It is not in his Warren Commission testimony. It is not in his 1996 book *Assignment: Oswald.*[71]

After Oswald's death, and without input or corroboration from Hosty, Bookhout took this section of his notes...

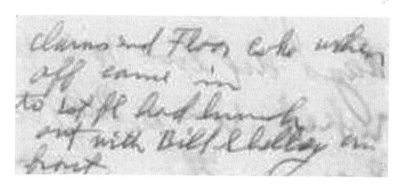

...and gave it a preposterous gloss that had the double merit of posthumously "confirming" the lunchroom incident Roy Truly was telling people about and making Oswald sound like a very bad liar:[72]

> Oswald stated that on November 22, 1963, at the time of the search of the Texas School Book Depository building by Dallas police officers, he was on the second floor of said building, having just purchased a Coca-cola form the soft-drink machine, at which time a police officer came into the room with pistol drawn and asked him if he worked there.

Mr. Truly was present and verified that he was an employee and the police officer thereafter left the room and continued through the building. Oswald stated that he took this Coke down to the first floor and stood around and had lunch in the employees' lunch room. He thereafter went outside and stood around for five or ten minutes with foreman Bill Shelly....

Member Bjørn Gjerde said this thread has reminded him of the poem "Antigonish" by William Hughes Mearns (1875–1965), also known as the song "The Little Man Who Wasn't There" as performed by Glenn Miller:

> *Yesterday upon the stair,*
> *I met a man who wasn't there.*
> *He wasn't there again today,*
> *Oh, how I wish he'd go away...*
>
> *When I came home last night at three,*
> *The man was waiting there for me*
> *But when I looked around the hall,*
> *I couldn't see him there at all!*
> *Go away, go away, don't you come back any more!*
> *Go away, go away, and please don't slam the door...*
>
> *Last night I saw upon the stair,*
> *A little man who wasn't there,*
> *He wasn't there again today*
> *Oh, how I wish he'd go away...*

Richard Hocking said there are several members who believe Prayer Man is holding a camera, mentioning an interesting story that lends support to that interpretation: Oswald's Imperial Reflex camera is unaccounted for that day, he said.

On the afternoon of November 22, 1963, the Ruth Paine residence became a beehive of Dallas Police activity, explained Richard. Her home and garage were thoroughly searched by a team of Dallas Police officers looking for anything that belonged to Oswald, any type of evidence that might have significance in the assassination. This team included Detectives Adamcik, Stovall,

Rose, Moore, Walthers, and Detective McCabe of the Irving Police Department. They actually searched Paine's residence on two days, November 22 and 23.

Richard said Oswald owned two cameras: a Minox, and an Imperial Reflex. The search team reported finding one camera that belonged to Oswald and one that belonged to Ruth Paine. The Dallas Police Department took pictures of Oswald's possessions. One of the pictures shows a camera:

The camera in this picture is not the Imperial Reflex. It does resemble the Minox.

Richard asked could Oswald have taken the Imperial Reflex to the TSBD on Friday, November 22, 1963. And more specifically, could that be the object in PM's hands.

The saga of the Imperial Reflex continues. On December 8, 1963, according to Robert Oswald,[73] he stops by the Paine's house to pick up the remainder of Lee's possessions. He takes a box out of the garage that contains several items—including the Imperial Reflex Camera. How did this slip past the Police search team? It is after all, the camera alleged to have taken the Backyard photos, said Richard.

In February and March of 1964, the FBI is trying to clean up the loose ends and questions regarding the camera issues. Robert Oswald turns over the camera to the FBI. James Hosty interviews McCabe. McCabe now remembers that he actually saw the Imperial Reflex and moved it onto a dresser because he did not think it belonged to Oswald. None of the other members of the police search team recalled seeing the Imperial Reflex while they were there. The FBI issued some reports to lay the issue to rest.

More coincidences and strange doings that must be mistrusted.

Sean said that it needs to be stated again that the theory he has been outlining posits an encounter involving Lee Oswald, Marrion Baker and Roy Truly that was perfectly simple and straightforward. Oswald is out front for the motorcade...

... and Marrion Baker very briefly addresses him as he—Baker—runs into the building...only to have Roy Truly intervene and offer his assistance as building manager.
All the complexity in the theory—*all of it*—pertains to the frantic attempts made in the hours, days and weeks ahead to cover up this simple event. For those attempts had one brutal aim: to deprive

Oswald of his all too clear alibi by displacing the Baker encounter to a location somewhere at or near the rear of the building, i.e., a location consistent with the notion of Oswald as the Sixth Floor shooter.

BAKER & TRULY ENCOUNTER OSWALD
AT FRONT ENTRANCE

⇩

BAKER & TRULY ENCOUNTER OSWALD BY
REAR STAIRWAY SEVERAL FLOORS UP

⇩

BAKER & TRULY ENCOUNTER OSWALD
IN SECOND FLOOR LUNCHROOM

The first incident above actually happened. The two incidents it morphed into are pure fiction. And it is in understanding the precise relationship between the one real event and each of the two fictions—as well as the precise relationship between the two fictions themselves—that we can come to account for the carefully coached nonsense of Baker and Truly's Warren Commission testimony, said Sean.

Richard Hocking said it seems like there are several unspoken assumptions in this thread. One is that Prayer Man cannot be on the top step/or entrance lobby when Baker goes by, and then also see Baker in the Second Floor lunchroom area. A second one is that Oswald could only have purchased one coke that day. In his own mind, he has not made those concessions just yet.

Richard says he understands that Sean has presented a comprehensive scenario that eliminates the Second Floor encounter. He has most definitely done an outstanding job providing news articles, photo and film evidence, witness testimony, and applied sound logic and critical thinking to make his case—a tremendous effort that he has shared with the JFK Research community.

But Richard added he also believes that we can begin from the same starting point (with Prayer Man on the steps, Baker and Truly coming in through the entrance) and entertain the possibility of some of the story unfolding in a different way, or in a slightly different form than Sean's scenario.

Richard is keeping an open mind here and that's good. But if somebody has a different way this may have unfolded, they'll need to lay it out exhaustively like Sean has done with his theory.

Sean thanked Richard for his kind words. He clarified his take on the Second Floor lunchroom encounter:

a) It almost certainly did not happen.
b) In the very unlikely event that it did happen, it most certainly cannot have involved Oswald/Prayer Man's hurrying upstairs for a coke: he must surely have been keeping tabs on Baker and Truly's progress.
c) Those conspiracy theorists who are open to the Prayer Man-Oswald identification but are dogmatically closed to any doubts whatsoever about the Second Floor lunchroom incident seem unaware of the accusation of complicity they are in effect leveling at Oswald.
d) That said, simultaneous acceptance that Oswald is Prayer Man and rejection of the Second Floor lunchroom story does not entail any necessary commitment to the view that Oswald is wholly innocent of any involvement in the assassination; it allows for arguments both ways.

As we have seen, Sean pointed out, Marrion Baker went to Dallas Police Department Headquarters the afternoon of the assassination and gave an affidavit stating that he had caught a man walking away from the rear stairway on the Third or Fourth Floor, but that he had let the man go when the building manager vouched for him as an employee.

This story—a fiction—would likely have formed the sensational centerpiece of Baker and Truly's Warren Commission testimony had it not been for two things:

a) The adverse and quite possibly principled reaction of Baker upon seeing Oswald being brought into the Homicide Office just as he was giving his affidavit
b) The bravery of one woman: Vicki Adams.

Regarding a), Sean says the document filed by or on behalf of Will Fritz at some point after Oswald's death made a false claim:

OFFICER WITNESSES:

M. L. Baker   Saw Oswald in building after shooting. Identified
Solo Motor Officer   him in line up. See affidavit.
Traffic Division

Baker attended <u>no such lineup</u>. He made <u>no such formal identification of Oswald</u>. Indeed, we have *good reason to believe he positively refused to do so*. And the crisis which his refusal was causing is reflected in the fact that the above note makes no mention of where in the building Officer Baker had seen Oswald.

All they had, and all they could clutch on to, was the crucial fact that Oswald's presence in the building just after the assassination was securely established by an officer's sighting of him. Given the collapse of the affidavit version of events, the precise where and how of this sighting *still had to be worked out*—and Baker *worked on*.

Regarding b), Sean said as Barry Ernest confirmed to him, the authorities heard very quickly indeed from Vicki Adams:

> Vicki told me she was questioned by several authorities when she returned to her office shortly after the assassination. She said she told each one about her trip down the stairs with Sandra. She and others in her office were dismissed around 2 p.m.
> I have not found a record of these "interviews" taken that early in the game. The first recorded interview of Miss Adams occurred by the FBI on 11/24/63. It was detailed and during part of that interview, it was said, "She [Miss Adams] and her friend then ran immediately to the back of the stairs."

Suddenly, maddeningly, the area by the rear stairway was off limits for an Oswald-Baker encounter, said Sean. And the authorities' Fourth Floor headache did not end with Adams and Styles. Let us remind ourselves again of what Adams' supervisor Dorothy Garner told Barry when he tracked her down in 2011:

> Did Miss Adams and Miss Styles leave the window right away, I asked her.
> "The girls did," she responded. "I remember them being there and the next thing I knew, they were gone."
> They had left "very quickly…within a matter of moments," she added.
> What did Mrs. Garner do after that?
> *"There was this warehouse or storage area behind our office, out by the freight elevators and the rear stairway, and I went out there."*
> Her move to that area clearly put her into a position where she could have observed activity on the back stairs as well as on the elevators. But how fast had she arrived there?
> Mrs. Garner said she immediately went to this area, following "shortly after…right behind" Miss Adams and Miss Styles. She couldn't remember exactly why she went out there, other than to say, "Probably to get something."
> Mrs. Garner said she did not actually see "the girls" enter the stairway, though, arriving on the fourth- floor landing seconds after. When I asked how she knew they had gone down, Mrs. Garner said, "I remember hearing them, after they started down. I remember the stairs were very noisy."
> Were the freight elevators in operation during this time?
> "I don't recall that," she answered. "They were very noisy too!"
> Mrs. Garner said she remained at that spot and was alone for a moment before "several came out back from the office to look out those windows there."

The rear of the Fourth Floor was getting horribly crowded, Sean said, so it had to be ruled out—subsequent to Baker's *disastrous affidavit statement!*—as a viable venue for the phony Baker-Oswald-Truly encounter.

Same went for the Third Floor: to put (or keep) the encounter there would be very dangerous, throwing a spotlight on the failure of anyone to see Oswald going down the stairs to three—and raising an awkward question as to whether any amongst these women had noticed Baker and Truly coming up. What if that question elicited the use of the taboo word "elevator" rather than "stairway"...?

Place the encounter any higher than the Fourth Floor, and things would just start getting silly. How on earth was Jesse Curry going to explain to the world how one of his men had had Oswald in his clutches in the most incriminating place imaginable—by the rear stairway, right in the shooter's escape route, way up in the building—only to let him loose? And how on earth was Marrion Baker going to be inveigled into testifying away his good reputation as an officer by signing up to that damning story?

What was needed, and urgently, said Sean, was a Baker-Oswald-Truly encounter away from the front entrance but also somewhere away from the stairs yet still within striking distance of Oswald's escape route down those stairs.

Sean said there was literally only one viable venue left: the Second Floor lunchroom. It was far from ideal. In fact it was pretty crappy. But it was the best they could come up with under trying circumstances.

And on Friday night a decision was made—by the FBI if not by Dallas Police Department—to run with this new location and somehow make the best of a bad situation.

From an FBI teletype sent from Dallas to Washington in the early hours of the Saturday morning:

PAGE FIVE

MR. ROY S. TRULY, WAREHOUSE SUPERINTENDENT, OBSERVED OSWALD AT WORK ON MORNING OF NOVEMBER TWENTYTWO. OSWALD HAD ACESS TO ALL FLOORS OF BUILDING IN HIS REGULAR OCCUPATION OF FILLING ORDERS FOR SCHOOL BOOKS. TRULY WAS ON SIDEWALK IN FRONT OF HIS PLACE OF EMPLOYMENT WITH PRACTICALLY ALL OTHER EMPLOYEES FROM BUILDING WHEN KENNEDY WAS SHOT. HE IMMEDIATELY ACCOMPANIED A POLICE OFFICER INTO THE BUILDING AND UP THE STAIRS TO THE SECOND FLOOR, WHERE THEY OBSERVED OSWALD ALONE IN THE COMPANY SNACK BAR. SNACK BAR IN CENTER OF BUILDING, HAS NO WINDOWS AND WAS UNUSUAL PLACE FOR ANYONE TO BE AT THAT TIME. AFTER SEARCH OF BUILDING COMPLETED, OSWALD COULD NOT BE LOCATED.

Larry Hancock said it seemed relevant for him to note the experience of his friend, Connie Kritzberg, a Dallas reporter. During the first 24 hours of the assassination, she wrote up an interview very clearly describing a shot from the front. She turned her story in at the end of the day, knowing it might be the most important news piece she would ever write, and was horrified to see the next morning, when it appeared in print, that the wording had been changed. Not a big change, simply a tweak in the wording to make the indication of a frontal shot less conclusive. She recognized the change immediately and called her editor who pushed back declaring he had not changed her wording. After she pushed him a bit more, he told her that if she had any issues about the whole thing she would need to contact the FBI.

Later, Larry said her research into the various iterations of her copy suggested that her story had been read over the phone to someone and edited outside the paper itself. Of course she has no solid proof of that but she is absolutely certain her copy was changed. Her editor denied he had done it, so as far as she is concerned, it remains a very open question.

Pat Speer said beyond that he thinks "Prayer Man" looks like a woman, he thinks those pushing that Prayer Man must be Oswald are missing something. The TSBD had a second building just up on Houston Street. The employees from that building had access to the TSBD and may very well have mingled with their co-workers on the steps. Now, he asked, is there a full accounting of those employees, so that we can see who was on Elm during the shooting? He said he's pretty sure the answer is no.

Richard Hocking replied to Pat saying all the known employees of both buildings were interviewed or accounted for.

Sean asked Pat which is more likely: a) Prayer Man would be a TSBD (Elm Street) employee, or b) Prayer Man would not be a TSBD (Elm Street) employee? And how likely is it that someone from the other building would "mingle with" co-workers and have their presence there noticed by not a single one of those co-workers? Why such resistance to the obvious explanation: it's Oswald?

Pat responded that he didn't think the explanation is "obvious." He said we have a blurry unidentified figure in a photograph that some think looks like Oswald. It could be any one of a number of people, the number of which is unclear. It could even be a woman. From what we have uncovered, nobody standing near this person ever said this person was Oswald. And the existing record suggests that Oswald himself never said he was in this location at the time of the shooting. "I mean, nothing," said Pat. If it was Oswald, he could have said "Don't worry, Marina,[74] I was out front when the shots were fired with lots of people nearby." But no, nothing.

So, there's no one saying it was Oswald...up against a number of people whose stories become problematic if it was Oswald.

And that's where it's likely to rest.

With that said, Pat admitted he still finds this topic intriguing and worthwhile. Why? A whole bunch of reasons: 1) it arouses interest in the case, 2) it invites study of the record, and 3) it may lead somewhere. Pat then relayed a story from personal experience. "Several years back", he said, "I had this vague notion that the paper bag photographed outside the building was not the paper bag in the FBI photographs. It sounded kind of loopy. But as I dug deeper, I found many indications that this was indeed the case. Did I prove it", asked Pat? "Probably not. But was it worthwhile? Yep," he said.

"In this instance, you have found some evidence supporting that Baker and Truly saw Oswald as they entered the building. Have you proved it? No. It would be almost impossible to prove it at this point. But have you succeeded in blurring the once accepted fact that after the shooting Oswald was first observed by Baker in the Second Floor lunchroom? And even raised the possibility Oswald was outside when the shots were fired? For many, the answer will be yes", said Pat.

Sean said if this were simply a matter of plucking out a rather blurry image and, solely on the basis of that image, rushing to the judgment, "Look, it's obviously Oswald!", then he said Pat's point would be well taken. But that is not what has happened here. Not even close. The Prayer Man images relate in a powerful way to a body of evidence putting Oswald, and the Oswald-Baker-Truly encounter, on the First Floor and at the front entrance of the First Floor.

Wiegman and Darnell show us:

1. a white man (Sean says he knows Pat doesn't agree, and we'll come to that)
2. who is neither wearing a suit nor wearing the white shirt of an office worker
3. who has short hair
4. who has dark hair
5. who appears to be holding at least one item
6. who appears to be holding at least one item up to his lower face area during the assassination sequence (Wiegman)
7. who appears to have lowered his right arm again just seconds after the shooting (Darnell)
8. who is right in Baker's entry route as Baker rushes up the front steps.

All things being equal, Sean asked Pat, which is the more likely scenario?

a) This is a TSBD (Elm St) person amongst lots of other TSBD (Elm St) people?
b) This is a non-TSBD (Elm St) person amongst lots of TSBD (Elm St) people?

It's a no-brainer says Sean: the more likely scenario, by far, is a).

There have been intensive efforts recently to propose a single viable candidate from amidst the ranks of the TSBD personnel. We've been told it's probably Lovelady, Frazier, Molina, Williams, etc. Sean said he's still waiting for someone to nominate the "confused" Jack Dougherty.

Every single effort along these lines has come up blank, said Sean. Except for one: TSBD (Elm Street) employee Lee Oswald. So we're left, by a process of simple elimination, with the explanation to the best and most obvious inference: *it's Oswald, eating his lunch*. And if you're saying that Prayer Man looks so unlike Oswald as to force us to look elsewhere for a more far-fetched explanation, well, Sean said he really must beg to differ. If an image this clear had been found at the Sixth Floor sniper's nest window, Sean believes (and he suspects most other conspiracy theorists would too) that you would have no choice but to wave the white flag and accept that Oswald was indeed the Sixth Floor shooter.

Sean said several times Pat has offered the suggestion that Prayer Man is in fact a woman. At one point he even suggested "she" was holding "a large purse in her hands." He asked Pat if he could—*with reference to actual images from Darnell*—back up this idea with data.

Bjørn Gjerde discussed FBI Director Hoover's narrative of the events in TSBD as told to President Johnson on November 29, 1963:[75]

> He then threw the gun aside and came down....at the entrance of the building he was stopped by police officers and some manager in the building told the police officers, "well he's allright...he works there...you needn't hold him." They let him go. That is how he got out.
> …
> ...he apparently had come down the five flights of steps—stairway—from the fifth floor...so far we've found out the elevator was not used...although he could have used it...but nobody remember whether it was or whether it wasn't.

So, according to Hoover on November 29, 1963, there had been no Second Floor lunchroom encounter between Oswald and Baker, said Bjørn.

There was no Second Floor encounter because it hadn't been fully cooked up yet.

Sean Murphy said this must surely rank as one of the most peculiar moments in the Warren Commission's many pages of witness testimony:[76]

> Mr. BALL - Do you have any idea how long it was from the time you heard those three sounds or three noises until you saw Truly and Baker going into the building?
> Mr. SHELLEY - It would have to be *3 or 4 minutes* I would say because this girl that ran back up there was down near where the car was when the President was hit.
> Mr. BALL - She ran back up to the door and you had still remained standing there?
> Mr. SHELLEY - Yes.
> Mr. BALL - Going to watch the rest of the parade were you?
> Mr. SHELLEY - Yes.
> Mr. BALL - The Vice President hadn't gone by, had he, by your place?
> Mr. SHELLEY - I don't know. I didn't recognize him. I did recognize Mr. Kennedy and his suntan I had been hearing about.
> Mr. BALL - How did you happen to see Truly?
> Mr. SHELLEY - We ran out on the island while some of the people that were out watching it from our building were walking back and we turned around and we saw an officer and Truly.
> Mr. BALL - And Truly?
> Mr. SHELLEY - Yes.
> Mr. BALL - Did you see them go into the building?

Mr. SHELLEY - No; we didn't watch that long but they were at the first step like they were fixin' to go in.

We know, said Sean, from the Darnell film that Shelley's sighting of Baker and Truly actually happened around half a minute after the shooting. Yet here we have Shelley himself giving us a time estimate that is extravagantly outsized. The peculiarity is only compounded, however, when we hear the person who was with Shelley out on the "island" backing him up in this time estimate:[77]

> Mr. BALL - You heard the shots. And how long after that was it before Gloria Calvary [sic][78] came up?
> Mr. LOVELADY - Oh, *approximately 3 minutes*, I would say.
> Mr. BALL - Three minutes is a long time.
> Mr. LOVELADY - Yes, it's—I say approximately; I can't say because I don't have a watch; it could.
> Mr. BALL - Had people started to run?
> Mr. LOVELADY - Well, I couldn't say because she came up to us and we was talking to her, wasn't looking that direction at that time, but when we came off the steps—see, that entrance, you have a blind side when you go down the steps.
> Mr. BALL - Right after you talked to Gloria, did you leave the steps and go toward the tracks?
> Mr. LOVELADY - Yes.

Three minutes, as Ball correctly notes, is indeed a long time for Lovelady to be estimating for his and Shelley's departure from the front steps. In fact it's plain absurd, said Sean.

Boy, I'll say.

While one might—at a stretch—credit one witness' memory going badly askew due to the shock of an assassination, being asked to believe that the time sense of this witness' companion was off precisely the same extent (3 minutes for the departure from the steps;

between 3 and 4 minutes for the sighting of Baker and Truly) will surely tax the credulity of even the most trusting of readers, Sean argued.

How do we explain this shared error on the part of Shelley and Lovelady? Why are both misremembering in such unbelievably synchronized fashion?

Their error, said Sean, cannot have come from Warren Commission prompting. Via a series of rigged time trials, the timeline the Commission had painstakingly put together already accommodated a realistically early entry into the building by Baker and Truly out of necessity.

Sean submits that Shelley and Lovelady are giving us evidence of very early coaching by Dallas Police Department men and/or FBI agents. For, as we have seen, the case/admission was made on the evening of the assassination that Oswald had been "stopped" by the officer at the front entrance. When Jesse Curry blithely announced this fact to news reporters that evening, he probably had no idea just how troublesome a hostage to fortune he was giving. The disastrous evidence of the Darnell film was not yet known at this stage, so the first tack was simply to delay Baker's entry into the building to a point that would give Oswald time to make his descent from the Sixth Floor and "escape." If this meant working on a couple of witnesses to Baker and Truly's entry, then so be it. (Recall what Sandra Styles told Sean about the authorities informing her that the first officers to reach the building did not arrive until some 15-20 minutes after the shooting.)

Sean said it was unfortunate that no one thought to mention to Shelley and Lovelady ahead of their Warren Commission appearances that they could revert to their real memories and just tell the truth: we left the front entrance less than half a minute after the last shot.

As we shall see, Sean said, the Warren Commission will have its own dirty work to do on Shelley and Lovelady, this time in relation to the Vicki Adams problem. But for now, let's turn to what happened in the first few days after the assassination to the original plan of extending the timeline so as to contrive a scenario consistent with Oswald's descent and guilt.

Sean said there was a second powerful reason why, in the immediate aftermath of the assassination, Billy Lovelady had to be artificially kept on the front steps: *he resembled Oswald*.

We underestimate at our peril the sheer panic that must have been abroad at Dallas Police Department Headquarters and at FBI Special Branch, said Sean. The suspect in custody was claiming to have been out front at the time of the assassination. He was describing events that only someone who had actually been there could have known. And there was every danger that a photo or film would emerge showing him at the front entrance.

The sum of all fears seemed to come true when people started looking closely at the doorway area in the Altgens 6 photograph which had gone out on newswire:

Cue an immediate investigation by the FBI, said Sean. They made a beeline for Billy Lovelady, as he would recall for Dom Bonafede several months later:[79]

> Lovelady maintains it is he standing in the door-
> way at the moment of the assassination. "I was stand-
> ing on the first step," he told me when I interviewed
> him two weeks ago in Dallas. "Several people in the
> picture saw me. That lady shading her eyes works here
> on the second floor."
>
> Lovelady said that the night following the assas-
> sination two FBI agents visited his home. "They said
> they had a blown-up picture they wanted me to see.
> Right away I pointed to me and they seemed relieved.
> One had a big smile on his face because it wasn't Os-
> wald. They said they had a big discussion down at
> the FBI and one guy said it just had to be Oswald."

The relief of the agents tells us all we need to know: Oswald's being out front at the time of the shooting was an all-too-live scenario, for it was the scenario that he himself was claiming in custody.

If Oswald was placing himself far from the front entrance—such as in or around the Second Floor lunchroom—then there would be no earthly cause for worry about what the assassination-time visual record might produce.

But he *wasn't*, so there *was*.

Sean said the authorities lucked out in a big way on it being Lovelady in Altgens, but what guarantee was there that another *Oswaldian* image would not show up over the coming days? And what better way—what other way—to indemnify themselves against this eventuality than to keep Lovelady on the steps for a good three minutes should he be needed to explain away any such image?

(That Lovelady has been seriously proposed as Prayer Man by several researchers over the past weeks has shown, this time rather farcically, the continued explanatory power he still holds for those intent on keeping Oswald away from that front entrance, said Sean.)

Continuing, Sean said the true incident at the front entrance involved Marrion Baker asking Oswald if he worked there. Later that evening, the Dallas Police Department (through Jesse Curry and Detective Ed Hicks) openly talked to the press about this incident, only they gave it a definite spin: Oswald had been "stopped" as he was "leaving" the building.

In reality, said Sean, he had been standing on the steps for the assassination itself, having (as the Hughes film suggests[80]) slipped out just as the President was approaching the turn onto Elm Street. It's possible—indeed likely—that not a soul had noticed Oswald there, and that he had only been noticed when Baker ran up to the entrance and addressed him.

Thus, Sean explained, we have **Phase One** of the suppression of Oswald's alibi: Pretend he was exiting the building and had the good fortune to be "let go" by the officer. This story collapsed, and quickly. It soon became apparent that too many people had witnessed Baker and Truly's extraordinarily early dash into the building. The timeline just didn't work. So the incident had to be relocated to the rear area of the building.

Phase Two: Baker's phony affidavit story of having caught a man "walking away from the rear stairway" on the "third or fourth" floor. That story collapsed too, and quickly, for reasons that have already been laid out (Vicki Adams and Baker himself). It gets buried, and not a word of this rear stairway encounter is ever breathed to the press.

Cue **Phase Three**: the Second Floor lunchroom story. It first comes into being in Roy Truly's FBI interview given late on November 22, 1963:

```
of these shots but believed they came from the area of the
railroad yards adjoining the depository building. He then
noticed a Dallas City Police officer wearing a motorcycle helmet
and boots running toward the entrance of the depository building
and he accompanied the officer into the front of the building. They
saw no one there and he accompanied the officer immediately up
the stairs to the second floor of the building, where the officer
noticed a door and stepped through the door, gun in hand, and
observed OSWALD in a snack bar there, apparently alone. This
snack bar has no windows or doors, facing the outside of the building
but is located almost in the center of the building. The officer
pointed to OSWALD and asked if OSWALD was an employee of the company
and he, TRULY, assured the officer that OSWALD was an employee. He
and the officer then proceeded onto the roof of the building, where
the officer conducted a thorough search but found nothing. They then
searched the 7th floor of the building and by this time many officers
```

Sean notes four things:

1. The impression given that the officer had to go through only one door off the landing in order to access the lunchroom.
2. The indication that Oswald was "apparently alone."

3. The lack of any description of Oswald's position in the lunchroom, i.e., was he sitting or standing?
4. The heavy emphasis on the lunchroom's lack of windows facing the outside; what a peculiar place for someone to be in when everyone else had been watching the motorcade.

Number 1 marks what will be an intractable problem at the heart of the lunchroom story.

Numbers 2 and 3 mark the hedging of bets as the details are still being worked out.

Number 4 discloses the game plan: the Second Floor lunchroom is the only available place anywhere near the rear stairway to which the incident can possibly be relocated and they're going to make the very best of it. Oswald's mooching around in the belly of the building will be portrayed as incongruous and suspicious, precisely the kind of place an assassin would take cover and try to act "normal" in. And this line will be taken up with enthusiasm by the constitutionally defensive Curry on Saturday, as he tries to make up for his gaffe of the day before.

> *No, folks, one of our men didn't let Oswald go as he was leaving the building. For Oswald, cunning killer that he was, took the kind of clever cover that no police officer could have been blamed for being fooled by.*

From the *New York Times* November 24, 1963:

The point of course, said Sean, is that Curry is telling the truth in this regard: he had been told, quite accurately, that Oswald had been "stopped" by the officer at the front entrance in front of other people. Now he's clumsily and/or cynically importing this detail up to the Second Floor lunchroom in order to deflect criticism of the decision by his officer to let Oswald go.

It would be tempting, said Sean, to write this off as Curry's singular error or embellishment. However the factoid lingers in an FBI report from December 10, 1963:

QUESTION: Did the police search the Texas School Book
Depository building immediately after the assassination? If
so, why did they let Oswald get out of the building?

ANSWER: The police began a search of the Texas School Book
Depository building immediately after the assassination. Oswald
was seen in a small lunchroom on the second floor by a police
officer and Roy S. Truly, warehouse superintendent. Oswald was
not questioned at the time inasmuch as Mr. Truly identified him
and other individuals to the police officer as employees of the

Interestingly, the original draft of this "answer" shows that the
"other individuals" was not a carelessly included detail but
something considered worthy of definite mention:

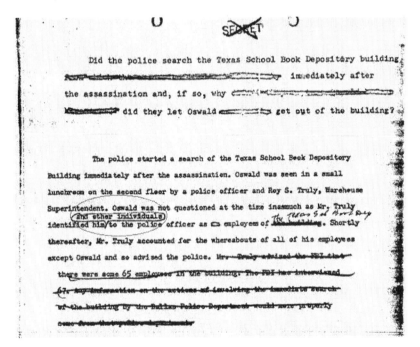

All of this is symptomatic of a story that stubbornly refuses to
stabilize, said Sean.

We will never be able to reconstruct exactly when and by whom each tweak to the Second Floor lunchroom story was produced. The broad evolution of the story is however fairly clear, and it centers on the problem of explaining **why Marrion Baker "popped his head" into the lunchroom in the first place**.

Roy Truly's first on-the-record statement (his FBI interview given late November 22) simply states that the officer saw Oswald in the lunchroom. No details are given as to what exactly he saw Oswald doing:

of these shots but believed they came from the area of the railroad yards adjoining the depository building. He then noticed a Dallas City Police officer wearing a motorcycle helmet and boots running toward the entrance of the depository building and he accompanied the officer into the front of the building. They saw no one there and he accompanied the officer immediately up the stairs to the second floor of the building, where the officer noticed a door and stepped through the door, gun in hand, and observed OSWALD in a snack bar there, apparently alone. This snack bar has no windows or doors, facing the outside of the building but is located almost in the center of the building. The officer pointed to OSWALD and asked if OSWALD was an employee of the company and he, TRULY, assured the officer that OSWALD was an employee. He and the officer then proceeded onto the roof of the building, where the officer conducted a thorough search but found nothing. They then searched the 7th floor of the building and by this time many officers

This same vagueness marks Truly's affidavit statement the next day:

AFFIDAVIT IN ANY FACT

THE STATE OF TEXAS

COUNTY OF DALLAS

BEFORE ME,_____ _____ Mary Rattan _____

a Notary Public in and for said County, State of Texas, on this day personally appeared ___ _____

Roy S. Truly, 4932 Jade Dr., 4R6 9893 _____

Who, after being by me duly sworn, on oath deposes and says: I am superintendent of the Texas School Book Depository, 411 Elm Street in Dallas, Texas. I was working in that capacity yesterday Friday November 22, 1963. I have 19 employees in the plant. Lee Harvey Oswald was one of these employees. We considered him a temporary employee. We work a lot of extra employees during the summer and fall. Mr. C. V. Campbell, one of the owners, and I started to lunch a few minutes after twelve o'clock. We saw that the parade was nearly down to us, so we stopped and watched the President go by. After the President passed, we heard what sounded like an explosion. I heard three such explosions. Then I realized that they must have been shots. I saw an officer break through the crowd and go into our building. I realized he did not know anything about the building, so I ran in with him. The officer and I went through the shipping department to the freight elevator. We then started up the stairway. We hit the second floor landing, the officer stuck his head into the lunch room area where there are coke and candy machines. Lee Oswald was in there. The officer had his gun on Oswald and asked me if he was an employee. I answered yes. We then went up the stairs to the 5th floor where we found the elevator open. We took the elevator to the 7th floor and out on the roof. We searched the roof and a small room, also checked the landings. We could look out over the tracks and street below. We did not find anything. We started down on the elevator. The officer took a hurried look on a couple floors on the way down. We then met some other officers on the 4th floor searching the building. I overheard someone say that the shot came from the window of our building. By that time there was several people in the building. Some fifteen minutes later I was checking our employees, and I did not find Lee. I asked Mr. Shelley if he had seen Lee. He said no. I then contacted Chief Lumpkin and told him Lee was missing. Then both of us went up on the sixth floor where Captain Fritz was and I told Captain Fritz about Lee being missing and where he lived. I did not see Lee Oswald any more. We don't run a thorough check on our temporary employees. They fill out an application form. In Lee Oswald's case, a lady from Irving called and said a neighbor had a brother working for me, and he had said we could use some more help. This woman said she knew a nice young boy

R S Truly

SUBSCRIBED AND SWORN TO BEFORE ME THIS. 23 DAY OF. November _____A.D. 1963

Mary Rattan
Notary Public, Dallas County, Texas Mary Rattan

CPS-GF-413

JRT.

Someone unfamiliar with the layout of the Second Floor would come away from reading this with the distinct impression that the lunchroom must have been straight off the landing, if not indeed in the officer's path as he made his way to the next flight of stairs—a scenario fitting not the rear stairway story but the very first story of Baker and Truly's having come up the *front* stairs and then taken a path through the office or corridor *leading right by the lunchroom.*

The FBI report on Truly's affidavit statement (*they sat in on the taking of the affidavit!*) studiously maintains the vagueness necessary to collapsing the earlier version (front stairs) on to the new version (rear stairs):

first floor, they ran up the stairway after he showed the officer where the stairway was. As they reached the second floor landing, the officer opened a door to a small lunch room next to the business office on that floor, and stuck his gun in the door. LEE OSWALD was in the lunch room. The officer asked him if he was an employee, to which OSWALD replied that he was. TRULY and the officer gave this no further consideration, inasmuch as OSWALD was an employee, and they ran up to the fifth floor of the

Lee Oswald was in the lunchroom: that's all we need to know, said Sean.

And we certainly don't need to be informed that the door leading off the landing was not the lunchroom door but an automatically self-closing door leading into a small connecting passage off of which there was another door belonging to the lunchroom. Again the reader is left with the erroneous impression that the officer needed only to take a peek through one door—*a door which he was passing in any case*—in order to see into the lunchroom.

A very large incompatibility between two stories is being evaded here, said Sean, and it will take more than a few days to sort it out.

Sean says it is our friend Jesse Curry who will fill in the gap in the meantime as to *what exactly* the officer did supposedly see when he looked into the lunchroom: **Oswald sitting at one of the tables**, the very picture of post-assassination nonchalance.

Truly will endorse this detail himself:

NEW YORK
HERALD TRIBUNE

FBI Sifts Oswald Data

**By Dom Bonafede and
Stuart H. Loory**
Of The Herald Tribune Staff

WASHINGTON

Lee Harvey Oswald, the 24-year-old ex-Marine rifleman accused of slaying President Kennedy, knew the Chief Executive would pay a Nov. 22 visit to Dallas when, on Oct. 15, he accepted a warehouseman's job in the Dallas book depository.

Further, Oswald had good reason to believe the seven-story building—the last in the downtown district—offered a good vantage point for shots into the Presidential limousine. The warehouse was the last building along the traditional downtown parade route, used to give visiting dignitaries maximum exposure to crowds in the city.

Oswald would have known, weeks in advance, that President Kennedy was planning to visit Dallas. A report on the proposed visit was published in the Dallas Morning News Sept. 26.

These facts emerged as the FBI pursued its investigation of the Presidential assassination, the attempt on the life of Texas Gov. John B. Connally Jr. and the subsequent murder of the accused gunman by Jack Ruby, the 52-year-old Dallas night spot proprietor. An FBI spokesman said the bureau's report, ordered by President Johnson, would be made public by the end of the week.

In Dallas, the city police announced they had turned over all their evidence in the case to the FBI.

R. S. Truly, head of the book depository, told The Herald Tribune in a telephone interview that Oswald was hired as an extra warehouseman at $1.25-cents-an-hour, without character references.

"Since he was only an extra we felt we didn't need recommendations," said Mr. Truly.

He said that Oswald noted in his application that he had been in the Marines but omitted the fact he had received an undesirable discharge or had sought to obtain Russian citizenship. The applicant was described to him as "a fine young man," by a woman who was caring for Oswald's wife and children.

Mr. Truly also reported that Oswald narrowly missed being captured immediately after the shooting.

I rushed into the building with a policeman. He thought the shooting came from the roof and we ran up the stairway. On the second floor he stuck his head into a snack bar we have and saw Oswald sitting at one of the tables. 'Does this man work here?' the policeman asked. I said, 'yes, he does,' and we continued up the stairs. Meanwhile, Oswald apparently left the building.

Oswald was seen on the sixth floor of the warehouse on the morning of the assassination, said Mr. Truly, but no suspicion was attached to it since he frequently was required to work there as he moved public school text books from one part of the building to another.

President Kennedy's slayer, according to police, fired from a sixth floor window in the warehouse.

Oswald had "never given any indication of being mentally ill or a subversive," the employer said. "He was a good worker, never seemed to stop. He was quiet and well-mannered but he didn't mingle a lot or talk much to the other men."

The President, Mr. Truly said, rode by during the lunch hour and all the employees went out to see him. No one noticed that Oswald had stayed behind.

He was seen carrying a large object wrapped in newspapers (presumably the murder weapon) into the warehouse the morning of the assassination. He could have hidden it almost any place in the building, Mr. Truly said.

"It is a big building filled with rows and rows of books. The men generally put their lunches and belongings anywhere they want and nobody thinks about it."

The shooting and its aftermath, he said, "has been a terrible ordeal, a fantastic nightmare, something I'll never forget as long as I live."

104

And it will be reflected in the culminating action of the Oswald stand-in in the Secret Service reconstruction film made within days of the assassination:

Sean said as far as he's been able to ascertain, this little tableau will survive until nearly the end of the month, along with its supporting fiction of the officer's just having—in a moment of inspiration—happened to have popped his head into the lunchroom.

By the start of December, however, Oswald will have been "brought to his feet." For, if the translation of the front-stairway-to-lunchroom story to the rear-stairway-to-lunchroom story is to be completed successfully, the officer needs to be given a reason for interrupting his flight upstairs, going all the way over to the passageway to the door to the lunchroom and checking out what's in that lunchroom.

I am spellbound by Sean's reasoning and logic here.

Member Vince Palamara said he thinks this is the most fascinating thread he has ever read here, at least since 2008 or so. He is most impressed with everyone's contributions. He admitted that he started out feeling that this was a bit like a Rorschach Test with a healthy dose of wishful thinking, but is so glad he kept reading! He is very compelled to believe that Prayer Man is indeed Oswald, and the Blu-ray stills are much better tools than the earlier grainy clips. Vince said his girlfriend, who is a non-researcher, is convinced Prayer Man is Oswald.

Sean said it's impossible to pinpoint with exactitude the moment that Lee Oswald was "brought to his feet" in the Second Floor lunchroom, but it seems to have happened on either the November 27 or 28.

From *The Evening Star*, November 29, 1963:

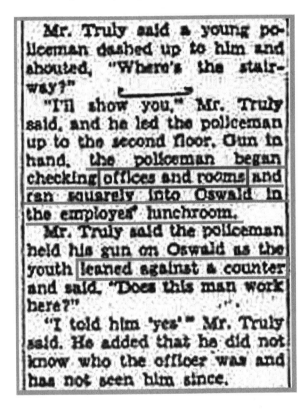

Mr. Truly said a young policeman dashed up to him and shouted, "Where's the stairway?"

"I'll show you," Mr. Truly said, and he led the policeman up to the second floor. Gun in hand, the policeman began checking offices and rooms and ran squarely into Oswald in the employes' lunchroom.

Mr. Truly said the policeman held his gun on Oswald as the youth leaned against a counter and said, "Does this man work here?"

"I told him 'yes'," Mr. Truly said. He added that he did not know who the officer was and has not seen him since.

Again, one notes the impression given that the lunchroom was simply a room—one of several here—passed by the officer en route to the rear stairway. But what Sean wishes to focus on here is the "counter" detail.

Note that Truly is the obvious and sole source of the "counter" detail.

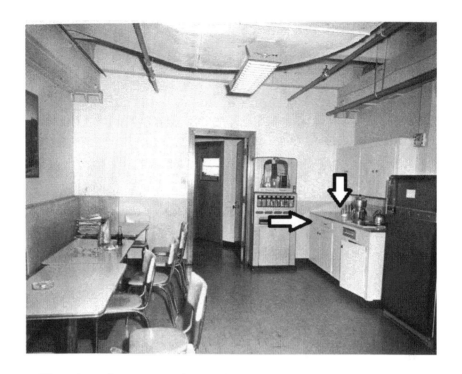

How does the reporter know there is indeed a counter in the lunchroom? Because Truly has told him. He has given the reporter a clear picture of Oswald leaning in all brazen nonchalance against the counter just inside the door.

Truly cannot possibly be inferring this image from having come on the scene just seconds after this, when Oswald is (as per his and Baker's Warren Commission testimony) at the door with Baker holding his revolver up to him. Nor can he have learned it from the officer, whom he "has not seen [him] since."

No, Sean said, just like the now discarded "sitting at one of the tables" image, this is an invention that Truly is giving—or has been directed to give.

But why has Oswald been brought to his feet? The answer comes in two parts.

Part one is *timeline*. It has become increasingly evident that Oswald, "the Sixth Floor assassin," needs to be made to appear as though he has only just arrived in the lunchroom.

Part two is *motivation for Baker to check out the lunchroom in the first place*. By the first of December, the second part becomes that much clearer as Oswald is moved from the "counter" over to the coke machine.

Again, bear in mind that Truly (as he will later tell the Warren Commission) was not supposed to have had any contact with Baker since they parted ways on November 22. Yet he was "guessing" with uncanny accuracy what Baker will months later testify to as to the location of Oswald in the lunchroom when he caught his first sighting of him in there.

From the *Sunday Bulletin* of Philadelphia December 1, 1963:

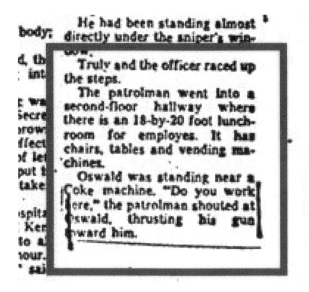

He had been standing almost directly under the sniper's window.

Truly and the officer raced up the steps.

The patrolman went into a second-floor hallway where there is an 18-by-20 foot lunchroom for employes. It has chairs, tables and vending machines.

Oswald was standing near a Coke machine. "Do you work here," the patrolman shouted at Oswald, thrusting his gun toward him.

From *The Washington Post* December 1, 1963:

"That's my building!" Truly shouted back. "I work in there."

He was quickly joined by a policeman, and they ran up the steps together, the officer with gun drawn. The two men scrambled up the stairs to the second floor. As they made their way to a back stairway, the policeman saw Oswald standing beside a soft drink machine, sipping "from a Coke bottle.

The officer ran toward Oswald and held the revolver at close range. "He's all right. He's one of my employes," assured Truly. The two men then continued on their way. Later, the employer described Oswald's demeanor in this incident as "cool as a cucumber —although he seemed a little bothered by the gun."

Oswald walked past a girl clerk who exclaimed, "Oh my land! the President has been shot!"

Why is Oswald now being put over by the coke machine? In order to push the explanation that Baker took his significant detour over to the lunchroom because of a noise he heard: *the noise of a coke machine in operation*, that's why.

If Charles Darwin was alive today, he might include the Second Floor lunchroom encounter story in his Theory of Evolution.

Sean then announced a "major development." Gary Mack,[81] curator at The Sixth Floor Museum at Dealey Plaza, said the following in an email:

> While the image is an interesting find, the Prayer Man question has probably been answered. I recently sent the Couch and Darnell frames to Buell Frazier and asked what he thought. First, he wouldn't confirm himself being on the top step because the image isn't clear enough. He then re-confirmed that Lovelady and Shelley were out on the steps with him, just as he has always said, but he couldn't confirm Shelley, either, due to the image quality.
> Next I asked about Shelley's appearance and learned he was a little taller than Lovelady (who was 5'8"), had red hair and a slender build. When I asked if Shelley usually wore a coat and tie to work Buell said no, he "dressed daily in slacks and sport shirts." And he repeated that he, Lovelady and Shelley stayed on the steps for "a short time" after the last shot, but he didn't estimate how long.
> So unless Buell Frazier is still part of the cover-up plot, **TSBD "Miscellaneous Department" manager William Shelley, by elimination, must be Prayer Man. According to Shelley's testimony, "I didn't do anything for a minute" following the last shot**, so the man was standing on the steps before, during and after the time Darnell and Couch filmed those brief scenes. – *Gary Mack*

This is a real breakthrough, said Sean, expressing his gratitude that Gary took the trouble to contact Buell Wesley Frazier. Why is it a breakthrough? Well, not because of the Shelley idea. For Shelley's own testimony, and that of the person with him Billy Lovelady, rules him out as Prayer Man:

> Mr. BALL - How did you happen to see Truly?
> Mr. SHELLEY - We ran out on the island while some of the people that were out watching it from our building were walking back and *we turned around and we saw an officer and Truly.*
> Mr. BALL - And Truly?
> Mr. SHELLEY - Yes.
> Mr. BALL - Did you see them go into the building?
> Mr. SHELLEY - No; we didn't watch that long but they were at the first step like they were fixin' to go in.
> Mr. BALL - Were they moving at the time, walking or running?
> Mr. SHELLEY - Well, they were moving, yes.

The Darnell film shows Baker just a couple of seconds away from the building entrance, said Sean. Prayer Man is still standing up on the steps. So Shelley is ruled out. Period. (Unless, that is, someone wants to accuse him and Lovelady of lying in their Warren Commission testimony about their run out on to the "island." Who wants to go first?)

Not me.

The reason Buell Wesley Frazier's response *is a breakthrough* is that Bill Shelley appears to be the only possibility Frazier himself can offer when presented with the Prayer Man image. (Although it's not quite clear from Gary's message whether Frazier himself nominated Shelley or whether that's Gary's own suggestion.)

Since Frazier is not giving us any new revelation as to the presence of anyone else on the steps at that time (i.e., a stranger to the building), and since Prayer Man cannot possibly be Shelley, we have just received startling confirmation that Prayer Man can only reasonably be Lee Oswald.

Buell Wesley Frazier probably knows it's Lee but—for the most understandable reasons in the world—cannot say so. However, to give him credit, he's just done the next best thing, said Sean.

I can't argue against that logic.

Richard Hocking commented it's excellent that we've finally heard from Buell Wesley Frazier. He agrees Frazier, who was standing a couple feet away at the time, has effectively limited the possibilities to Shelley and Lovelady. This is a powerful statement against any other employee or any stranger being at Prayer Man's location. And the possibilities of either Shelley or Lovelady being Prayer Man have been thoroughly covered previously. This thread just got a turbo boost, said Richard.

Bill Kelly doesn't see much difference in Baker's statement and testimony, other than the mention of the Fourth Floor encounter with someone, which he later said was a reference to the Second Floor lunchroom encounter. Baker pretty much sticks to his story of seeing

Oswald through the door window, and Truly did not see him, therefore Oswald must have been on the other side of the closed door and did not go through it, as he would have had to if he was the Sixth Floor sniper. Bill cited much evidence that the Second Floor encounter rules out Oswald as Sixth Floor shooter. Bill added that none of this eliminates Oswald as Prayer Man, as that is a distinct possibility.

Sean replied that there's no mention of a "door window" in Baker's November 22 affidavit story. There's no mention of a door, there's no mention of a room. Instead we hear about a man Baker catches "walking away from the stairway" several floors up the building. According to Marvin Johnson, who took the affidavit, Baker even talked about searching the man. This is not the lunchroom story that Baker will tell the Warren Commission.

As for Baker and Truly's Warren Commission story exonerating Oswald, all a Warren Commission defender has to do is argue the following:

- Oswald shoots JFK
- Oswald comes down the stairs
- Oswald on the Second Floor, hearing the noise of someone on the way up, hurries over to the Second Floor landing door and goes through it
- Oswald looks through the door window as Truly crosses the landing
- Oswald is about to go back out onto the landing when he is surprised to see an officer hit the landing
- Oswald spins around to head for the lunchroom
- But the officer notices the movement.

Now this scenario he outlined is pure crap, said Sean. But that doesn't matter. The lunchroom story makes it *possible*. Just tweak the timeline here and there, invent extra seconds for Truly and Baker to show up, and presto!—you have all the make-believe ambiguity you need to keep the fable of Oswald's guilt alive. That's what the Second Floor lunchroom fiction achieves: *it gets Oswald away from the front entrance.*

Does the lunchroom incident eliminate Prayer Man, Sean asked? No, quite the opposite! Prayer Man eliminates the lunchroom incident. Why? Because it *tells us where the real Baker-Oswald-Truly encounter happened*: at the front entrance.

This is what the Darnell film is telling us: **Look! Here's Baker, Truly and Oswald—*in the same frame together!***

No need to bustle Oswald upstairs for a phony second encounter, said Sean.

Chapter Seven Recap

Over five weeks into this thread and I'm getting the sense that Sean Murphy has now provided most of the bulk of his research on Prayer Man. He seems to be shifting over from instructing us to defending his claims and assertions. We'll see how that plays out going forward. In this chapter we have seen:

- Improved, higher-resolution Darnell frames show Prayer Man has the hairline and general appearance of Lee Oswald.
- The same frames unmistakably show Buell Wesley Frazier standing exactly where he testified he was.
- Oswald's presence at the front entrance at the time of the assassination is confirmed by multiple first-day/early affidavits and news reports.
- Careful analysis of Fritz's handwritten notes reveal Oswald said he:
  - didn't own a rifle
  - he saw a rifle in the building
  - was a member of the ACLU along with Mrs. Paine
  - got a Coke on the Second Floor
  - was having lunch out in front with Bill Shelley when the motorcade passed by.
- The Darnell images confirm Oswald was indeed telling the truth as to what he was doing and his whereabouts.
- The initial accounts describing a Baker-Truly encounter at the front entrance which were later revised to show the encounter taking place several floors up, with the Second Floor lunchroom encounter ultimately ending up as the official version, do one thing: they deprive Oswald of his 100 percent airtight alibi.
- When FBI Director J. Edgar Hoover briefed President Johnson on the status of the investigation on November 29, 1963, he did not mention a Second Floor encounter between Baker and Oswald.
- There is evidence that Shelley and Lovelady were coached on what to say by the Dallas Police Department and/or the FBI on when they saw Baker and Truly.
- The broad evolution of the Second Floor lunchroom encounter story centers around the problem of explaining why Baker "popped his head" into the lunchroom in the first place.
- Early accounts have Oswald sitting at one of the tables in the Second Floor lunchroom when Baker confronted him.

- The Secret Service assassination reconstruction film has the Oswald "actor" sitting at a table.
- Later, the story evolved to where Oswald is now on his feet, leaning against a counter.
- Next, Oswald is moved from the counter over to the Coke machine.
- All of these revisions provide greater reason for Baker to interrupt his flight upstairs to check out a noise he heard: the noise of a Coke machine in operation.
- When shown the improved Darnell image in September 2013, Buell Wesley Frazier would not identify himself, and said Shelley, possibly Lovelady, were the only two people he suggested Prayer Man could be.
- Frazier saying Prayer Man was Shelley or Lovelady rules out a stranger being Prayer Man.
- Since neither Shelley nor Lovelady are Prayer Man, the only reasonable conclusion is that Prayer Man is Oswald.

The pictures of Prayer Man tell a story—the story of Lee Oswald. Narrated by Sean Murphy.

CHAPTER EIGHT – PREY MAN

Starlings are tough but the lions are made of stone.

– Mark Knopfler

September 21, 2013. While the interest in the Prayer Man thread remains sky high, the pace seems to be slowing a bit in terms of new research presented by Sean Murphy. I see a lot of discussion that touches on more tangential issues and not so much on the central questions of the identity of Prayer Man and the evolving First-Third/Fourth-Second Floor Table-Counter-Coke Machine Whack-A-Mole story.

Also, I discovered that a Prayer Man thread was started at another popular JFK research forum (I'll refer to it as "The Popular Forum") and Sean has involved himself in those discussions.

While there are many supporters of Sean's research, I'm seeing people attack his work—and him—as well.

Pat Speer told Sean extraordinary claims demand extraordinary evidence. He said Sean has moved beyond raising the question of Oswald being Prayer Man, to claiming it's obvious. But it's only obvious to Sean (and perhaps a few others) because he has dismissed the possibility it could be anyone else, based upon the vague statements of people made days, weeks, and years after the shooting, that suggest (at least to Sean) that all the other people standing on the steps were standing somewhere else.

If these vague statements are trustworthy and reliable enough to support Sean's claim, Pat says, then they ought to be trustworthy and reliable enough to identify all the people standing on the steps in Altgens, Wiegman, and Darnell. This is something that needs to be done, in Pat's opinion, before Sean claims that Prayer Man as Oswald can be considered a reasonable possibility, let alone an obvious fact.

Pat suggested starting with Sarah Stanton. Where is she in the Altgens photo? Frazier indicates that she was standing by him in the aftermath of the shots. I think you've found Frazier in Darnell, but where is she in that film? To his left? If so, where is she in Altgens? Pat said if Sean can do this—go through the people claiming to have been on the steps one by one and identify them in the films and photos—it seems probable he will still have a few left over. If so, he would have to find photos of these people and compare them to Prayer Man before you could reasonably rule them out as Prayer Man.

It's a long road, but it might lead somewhere, said Pat.

Sean told Pat that he seems to have the thing topsy-turvy. If Wiegman or Altgens were showing us twenty people in the front entrance, then we would have to conclude that a number of non-TSBD employees must have gone unnoticed. But Wiegman and Altgens do no such thing, leaving any claim that the front steps may have played host to supernumerary persons not connected with the building arbitrary, gratuitous and extraordinary. If Pat wants to press such an extraordinary claim, let's see what he has to offer in that line.

Thus far anything he's had to suggest (Houston Street TSBD warehouse) has come to naught.

Sarah Stanton might be Prayer Man? I know one person who doesn't believe that extraordinary idea for a minute, said Sean. His name is Pat Speer.

From a large chunk of text from Pat's website that he copied and pasted in another post, Pat said:

> Although Mrs. Saunders [sic] tells us almost nothing on how the shots were fired, *her brief statements are at least of some assistance in clearing up some other mysteries.* For one, she says she left the lunch room at 12:20, but has no recollection of seeing Oswald on the day of the shooting. This works against Oswald's being in the second floor lunch room at that time. *For two, she says she stood on the east side of the top step,* and worked on the second floor. This, along with Billy Lovelady's claim the woman shielding her eyes in the Altgens photo worked on the second floor, suggests the

possibility Saunders was this woman. *If not her, then Stanton.*

Now, said Sean, if Pat wants to press an extraordinary claim, e.g. that—

- Prayer Man is a woman
- there is a woman standing beside Prayer Man
- Pauline Sanders hallucinated the presence of Sarah Stanton beside her
- Pauline Sanders completely misremembered which side of the TSBD entrance she was on

—then by all means let's see some extraordinary evidence to back it up. A photo of Sarah in her cross-dressing testosterone-injecting late-63 phase would be a good start. Until then...

~~Sarah Stanton~~

Sean asked "Who's next on your list?"

Sarah Stanton, said Pat. You still haven't shown us where she is in the footage with Frazier standing near the top of the steps. Frazier said he spoke to her just after the shots. Where is she?

Pat said it appears Sean is cherry-picking his way through a bunch of statements in order to arrive at his preferred conclusion. Sean cannot reasonably claim that Prayer Man is Oswald when he can't even say for sure Prayer Man is a man, said Pat. So that's one person on the steps who could be "Prayer Man." Shall we go for another?

How about Roy Lewis? He said he was alone in the entrance of the building when the shots were fired and that Oswald wasn't with him at the time of the shooting. If he's not Prayer Man, and Oswald was, then he would have to be considered a part of the cover-up.

Could he be Prayer Man? Why not? Because he's a Negro? Couldn't he have been a light-skinned Negro? I honestly don't know Lewis' skin tone. Do you, Sean?

What is it about Prayer Man that makes you so sure it's a white male? And Oswald? It's hard for me to believe that a number of people not involved in the conspiracy (Baker, Truly, Frazier, Lewis, Reid and ???) would all pretend they either didn't see Oswald at the front of the building after the shots, or that they did see him elsewhere in the building, and then keep this secret for decades.

I don't know who Prayer Man is. If you could identify all the people on the steps, and show how they were all employees of the TSBD, that would be a solid start toward making the case Oswald was Prayer Man, and that a number of people lied to cover it up.

There are no short-cuts around this, in my opinion, said Pat.

Sean exclaimed, "I'm cherry-picking my way through a bunch of statements, Pat?" All he did, Sean said, was quote, without omission, the relevant text from Pat's website. If Pat now suddenly disagrees with the following analysis...

> Although Mrs. Saunders [sic] tells us almost nothing on how the shots were fired, *her brief statements are at least of some assistance in clearing up some other mysteries.* For one, she says she left the lunch room at 12:20, but has no recollection of seeing Oswald on the day of the shooting. This works against Oswald's being in the second floor lunch room at that time. *For two, she says she stood on the east side of the top step,* and worked on the second floor. This, along with Billy Lovelady's claim the woman shielding her eyes in the Altgens photo worked on the second floor, suggests the possibility Saunders was this woman. *If not her, then Stanton.*

...then Sean said he suggests Pat take the matter up with himself and the two of him work up an amended version of the text. Sean said he's in a helpful mood so here's a first draft:

Although Mrs. Saunders [sic] tells us almost nothing on how the shots were fired, *her brief statements are **of no real** assistance in clearing up **any** other mysteries.* For one, she says she left the lunch room at 12:20, but has no recollection of seeing Oswald on the day of the shooting. This works against Oswald's being in the second floor lunch room at that time. *For two, she says she stood on the east side of the top step,* and worked on the second floor. ***But can we believe her? Her statement***, along with Billy Lovelady's claim the woman shielding her eyes in the Altgens photo worked on the second floor, ***may*** suggest [] the possibility Saunders was this woman. ***If not her, then Stanton.*** *However, it is perfectly possible and cannot be disproven that Stanton herself got down on her hands and knees, crawled over to the west side of the front entrance in order to secure a lousier view of the motorcade's progress and was subsequently too embarrassed to mention this fact to anyone. ANALYSIS: There is no hard evidence on record that Stanton was a feminine female, but every possibility she was a masculine female.*

As for Sarah Stanton showing up in Altgens or Wiegman, why should she? Witness statements place her back in the shadows with Frazier and Pauline Sanders, said Sean. This may well be her to Frazier's immediate left in Darnell:

231

We have no earthly reason to believe that Sarah Stanton could possibly be Prayer Man. Yet Sean said Pat insists on raising this profoundly silly idea. Why? And Prayer Man a "light-skinned

Negro"? You cannot possibly be serious, said Sean. What's next? Buell Wesley Frazier is a "dark-complected Caucasian"?

Sean asked "Who's next on your list, Pat?"

Avery Davis
Judy McCully
Ruth Dean
Madie Reese
~~Carl Jones~~
~~Roy Lewis~~
Joe Molina
Otis Williams
Pauline Sanders
~~Sarah Stanton~~
Bill Shelley
Billy Lovelady
Buell Wesley Frazier

He asked Pat, "Perhaps you'd like to make the case for Billy Lovelady again?"

On the day of the assassination, Sean said Oswald's supervisor Bill Shelley gave an affidavit in which he mentioned the name of Gloria Calvery:

AFFIDAVIT IN ANY FACT

THE STATE OF TEXAS
COUNTY OF DALLAS

BEFORE ME, _____ Mary Rattan

a Notary Public in and for said County, State of Texas, on this day personally appeared _____

William H. Shelley w/m/37 of 126 S. Tatum, FE7 1969. Bus: 411 Elm, RI7 3521

Who, after being by me duly sworn, on oath deposes and says: Today approximately 12:30 pm November 22,
1963 I was standing on the front steps at 411 Elm watching the President in the parade.
The President's car was about half way from Houston Street to the Triple Underpass
when I heard what sounded like three shots. I couldn't tell where they were coming from.
I ran across the street to the corner of the park and ran into a girl crying and she
said the President had been shot. This girl's name is Gloria Calvery who is an employee of this same building. I went back to the building and went inside and called
my wife and told her what happened. I was on the first floor then and I stayed at
the elevator and was told not to let anyone out of the elevator. I left the elevator
and went with the police on up to the other floors. I left Jack Dougherty in charge
of the elevator.

William H. Shelley

SUBSCRIBED AND SWORN TO BEFORE ME THIS __22__ DAY OF _____November_____ A.D. 196 3

Mary Rattan Mary Rattan
Notary Public, Dallas County, Texas

CPS-GF-413

The affidavit leaves no room for ambiguity. Shelley "ran into" Gloria *after* leaving the front steps of the building and running "across the street to the corner of the park." By the time of his and Billy Lovelady's April 7, 1964 Warren Commission testimony, however, the encounter with Gloria has been mysteriously transplanted to the front steps.

Shelley:

> Mr. SHELLEY - Gloria Calvary [sic] from South-Western Publishing Co. ran back up there crying and said "The President has been shot" and Billy Lovelady and myself took off across the street to that little, old island and we stopped there for a minute.
> ...
> Mr. BALL - She ran back up to the door and you had still remained standing there?
> Mr. SHELLEY - Yes.

Lovelady:

> Mr. BALL - Now, when Gloria came up you were standing near Mr. Shelley?
> Mr. LOVELADY - Yeah.
> Mr. BALL - When Gloria came up and said the President had been shot, Gloria Calvary [sic], what did you do?
> Mr. LOVELADY - Well, I asked who told her. She said he had been shot so we asked her was she for certain or just had she seen the shot hit him or--she said yes, she had been right close to it to see and she had saw the blood and knew he had been hit but didn't know how serious it was and so the crowd had started towards the railroad tracks back, you know, behind our building there and we run towards that little, old island and kind of down there in that little street.

It couldn't be clearer. The two men don't run into Gloria out across the street, she now runs up to them and becomes *the reason why they leave the steps.*

Most bizarrely of all, as we have seen earlier in this thread, both Shelley and Lovelady are now timestamping their departure from the front steps to some *3 minutes* after the shooting. Even Ball is taken aback by the extravagance of their over-estimation, said Sean. And it in turn yields the wildly implausible timestamp of between 3-4 minutes for their looking back from the "island" and seeing Baker and Truly about to enter the building.

It's clear that somebody at some point—somebody other than the Warren Commission folk—prevailed upon Shelley and Lovelady to delay their departure from the front steps by several minutes. But why?

Sean said he's already suggested two likely reasons:

1. The police were initially admitting that the Baker-Oswald-Truly encounter happened on the front steps just after the assassination. In order to make this story work, the timeline had to be stretched to minutes rather than seconds: Oswald was "stopped" on his way out of the building some 3-4 minutes after the shooting. He had time to make his descent from the Sixth Floor.
2. Billy Lovelady needed to be kept on the steps for a little while to help explain away any *Oswaldian* images that might show up in photos or films of the TSBD front entrance in the immediate assassination aftermath.

Sean said he thinks we can reasonably offer a third reason why the authorities, in the very early part of the "investigation," would have wanted to distort the Shelley-Lovelady timeline: ***Oswald was still alive***. The prospect of his going to trial was still a real one. And he, as defendant, was going to make a very damaging claim from the dock: *"I was out front with Bill Shelley."*

How, Sean asked, if Oswald was the Sixth Floor shooter, could he have known exactly where Bill Shelley was at the time of the assassination? How was the prosecution to explain away his description of Shelley (and others) on the steps?

The intended solution was to shift Oswald's sighting of Shelley to several minutes after the assassination. The front-entrance Baker incident having been transplanted up to the Second Floor lunchroom, Oswald would now be said to have spotted Shelley at the front entrance on his (Oswald's) way out of the building. To this end, Shelley needed to be kept on the front steps just long enough for this story to be plausible. Three minutes would do it.

Shelley's name is not mentioned in the joint Bookhout-Hosty interrogation report, written while Oswald is still alive. It does however make it into Bookhout's solo report,[82] written after Oswald has been murdered: "out with Bill Shelley in front" is glossed as a post-lunchroom incident event:

```
He thereafter went outside and stood around for five or
ten minutes with foreman BILL SHELLEY, and thereafter went
home. He stated that he left work because, in his opinion,
based upon remarks of BILL SHELLEY, he did not believe that
there was going to be any more work that day due to the
confusion in the building. He stated after arriving at his
```

All that now remains, said Sean, is for Shelley to be asked whether this had ever happened—and for Shelley to answer with an honest "no." Thus the ***Quadruple Switcheroo***:

   i.   Oswald, in the Domino Room, sees Jarman and Norman come in the back door of the First Floor <u>BECOMES</u> Oswald claimed to have eaten his lunch with Jarman and Norman.

   ii.   Oswald claims to have gone up to the Second Floor lunchroom to buy a coke shortly before the assassination <u>BECOMES</u> Oswald claimed to have gone up for the coke just after the assassination.

   iii. Oswald claims to have been eating his lunch and/or drinking the coke out front when the officer came in to the First Floor <u>BECOMES</u> Oswald claimed the officer came into the Second Floor lunchroom just after he had bought his coke.

   iv.   Oswald names Bill Shelley as one of the people he was out front with at the time of the assassination <u>BECOMES</u> Oswald named Bill Shelley as someone he spoke with out front several minutes after the assassination.

"That lying bastard, Oswald. We have him [literally] dead to rights."

One thing's for sure: Sean hasn't run out of ammunition yet.

Sean provided a quick recap:

Once it became clear that the police urgently needed to stop talking about the Oswald-Officer-Truly encounter at the front entrance, the encounter was moved deep into the building, at or near the rear stairs. The Third/Fourth Floor rear stairway story was quickly superseded by the lunchroom story. This became: the lunchroom stor*ies*.

The initial plan was simply to transplant Oswald up to the lunchroom, stretch the timeline and worry about the details later. Oswald was still alive and had every prospect of going to trial, so his damaging ability to describe an officer and Mr. Truly coming in to the First Floor needed to be preempted by a story involving the officer and Mr. Truly coming into the lunchroom. Truly's inflated time estimate in his first on-the-record account of the lunchroom incident (November 22, 1963 FBI interview) tells us how the thing was going to be played:

> searched the 7th floor of the building and by this time many officers were swarming through the building, and he returned to the first floor of the building. The time that he and the officer saw OSWALD in the snack bar could not have been more than two or three minutes after the shooting of President KENNEDY and they saw no one else in the building at that time. He has not seen OSWALD since that time, and shortly after, he, TRULY, had returned to the first floor of the building,

Two or three minutes? Yeah, right. The Warren Commission would struggle badly—even with the help of numerous time-trial shenanigans—to stretch the time to 90 seconds. But as of the night of November 22, the gambit was to inflate the time enough to give Oswald a chance to descend from the Sixth Floor but not enough to delay overmuch his exit from the building. Then all the Oswald accusers had to do was drive home the incongruity of a man alone and palely loitering in a lunchroom while everyone else was either outside or looking outside.

But what was Oswald actually *doing* in the lunchroom when Baker spotted him?

At first the question was fudged: Truly in a suite of statements simply has him "in" the lunchroom, specific location and activity left vague. Then, very quickly, the incongruity of Oswald's behavior gets sharpened up by the detail of his *sitting at one of the tables*. Within about a week, Oswald is brought suddenly to his feet: Truly describes him, first, as leaning against the counter and, then, as standing right over at the coke machine.

Why the coke machine? Because Oswald had talked about purchasing a coke before the assassination—having him over by the coke machine turned this into a cool post-assassination act.

But there was a second reason.

In February 1964, French writer Leo Sauvage contacted Roy Truly and grilled him about the lunchroom incident. Truly revealed the game plan as he and Baker headed in to March 1964 and their rendezvous with the Warren Commission at the TSBD: the officer (name still unknown to Truly!) evidently had heard a noise coming from the lunchroom, the noise, evidently, of a coke machine delivering up its product to the man who had just shot the President.

This was a crucial addition, for it gave Baker a reason for checking out the lunchroom—*a reason he badly needed*—as the lunchroom was nowhere near being in his line of sight as he came off the landing. Just look how far he would have had to swing over to the right to get a line into the lunchroom:

The door of the lunchroom being open, the noise of the coke machine would have been heard by Baker. Except... it wouldn't. For there was another door between Baker and the coke machine, and—disastrously—it was an automatically **self-closing** door.

The news story as told in *The Washington Post* December 1, 1963…

> "That's my building!" Truly shouted back. "I work in there."
>
> He was quickly joined by a policeman, and they ran up the steps together, the officer with gun drawn. The two men scrambled up the stairs to the second floor. As they made their way to a back stairway, the policeman saw Oswald standing beside a soft drink machine, sipping from a Coke bottle.
>
> The officer ran toward Oswald and held the revolver at close range. "He's all right. He's one of my employes," assured Truly. The two men then continued on their way. Later, the employer described Oswald's demeanor in this incident as "cool as a cucumber —although he seemed a little bothered by the gun."
>
> Oswald walked past a girl clerk who exclaimed, "Oh my land! the President has been shot!"

…seemed beautifully clean and convincing. However its lack of acoustic plausibility meant that a further refinement would be in order.

Sean Murphy's research is the gift that just keeps on giving.

We have seen, said Sean, Roy Truly's lunchroom story evolving over the first ten days or so through the following stages:

- The officer saw Oswald in the lunchroom...
- The officer saw Oswald *sitting at one of the tables* in the lunchroom...
- No...make that the officer saw Oswald *leaning against a counter* in the lunchroom...
- No...make that the officer saw Oswald *standing at the coke machine sipping a Coca-Cola* in the lunchroom...

Yet Truly's Warren Commission testimony will make it clear that he himself could have seen *none of these things*. All he *actually saw* was the officer standing at the lunchroom door with his gun up against Oswald, who was standing just inside the lunchroom door.

Those who still cling to the veracity of Baker and Truly's Warren Commission story can brush away these discrepant stories with a simple explanation: Truly made a number of erroneous but innocent inferences. He just filled in the gaps by making a series of guesses.

Perhaps this line of argument might be developed:

- At first Truly just assumed Oswald had been sitting at a table when the officer first burst in and then rose to his feet and came towards the door.
- Maybe a reporter or two just misattributed certain statements to Truly.
- Maybe the whole thing is just a case of Truly's guesswork meeting journalistic Chinese whispers.
- And maybe Truly refined his guesswork towards the end of November on the basis of information passed on to him by investigators that the officer back at Dallas Police Department Headquarters was saying that Oswald had been over at the coke machine by the time he had taken a look inside of the lunchroom.

- Maybe Truly just assumed Oswald had already bought the coke.
- Or maybe Truly said nothing about a coke—we have no direct quote from him mentioning a coke—but a reporter or reporters had embellished on the basis of picking up word of Mrs. Reid's sighting of Oswald with a coke in his hand just after that.

Thankfully (so the lunchroom believer will conclude) all of this was cleared up when Truly and Baker finally met up in March 1964 and Truly was able to learn first-hand from Baker the true circumstances of his first glimpse of Oswald behind the closed door.

Sounds plausible, no?

Well, there are two very large problems with this explanation.

First: It must ignore the fact that we have absolutely nothing on-the-record from Baker himself between end-November 1963 and March 1964. Are we seriously to believe that not a single investigator thought to ask Baker for his version of events? That no attempt was made by the Dallas Police Department, the FBI or Secret Service in the pre-Warren Commission phase to nail down the basic facts of this exquisitely important first post-shooting sighting of the alleged assassin?

Second: It must ignore this:

September 23, 1964
Dallas, Texas

I, Marrion L. Baker, do hereby furnish this voluntary signed statement to Richard J. Burnett who has identified himself to me as a Special Agent of the Federal Bureau of Investigation.

I am employed as an officer with the Dallas police department and was so employed as of November 22, 1963.

On the early afternoon of that day after hearing what sounded to me to be bullet shots, I entered the Texas School Book Depository Building on the northwest corner of Elm and Houston Streets in downtown Dallas.

I had entered this building in an effort to determine if the shots might have come from this building.

On the second floor MLB ~~main lunch floor~~, where the lunch room is located, I saw a man standing in the lunch room. ~~drinking a coke~~ MLB. He was alone in the lunch room at this time.

I saw no one else in the vicinity of the lunch room at this time.

M L Baker

Baker and Truly have been brought in—*on the eve(!) of the Warren Commission's findings being presented formally to President Johnson*—to clarify once and for all that Oswald was on his own in the lunchroom at the time of the incident. Yet, even as Baker dutifully clarifies this important point, he does something that is quite inexplicable on the lunchroom believer argument outlined above: He offers a version of events that **chimes perfectly with the "erroneous" "guesswork" version of events everyone had been told at the end of November 1963**:

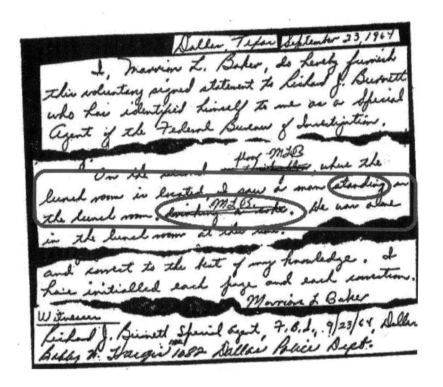

There is no wiggle room here. No Truly to distort the story. No reporter to distort Truly's distortion of the story. Just Marrion Baker himself, talking about Oswald "standing in the lunchroom drinking a coke." The coke "error" is pointed out to him, or he has second thoughts about it himself, and it's crossed out. But it's still there, a glaring anomaly in the statement.

The other glaring anomaly—Oswald "standing" in the lunchroom—is allowed to, well...stand.

It's as though Baker has brought the wrong, outdated memo with him to Dallas Police Department Headquarters and has very foolishly worked off it for his final statement on the lunchroom incident. His Warren Commission appearance being months in the past, he has forgotten to forget the details of this earlier version he had at one point been asked to support.
What a gaffe!

And I say to you, Mr. Murphy, what brilliance!

Bjørn Gjerde pointed out that Baker actually doesn't say a word about Oswald in this statement! He just saw "a man" standing in the lunchroom. And Truly was apparently not in the vicinity either ("I saw no one else in the vicinity of the lunch room at the time"). It may suggest that Baker is uncomfortable with the whole story and is deliberately vague, he said.

Yes, just "a man." Sean said the main body of Baker's September 23, 1964 statement...

September 23, 1964
Dallas, Texas

I, Marvin L. Baker, do hereby furnish this voluntary signed statement to Richard J. Burnett who has identified himself to me as a Special Agent of the Federal Bureau of Investigation.

I am employed as an officer with the Dallas police department and was so employed as of November 22, 1963.

On the early afternoon of that day after hearing what sounded to me to be bullet shots, I entered the Texas School Book Depository Building on the northwest corner of Elm and Houston Streets in downtown Dallas.

I had entered this building in an effort to determine if the shots might have come from this building.

On the second floor MLB, where the lunch room is located, I saw a man standing in the lunch room. MLB. He was alone in the lunch room at this time.

I saw no one else in the vicinity of the lunch room at this time.

M L Baker

...reads to him like a very early text, as though it has been lifted straight out of a late-November 1963 statement drafted for or by Baker. No mention of Oswald's name. No mention of Truly's. The hesitancy between Second and Third Floor, as though this statement is being delicately harmonized with Baker's disastrous November 22 affidavit statement ("third or fourth floor"). And, of course, "drinking a coke." No wonder certain bits had to be crossed out in September 1964 before the thing got filed for typing, he said.

Bill Kelly said, as Sean is still trying to convince us that the Second Floor lunchroom encounter never occurred and was the result of Baker and Truly being told what to say by the nameless screenwriter of the epic JFK assassination cover-up, Bill calls our attention to the fact that the date on the handwritten statement that Sean refers to (with the crossed out "drinking a coke"), is dated September 24, 1964, after the Warren Report was written and the day before it was publicly released. What the heck?

Why are they still concerned about this? Because they know its significance, and the fact that if it is reviewed in detail, as the Secret Service did, it exonerates Oswald as being the Sixth Floor Assassin. If Baker saw Oswald through the window of the closed lunchroom door, and Truly *ahead* of Baker didn't see him go through that door, then he didn't enter the lunchroom through that door. Instead, he went through the other door that leads to the offices which he left by, said Bill.

Truly testified that he didn't know Baker saw Oswald through the window of the closed door until sometime later, and heard it through the grapevine, just as Baker later heard that Oswald bought the now famous coke and Mrs. Reid saw him with it in his hand.

The clincher however, is when they called Truly back to the Post Office Annex to get him to answer one question under oath—does the lunchroom door with the window through which Baker saw Oswald—does that door have an automatic door closing mechanism—and the answer is yes, it does, securing the fact that the door was tightly closed when Baker saw Oswald on the other side of it—and Truly didn't see Baker go through it.

So Bill said Sean would have us believe that the master cover-up artists—the author of the fictional Second Floor encounter—made all this up in order to hide an even more telling truth—that the Baker-Oswald-Truly encounter occurred at the front door.

Now it's possible that Oswald is "Prayer Man" and he was like an invisible fly on the wall on the top steps by the front door. *Maybe*

"Prayer Man" even held the door open for Baker, but if that's the case, when Baker and Truly went to the rear of the building, Oswald, whether Prayer Man or not, went up the front steps and entered the vestibule of the lunchroom from the south door—so Baker saw him through the window of the closed door—and while Truly continued up the steps to the Third Floor, Baker investigated and confronted the man—Oswald.

Now if this story was concocted by anyone, says Bill Kelly, why wouldn't they tell Truly that he had to see Oswald go through the door ahead of Baker? Why would they tell Baker that he saw Oswald through the window of the closed door—and why would they create a scenario that exonerates Oswald?

Sean replied that he's not trying to convince Bill of anything. Bill's devotion to the lunchroom story is total, and that's fine. Bill is also perfectly free to mock the notion that the "investigating" authorities would have worked very hard to cover up inconvenient facts in the case, he added. But Bill should be aware that when he does so, he sounds more like Warren Commission defender David Von Pein than his own good self.

Now Sean said the question Bill asks is easily answered: Truly, by the time the "walking away" element was incorporated into the lunchroom story, had already gone on the record over and over again to the effect that his own first sighting of Oswald post-assassination was of Oswald in the actual lunchroom. It was too late to embellish along the lines Bill is suggesting.

Sean asked Bill why he keeps claiming that the lunchroom scenario, as told by Baker and Truly to the Warren Commission, "exonerates Oswald"? Please show us, Sean requested, how the following Oswald-as-lone-nut scenario is ruled out by Baker and Truly's testimony:

- Oswald shoots JFK
- Oswald comes down the stairs
- Oswald on the Second Floor, hearing the noise of someone on the way up, hurries over to the Second Floor landing door and goes through it

- Oswald looks through the door window as Truly crosses the landing
- Oswald is about to go back out onto the landing when he is surprised to see an officer hit the landing
- Oswald spins around to head for the lunchroom
- But the officer notices the movement.

Sean asked Bill to please give him his own analytical refutation of the above scenario with close reference to Baker and Truly's testimony.

Bill responded saying Oswald never looked through the window so he didn't know Baker was there until Baker walked over and opened the closed door and pointed his gun at Oswald's belly. Additional evidence, at least for Bill, that Oswald didn't go through that door was Baker and Truly's description of Oswald's demeanor—cool, calm and collected. This indicates he didn't just blow somebody's head open less than two minutes earlier because anyone who has killed someone and ran down four flights of steps would be hyper, heart pumping, breathing heavily, sweating, etc. The Second Floor encounter exonerates Oswald as a suspect, as Truly recognized and gave Oswald a pass.

Sean replied *"Proof—at least for me...X indicates not-Y...."* Sorry, he told Bill, but this is thin gruel. At best Bill's argument establishes that Truly and Baker's testimony is strongly indicative that Oswald was coming from the corridor to Baker's right. But it doesn't prove that scenario to the exclusion of all others, said Sean. It doesn't disprove the scenario he laid out, for instance. It leaves Baker's first glimpse of Oswald ambiguous. The thing can be—and has been—argued both ways. And Roy Truly recognized that the incident exonerated Oswald? He did no such thing, said Sean.

There is more back and forth discussion between Bill and Sean on the Second Floor encounter, but in the interest of space, I decided not to include these exchanges. I think what I've added here is sufficient to make up one's mind. If more detail is desired, one can visit The Education Forum and read the "Oswald Leaving TSBD?" thread.

Richard Hocking said Sean Murphy has created a persuasive analysis showing the evolution of the Second Floor lunchroom story. And he has used that analysis to conclude that the Second Floor lunchroom encounter is a fabrication. Bill Kelly feels that the officially sanctioned and widely accepted lunchroom story is strong enough to stand on its own to vindicate Lee Oswald. Richard thinks there is another option.

We cannot exclude the possibility, he said, of Prayer Man/Oswald going up to the Second Floor after Truly and Baker had passed through the lobby, and perhaps after Campbell had ascended the Lobby stairs to the Second Floor (to vindicate the sighting by the storage closet). Getting Oswald from the Sixth Floor to the lunchroom in time to see Baker is problematic. Getting Oswald from the front lobby to the Second Floor is not. We know a group of employees went up to the Second Floor offices right after the assassination. It is entirely possible Lee Oswald also decided to go. We have no evidence that precludes this possibility. Could he have made it all the way to the lunchroom? Possibly. A simple sighting of Oswald on the Second Floor would give strength to any lunchroom story, whether it happened as advertised by the Warren Commission or was simply a last resort fabrication by the conspirators to get Oswald as close to the rear stairs as possible, he said.

Earlier in this thread, Sean mentioned the note by the *Dallas Morning News* reporter Kent Biffle on March 1964 about the nature of the Truly-Baker-Oswald encounter:

The [TSBD] superintendent [Truly] would recall later that he and a policeman met Oswald as they charged into the building after the shots were fired.

Biffle is not talking off the top of his head here, said Sean. He got closer to Truly in the TSBD in the immediate aftermath of the assassination than any other news reporter. And here he is reporting exactly what happened. They met Oswald/Prayer Man at the front entrance to the building as they charged into it. Baker didn't challenge Oswald or stop him, he simply asked him for help.

Shortly after this, a second man would ask Oswald for help at the same front entrance, said Sean. His name was Pierce Allman, manager of programming and production at WFAA radio, and here's his 1998 recollection of the incident:[83]

> And then I turned around, ran back down the hill, ran up the sidewalk, went into the depository building, *asked the guy where the phone was,* went inside, got on the phone, called the station, and had trouble getting through.

The "guy" in question was, of course, Lee Oswald, who would later erroneously recall the crew-cut credentials-flashing Allman as a Secret Service man whom he had directed to the phone on the First Floor located towards the rear.

Now Allman was noticed shortly after this by Army Intelligence Special Agent James W. Powell:

Street. I took a photograph of the building at that instant.
Several policemen, men from the Dallas County Sheriff's Office, and
newspaper and television reporters, were rushing toward the railroad
switching yard behind the TSBDB. I followed them in order to learn
what had happened. One of the television reporters, whose name I
did not get, said that he heard that someone had fired a gun at
Kennedy. I rushed back to the TSBDB, through the lobby, and into
the first-floor offices. There I overheard Pierce Almond (phonetic),
a newscaster for WFAA Television Station, Dallas, who was telephoning
his office. Almond said that he heard that Kennedy had been fired at
and hit, and that the shots may have come from the TSBDB. Almond had
just talked with a construction worker who supposedly witnessed the
accident. I went upstairs to the second floor and telephoned my
office. I reported what I had heard to Lt. Col. Roy H. Pate, Region
Commander. I then returned to the first floor, where I met and
interviewed the aforementioned construction worker, an employee of
Wallace Beard, Oil and Gas Building, Dallas. I did not have time to

Powell went up to the second floor to use the available telephone there. He is surely the "policeman" recalled by Geneva Hine:[84]

There is an uncomfortable moment in Hine's Warren
Commission testimony, said Sean, where she is asked about
Jeraldean Reid, who was claiming to have gone up to the Second
Floor office area very shortly after the assassination and to have
encountered Lee Oswald there:[85]

> Mr. BALL. When you came back in did you see Mrs. Reid?
> Miss HINE. No, sir; I don't believe there was a soul in the
> office when I came back in right then.
> ...
> Mr. BALL. Did you see Mrs. Reid come back in?
> Miss HINE. Yes, sir; I think I felt sure that I did. I thought
> that there were five or six that came in together. I thought she
> was one of those.
> Mr. BALL. Mrs. Reid told us she came in alone and when
> she came in she didn't see anybody there.
> Miss HINE. Well, it could be that she did, sir. I was talking
> on the phones and then came the policemen[86] and then came
> the press. Everybody was wanting an outside line and then
> our vice president came in and he said "The next one that
> was clear, I have to have it and so I was busy with the phone.
> Mr. BALL. From the time you walked into the room you
> became immediately busy with the phone?
> Miss HINE. Yes, sir; sure was.

Hine in the above exchange is clearly trying to be helpful,
offering as an explanation for her having missed Reid the

circumstance that she (Hine) was so busy with the phones. But Sean said it just doesn't work.

For one thing, how could Reid have missed her and the "policeman" with her? For another, and even more calamitously for Ball's line of questioning, how could Hine have missed both Reid and Oswald when *the desk she was manning the phones at was in the front row of desks facing right where Reid is supposed to have come in and Oswald to have gone out?*

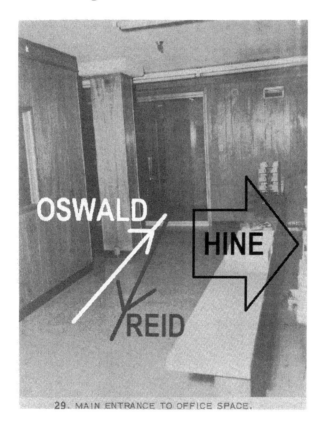

29. MAIN ENTRANCE TO OFFICE SPACE.

Continuing:

> Mr. BALL. Did you have to change your desk over to
> another desk [in order to watch the phones that day]?
> Miss HINE. Yes, sir; to the middle desk on the front row.
> ...

Mr. BALL. Did you see Oswald come in?

Miss HINE. My back would have been to the door he was supposed to have come in at.

Mr. BALL. Were you facing the door he is supposed to have left by?

Miss HINE. Yes, sir.

Mr. BALL. Do you recall seeing him?

Miss HINE. No, sir.

How in heaven's name can Hine—desperate for information as to what has happened outside—possibly have missed Reid and Oswald? And how can Reid possibly have seen Oswald but missed Hine (and the policeman)?

Might it be that the Reid-Oswald encounter happened before Hine reentered the office space?

For anyone wishing to preserve the Second Floor lunchroom story, it's a tempting idea. But it causes a whole new set of problems.

Wee doggies. Does it ever!

Acting as a "Gunga Din water boy," Bill Kelly presents Gary Mack's comments (Sean Murphy's responses are in bold):

> Sorry, folks, you cannot use Pierce Allman to turn Oswald into PM. I've known Pierce for many years, and this account is the story he has always told and sticks with today:[87] (The report has one error I know of: Pierce was program director of WFAA radio, not TV, and once Oswald pointed to the phone, Pierce called the radio station.)
> **Based on his travel down to the Newmans TWICE from the Elm-Houston intersection, he could not have gotten to the TSBD door for 2, 3, maybe 4 minutes depending on how long he spoke to them, whether he spoke to others, or just looked around before heading to the building and dodging traffic. For Oswald to be PM, he would have had to hang around the front door for several minutes from the moment of**

the shooting until he was met by Pierce, and that is highly unlikely. One or more fellow employees would have seen him and eventually reported it.

In case you haven't been following closely, Gary, the claim is <u>not</u> that Oswald just hung around the front door for several minutes. It's that he popped in to the "small storage room" just off the lobby and <u>was seen there</u> by Ochus Campbell (and possibly Jeraldean Reid too) as he (and possibly she) headed for the front stairs up to the second floor: that's the sighting Ochus Campbell himself was telling news reporters in the TSBD within just two or three hours of the assassination. Allman's reaching the front door of the TSBD within 2 or 3 minutes of the shooting in no way undermines the case for Oswald as Prayer Man.

Instead, Pierce stopped Oswald as Oswald left the building following the lunchroom encounter, for no other explanation makes sense.

It's important that you not put words in Pierce's mouth, Gary. He did not say he "stopped" Oswald; he merely said he spoke with him. Precision, please.

Pierce may have flashed his press pass to Oswald, but he didn't remember doing that nor did co-worker Ford say he did....but he certainly could have done so and it would have been a natural thing to do at the time.
As for Oswald's belief Allman was a Secret Service man, the notes and recollections say he said the man had a crew cut hair style. Pierce appeared on WFAA-TV later that afternoon, the tape exists, and he certainly did have that hair style. Although Manchester and other books often attribute the TSBD encounter to NBC's Robert MacNeil, that's simply wrong. Tapes of MacNeil that day show his hair was much, much longer than Allman's and it was even longer then than it is today.

I quite agree: Allman is the most likely candidate for the crew-cut man Oswald helped.

Folks will have to look elsewhere to ID the Prayer Man, for he certainly wasn't Oswald.

Oh dear, Gary, such categorical ruling out of something you simply cannot categorically rule out. Given the certainty with which you issued your erroneous declarations that Prayer Man was (first) Lovelady and (then) Shelley, perhaps a little humility and tentativeness might have been hoped for from you with respect to further suggestions as to the identification of Prayer Man?

(Unless, of course, one subscribes to the theory that the polite, ever-trusting killers allowed all TSBD workers who could have seen Oswald on the steps to live for years if not decades after the assassination, hoping they would never tell anyone.)

Who says the killers of JFK would have been bothered by the revelation that Oswald was not the sixth floor shooter? Again, please address the Prayer Man theory that is being put forward, not a straw man simplification of it.

Gary Mack

Question for you, Gary: who do you believe Prayer Man is?

Two days later, Sean Murphy said that Gary Mack has not responded, adding it seems to him there's no hard evidence that

Gary's job allows him to even consider the possibility that Lee Oswald was not the Sixth Floor shooter.

Bill Kelly said Gary Mack says he can think whatever he wants and that history has placed Oswald elsewhere, whether Sean agrees with that or not.

Oookay then. I reckon that settles it, huh?

Sean said Jeraldean Reid's November 23, 1963 affidavit is an impressive document, for it manages with great economy to tick every box Roy Truly and the FBI so very badly needed ticked:

1. *Just* as Jeraldean entered the office area, she noticed Oswald coming through the back door into the office area
2. This back door was located near the lunchroom *and the rear stairway*
3. The encounter was unmistakably post-assassination because Jeraldean *said something to Lee about the President's being shot*
4. Lee had a *coke* in his hand
5. She saw Lee *walk out of the office* just after their paths had crossed.

The last item here...

AFFIDAVIT IN ANY FACT

THE STATE OF TEXAS

COUNTY OF DALLAS

BEFORE ME, _____ Patsy Collins

a Notary Public in and for said County, State of Texas, on this day personally appeared _____

Mrs. R. A. Reid, 1914 Elmwood, FE-1-6617

Who, after being by me duly sworn, on oath deposes and says: I work for the Texas School Book Depository
I have worked for them seven years, at 411 Elm Street.
Yesterday November 22, 1963 I was working, we took our lunch period from 12 to 1pm
I went out side to watch the parade go by. I was standing on the front steps of
our Building, as the parade drew near I walked closer to the street. Just after
the President passed by I heard three shots. The first thing I thought of was
someone was shooting at the President. I remarked to Mr. Campbell who was
standing near by that I thought the shots had come from our building. But I
heard someone else say no, I think it was farther down the street. I went
back into our building and up to the second floor to our office, just after
I entered the office I saw one of the men who work in the warehouse come through
the back office door. This door is located near the lunch room and the rear stairway. I did not know this man's name at the time for he had not worked there long.
However I now know his name to be Lee Oswald. I said to Lee, Oh! someone has
shot at the President. I hope they didn't hit him. Lee mumbled something and
walked on out of the office. I did not understand what he said, he had a coke
in his hand. When I saw him he was dressed in a white T-shirt and I don't
recall what his trousers was like. I did not see him anymore after that.XXXXXXXX
XXXXXXXXXX

Mrs. R. A. Reid

SUBSCRIBED AND SWORN TO BEFORE ME THIS 23 DAY OF November _____ A.D. 196 3

Patsy Collins
Notary Public, Dallas County, Texas

jrl
CPS-OF-413

...is of particular note for it will become weirdly muddled in
Jeraldean's Warren Commission testimony. There, she and Belin will
go on an elaborate and silly detour as to the possible routes Oswald
might have taken just after passing Reid near her desk.

For some unknown reason, Jeraldean now refrains from telling us authoritatively that, after Lee mumbled something, he "walked on out of the office."

And yet she take pains to eliminate the possibility that the door through which he walked on out of might have been the back door through which he had just come in:[88]

    Mr. BELIN - Did Lee Harvey Oswald walk past you?
    Mrs. REID - Yes; he did.
    Mr. BELIN - Kept on walking in the same direction?
    Mrs. REID - Yes, sir.
    Mr. BELIN - How far did you see him go?
    Mrs. REID - I didn't turn around to look. He went on straight, he did not go on past the back door because I was facing that way. What he did after that—
    Mr. BELIN - But you know he did not go out the same back door he came in?
    Mrs. REID - No; he did not.

But where exactly was Jeraldean so that she could rule out the possibility of Oswald's having gone out the back door? Let's look at the layout of the floor, with Oswald's alleged post-shooting route from the Sixth Floor drawn in:

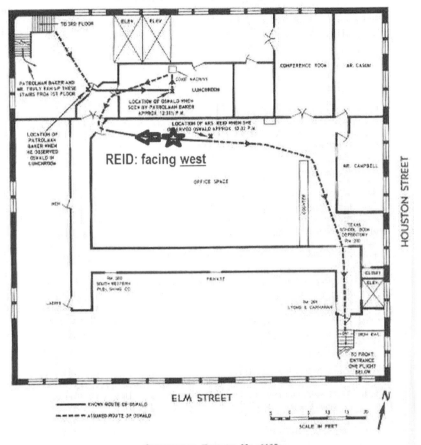

TEXAS SCHOOL BOOK DEPOSITORY
DIAGRAM OF SECOND FLOOR
SHOWING ROUTE OF OSWALD

REID: facing <u>west</u>

ELM STREET

COMMISSION EXHIBIT No. 1118

The natural assumption would be that Jeraldean was at her desk. But she explicitly rules that idea out:

> I met him by the time I passed my desk several feet and I told him, I said, "Oh, the President has been shot, but maybe they didn't hit him."

Why did she pass her desk? Where was she going? Did she keep walking and leave the office area through the same back door which

Oswald had just entered? Did she perhaps want to recover from the shock of the shooting by making a beeline for the ladies' room?

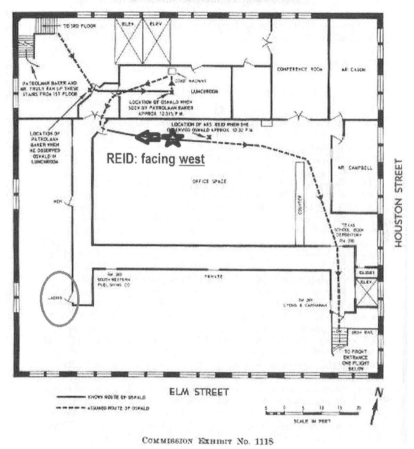

TEXAS SCHOOL BOOK DEPOSITORY
DIAGRAM OF SECOND FLOOR
SHOWING ROUTE OF OSWALD

COMMISSION EXHIBIT No. 1118

No, her testimony rules all this out because she is in the office long enough to preclude the possibility that Oswald could have turned around and gone out the back door at some point after Reid herself had left it.

Thus we are left with the very strange image of Jeraldean Reid standing frozen in space several feet away from her desk, resolutely facing west and not going anywhere. Why is she fudging the issue of

263

her actions after the Oswald exchange? Because she needs to do two irreconcilable things:

a) Be in the office for a long enough time to rule out Oswald's having exited the office via the back door
b) Sustain the impression that she is herself perfectly positioned to exit the office by the back door.

The reason for b? *Geneva Hine, who is about to <u>reenter the office</u>—via the corridor and through the back door.*

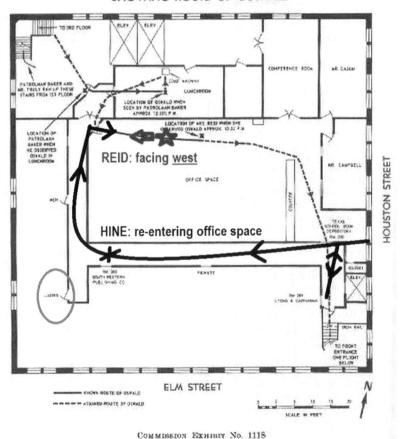

TEXAS SCHOOL BOOK DEPOSITORY
DIAGRAM OF SECOND FLOOR
SHOWING ROUTE OF OSWALD

REID: facing <u>west</u>

HINE: re-entering office space

ELM STREET

COMMISSION EXHIBIT No. 1118

My earlier impression that Sean had already provided the bulk of his research on Prayer Man was wrong. He seems to have a bottomless pit of info! He keeps rolling right along like a freight train.

Sean provided an update from Gary Mack:

> Cheap shot, Sean, cheap shot. I can think whatever I want. History has put Oswald elsewhere whether you agree with that or not. As to your question, I think Prayer Man is NOT Lee Harvey Oswald. Clear enough?
> – Gary Mack

Sean replied:

> Gary, we already know you think Prayer Man is NOT Lee Harvey Oswald. History has evidently placed you in a position where you are professionally compelled to rule that possibility out. But in answer to your question: no, not clear enough.
> Who do you think Prayer Man is? Are you still, by process of elimination, backing the slender white male TSBD employee Bill Shelley?

On December 6, 1963, *Time* magazine carried a story titled "The Man Who Killed Kennedy." It contained the following account of the Oswald-Reid encounter:

> Carrying his Coke, Oswald ambled into a nearby office. A switchboard operator said, "Wasn't that terrible—the President being shot?" Oswald mumbled something unintelligible, went out of the office, walked down the steps and slipped through the crowd outside.

French researcher Leo Sauvage was puzzled by the reference to a "switchboard operator," and in February 1964, asked Roy Truly about it:[89]

> Yes, he confirmed, that was the story told to the FBI when—on the following week—they finally began questioning everyone who works in the School Depository. But, he added, **it wasn't the switchboard operator who spoke to Oswald. It was another woman working in the same office**, and yes, that office is "right next to the lunchroom." Did either of the two women notice the noise Oswald must have made in the corridor rushing in from the sixth floor? Mr. Truly didn't know.

How very odd, Sean said. One would expect Truly to simply correct the idea that Mrs. Reid was a switchboard operator and leave it at that. But the specter of Geneva Hine looms too large. Technically speaking, Geneva wasn't a switchboard operator (there was no switchboard proper in the Second Floor office). She did however volunteer to keep an eye on incoming phone calls while her colleagues went outside to watch the motorcade. And, given the fact that she and she alone was in the office area around the time of the motorcade, it is simply not credible that the *Time* magazine reporter in referring to a switchboard operator meeting Oswald there had just made a lucky mistake.

Clearly the reporter had gotten wind of the fact that someone was in the office at the time looking after the phones and that this person had had an interaction with Oswald. And the reporter, hearing also about a conversation between a female employee and Oswald in that same office area just after the shooting, assumed that said female employee must have been the switchboard operator.

So Truly is in a real bind when asked about the *Time* reference to a switchboard operator. He has to admit that Jeraldean Reid was not the only woman in the office area immediately after the assassination. Yet the Reid story—which she was given on November 23—**requires the office to be empty at the time of the encounter.**

On September 17, 2011, Sean said Robert Groden made the following remarks in a radio interview with Len Osanic:[90]

> I actually found a woman some years ago. She was terrified. She did not want to come forward. And she finally agreed to give an interview, and I did interview her. When the shots actually went off, she was talking to Lee Oswald on the second floor. [...] We always assumed that Lee had the change, that he had had the change for the machine. He didn't. He went into the office across from the snack room with a dollar bill and asked for change. He said, "No pennies, please." And, as the change was being counted out into his hand, the shots went off. And they looked at each other, this woman and Lee, and [asked], "What was that?" Backfires, firecrack[ers], who knew? He got the rest of the change, walked back across the hall, bought the Coke and then just a little over a minute later there was a gun in his ribs held by Officer Baker. Lee had an airtight alibi. He could not possibly have done this. She told this story to the Warren Commission. They told her to keep her mouth shut. And she did. She told very few people. Very few people. I was one of the few that she did. So I got to speak to her because I had a friend who knew a friend of hers. I had to promise her I would never reveal any of this until after she was gone. And now she is. The whole story, including her name, will be in the next book.

Groden's book has not yet been published, said Sean, and it is a cause of real regret that he has chosen to hold back these potentially case-breaking details for so long. The woman he spoke with must surely be Geneva Hine (who died at the age of 100 just over a decade ago).

What are we to make of Groden's claim?

Sean said his belief is that Lee Oswald is Prayer Man and that he had already descended from his coke-purchasing visit to the Second Floor lunchroom in time to catch the motorcade from the front steps. This is the chronology of events implied in the crucial first interrogation report written jointly by FBI Special Agents Bookhout and Hosty:

- Broke off work and went down for lunch in Domino Room

- Went up to Second Floor lunchroom to purchase a Coca Cola
- Back down to First Floor, which is where he was at the time of the assassination.

If—as Sean said he believes—Oswald really did claim to have been on the First Floor at the time of the shooting, then the story as relayed by Groden does not make sense. Hearing the loud bangs in the Second Floor office, he may conceivably have mistaken them at the time for motorcycle backfires or firecrackers, but there is no way he would have failed to grasp their true meaning by the time of his arrest. And yet he appears to be placing himself on the First, not Second, Floor "when President Kennedy passed this building."

This is not to say that Groden's witness story is without significance, said Sean. It may in fact be of huge importance. Here— pending disclosure of the full details from Groden—is what Sean believes may have happened:

1. Oswald got change for the coke machine from Hine a very few minutes before the shooting.
2. Oswald and Hine did hear bangs as she was giving him his change, but they were not shots--they were motorcycle backfires, the same motorcycle backfires which Buell Wesley Frazier told Gary Mack he heard in Dealey Plaza while everyone was awaiting the motorcade.
3. Oswald then went to the Second Floor lunchroom and got his coke.
4. Oswald after this went down to the First Floor and caught the motorcade (in Sean's opinion, Prayer Man is holding the coke in his immobile left hand).

Sean says he hesitates to say this, but his suspicion is that Groden has (for understandable reasons) slightly "sexed up" Hine's account by unequivocally identifying the "bangs" she said she and Oswald heard as the shots that were fired at Kennedy. Groden is also joining the dots between Hine's story and the fictitious lunchroom story in a way not strictly sanctioned by Hine's account.

If Hine was indeed the woman Groden spoke with, and if her story was basically factual, then we have another explanation for

Reid's being drafted in on Saturday as a supporting witness for Truly's damage-limitation lunchroom story:

- Oswald is still alive.
- He is expected to go to trial.
- He is going to be talking about an interaction with a female employee in the Second Floor office area just before the assassination.
- Hine must be told to shut up about giving Oswald change for the coke machine, for her story would blow the lid on the lie that his visit to the lunchroom was post-assassination.
- And in order that Oswald's testimony at trial about speaking with a female employee in the office area can be explained away, Reid must be enticed into coming forward with a phony post-assassination Oswald-in-office-area story.

If the above outline of events is correct, said Sean, then why was Hine not simply pressurized into testifying to the Warren Commission that she had witnessed the Reid-Oswald encounter? Because she had already been pressurized into going on the record several times to the effect that **she had not seen Lee Oswald at all on the day of the assassination**.

The result of all this?

The relationship between Hine's Warren Commission testimony and that of Reid is horribly messy and contradictory. The best Reid can do—can be made to do—is leave open the impression that she may have left the office area shortly after the Oswald encounter, said Sean.

Where might she have gone to?

Ironically enough, there is only one possible place available if she is to avoid running into Hine in the corridor: the Second Floor lunchroom...

TEXAS SCHOOL BOOK DEPOSITORY
DIAGRAM OF SECOND FLOOR
SHOWING ROUTE OF OSWALD

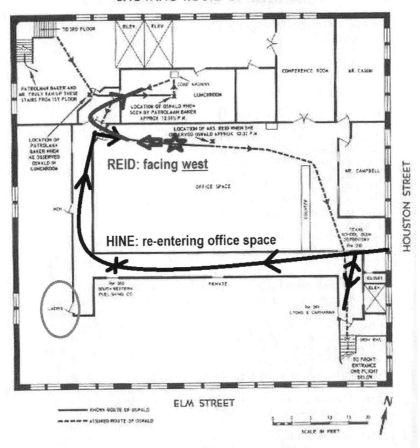

REID: facing west

HINE: re-entering office space

COMMISSION EXHIBIT No. 1118

Sean said Marrion Baker testified before the Warren Commission that Lee Oswald was just behind the door with the glass pane when he first glimpsed him:[91]

> Now, through this window you can't see too much but I just caught a glimpse of him through this window going away from me and as I ran to this door and opened it, and looked on down in the lunchroom he was on down there about 20 feet so he was moving about as fast as I was.

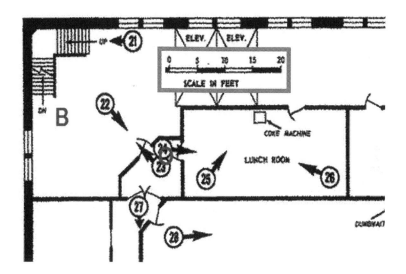

Oswald was "moving about as fast" into the lunchroom as Baker was moving from the landing just off the stairway to the door? It's hard to see how, Sean said. Baker's story is that he "ran" to the door in order to go after a man he had glimpsed "walking away." Yet we are to believe that they covered <u>about the same distance in the same time</u>—i.e., that Baker running did not cover more ground than Oswald walking.

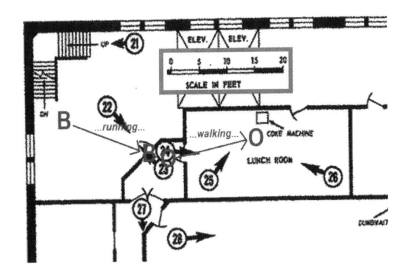

It's a nonsensical scenario, said Sean, so nonsensical that one wonders why Baker is making such a transparently unrealistic claim. Why doesn't he just say that Oswald was running? Or, alternatively, that Oswald was only a few feet into the lunchroom by the time he himself opened the door and looked into the lunchroom?

The short answer is Baker has to merge by force two stories that cannot easily be merged:

1. I saw a man walking away (as per Baker's November 22 affidavit).
2. I saw Oswald standing by the coke machine (as per a later draft of the story, as told by [or to?] Roy Truly).

As we have already seen, Baker in September 1964 will go on the record again with a careless reversion to the "standing" version of the story:

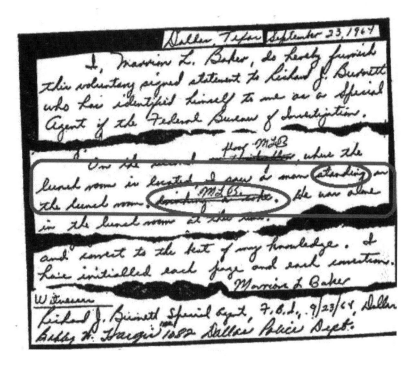

Yet his own Warren Commission testimony has both of his sightings of Oswald being of a man who is moving, walking:

> I just caught a glimpse of him through this window going away from me → I ran on up here and opened this door and when I got this door opened I could see him walking on down.

He has a real problem here: his November 22 affidavit talked of "a man walking away from the stairway." For Oswald, just behind the glass pane, to be "walking away" in any commonsense meaning of the words, he would need to be walking into—a wall.

The lunchroom was sharply off to the left, it was not straight ahead—not even close. So Baker, in his Warren Commission testimony, has to split his affidavit's single description of a man "walking away" into two incidences of walking away. The result, as one would expect said Sean, is a horrible muddle.

The one thing Baker desperately needs to say—that his first glimpse of Oswald had him "walking away from the stairway"—is the one thing the layout of the landing/door/lunchroom disallows him from saying. And so we get a hesitation around the words "walking away":[92]

> Mr. BAKER - As I came out to the second floor there, Mr. Truly was ahead of me, and as I come out I was kind of scanning, you know, the rooms, and I caught a glimpse of this man *walking away from this*—I happened to see him through this window in this door. I don't know how come I saw him, but I had a glimpse of him *coming down there*.
> Mr. DULLES - Where was he coming from, do you know?
> Mr. BAKER - No, sir. All I seen of him was a glimpse of him *go away from me*.

"I caught a glimpse of this man walking away from this—": if only Baker could finish the thought with the magic word: "stairway"!

But Sean said he can't, for to do so would be to make a ludicrous claim that would only draw attention to the discrepancies between his current story and the story told in his affidavit.

Excruciatingly, the money shot—the shot of Oswald actually walking directly away from Baker's position such that Baker can call to him and have him turn around and come back to where Baker is—has to be held back until Baker has left the stairway and gone over to the door:[93]

> Mr. BAKER - ... There is a door there with a glass, it seemed to me like about a 2 by 2, something like that, and then there is another door which is 6 foot on over there, and there is a hallway over there and a hallway entering into a lunchroom, and when I got to where I could see him he was *walking away from me* about 20 feet away from me in the lunchroom.
> Mr. BELIN - What did you do?
> Mr. BAKER - I hollered at him at that time and said, "Come here." He turned and walked right straight back to me.

Baker is now, at last, giving a story that sounds a little more like his November 22 affidavit story:

> *As we reached the third or fourth floor I saw a man walking away from the stairway. I called to the man and he turned around and came back toward me.* – Baker, November 22 affidavit.

But only a little, said Sean.

The two stories—November 22 affidavit plus his Warren Commission testimony—are still irreconcilable. Even after the heavy coaching that Baker has been put through ahead of his Warren Commission appearance. We still are being asked to believe that an indeterminate glimpse of a man moving behind a door located well off the stairway could be described as a sighting of "a man walking away from the stairway."

The plain sense of those words in Baker's November 22 affidavit cannot be ignored, Sean stressed: the man had just left the stairway and was putting distance between it and him. That's what "walking away from" means, and it's how Baker himself is using those words in his Warren Commission testimony.

No amount of special pleading (Baker in his affidavit was being economical with language; he used an unfortunate choice of words; etc.) can change the plain sense of those words. Especially as there is nothing—*nothing*—in the rest of Baker's November 22 account to particularize the scene of the encounter as the Second Floor, let alone a room on the Second Floor, let alone a room on the far side of a closed door on the Second Floor, let alone a lunchroom on the far side of a closed door on the Second Floor.

If a witness were to say, "Just after the shooting I saw a car driving away from the Triple Underpass," would anyone dare to suggest that this could mean anything other than that the car had been at or by the Triple Underpass and was now increasing its distance from it? Yet that is the offense against common sense and the English language that those arguing for the veracity of the lunchroom story would have us commit.

Just how many impossible things are we expected to believe before breakfast?

As many as it takes to sell a fiction, I suppose.

Member B. A. Copeland asked Sean if he believes that if anyone had actually seen Oswald himself in the front, would they have remained silent about such "guilty knowledge."

Sean said he doesn't believe a single soul noticed Oswald taking his place back in the shadows just as the motorcade was arriving—their attention was riveted elsewhere. He believes Oswald was noticed, and remembered, by at least two people just after the shooting: Roy Truly and Marrion Baker—and that they told the Dallas Police Department and the FBI about this within minutes (Truly) and hours (Baker) of the shooting.

Sean said he also believes Buell Wesley Frazier, and possibly Joe Molina, noticed Oswald there but were put through intense pressure by the authorities (i.e., on pain of being charged with the capital offense of co-conspiracy in the murder of the President) to keep quiet about this. Additionally, Sean believes Buell Wesley Frazier knows that Lee didn't shoot President Kennedy.

Richard Hocking told Sean in the Darnell cropped image posted earlier, Frazier has his head turned towards the right. Prayer Man/Oswald is well within his field of vision.

Sean agreed. He said it seems a stretch that Frazier would not notice Prayer Man standing there.

It's "highly, highly significant" that Buell Wesley Frazier was unable to identify Prayer Man as someone other than Lee Oswald when Gary Mack showed him the Darnell image, he added.

I'd say so.

As we have seen, Jeraldean Reid's story of reentering the TSBD and arriving up in the Second Floor office area some two minutes after the shots doesn't add up, Sean reminded us. It is contradicted by Geneva Hine's description of the empty office area she found herself reentering very shortly after the shooting. A comparison of Reid's story with that of a colleague, Sarah Stanton, is instructive:

1
DL 89-43
NAP:gmf   .

         The following investigation was conducted by Special
Agents NAT A. PINKSTON and GEORGE W. H. CARLSON:

         SARAH STANTON, 227 North Ewing, Apartment A-4, on
November 23, 1963, advised that she is employed in the second
floor office of the Texas School Book Depository, 411 Elm
Street, Dallas, Texas, and at about 12:30 P. M., on November
22, 1963, she was standing on the front steps of the building
as the President passed and shortly thereafter she heard three
explosions, however, she did not know where they came from
and immediately went into the building, caught the elevator
and went to the second floor offices and into the office of the
Southwestern Publishing Company, located there, to try to look
out the window and see what was happening. She then went to
the restroom and later returned to her desk. She knows LEE
HARVEY OSWALD by sight, being employed by the same concern, but
is not personally acquainted with him and did not see OSWALD
on November 22, 1963, and has never seen him with a gun.

The detail about the Southwestern Publishing Company—she went into it, rather than just knocking futilely on the locked door as Hine did—helps us plot Stanton's movement in terms of the Hine timeline in a way that allows their two stories to harmonize, said Sean:

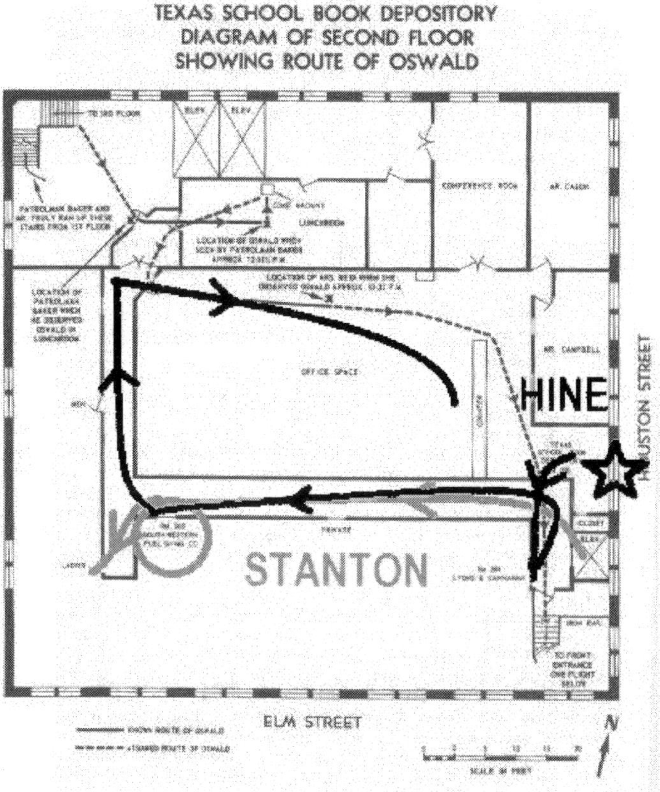

TEXAS SCHOOL BOOK DEPOSITORY
DIAGRAM OF SECOND FLOOR
SHOWING ROUTE OF OSWALD
HINE
HOUSTON STREET
STANTON
ELM STREET
N

Commission Exhibit No. 1118

It would seem that, by the time Stanton (light gray) came off the passenger elevator and went down the east-west office corridor, Hine had already tried to gain entry to the Lyons & Carnahan and South-Western Publishing offices. Hine says she saw/heard a female employee on the phone behind the locked door of the South-Western office: presumably this woman was off the phone and had unlocked the door by the time Stanton arrived.

What's crucial here is that Stanton says she went to the ladies' room after this: this visit explains her delay in reentering the office area in which Hine is now located.

Reid's story, by contrast, leaves completely hanging the question of where she went after she and Oswald had crossed paths.

Did Reid remain in the office?

Not possible, or the re-entering Hine would definitely have noticed her and pumped her for information about what had just happened outside.

Did Reid pay a visit to the ladies' room?

Not possible, or she would have been noticed by Hine who was herself in the corridor.

Unless Reid climbed into the dumbwaiter in the office area and hid there for several minutes, there appears to be only one place she could have gone in order to miss Geneva Hine: the Second Floor lunchroom.

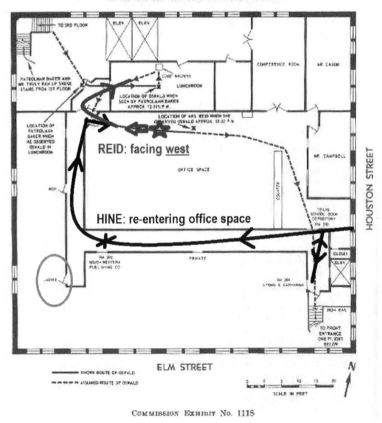

TEXAS SCHOOL BOOK DEPOSITORY
DIAGRAM OF SECOND FLOOR
SHOWING ROUTE OF OSWALD

COMMISSION EXHIBIT No. 1118

Which is surely, and for pretty obvious reasons, a non-starter, explained Sean.

The two minute result of the time trial Jeraldean Reid did for the Warren Commission on March 20, 1964 was a foregone conclusion: it had already been carefully arrived at months earlier by the FBI.

Sean said we know this from item #6 in a November 30, 1963 document researcher Colin Crow has drawn attention to:

FD-302 (Rev. 3-3-59)   FEDERAL BUREAU OF INVESTIGATION

1   Date   11/30/63

A survey was made at the Texas School Book Depository building, Dallas, Texas, in an effort to determine the time required to go from the window on the sixth floor where it is believed that shots were fired in the assassination of President JOHN F. KENNEDY to the front door of the Texas School Book Depository building. Several methods of travel were utilized in this survey and the travel was done at a fast walk except in areas where an individual would have walked at a normal pace so as not to arouse suspicion. The following results were obtained from the methods of travel described.

1. Walking from window on sixth floor to stairway, walking down stairway to first floor, and walking from stairway to front door: 1 minute 45 seconds

2. Walking from window on sixth floor to freight elevator which was on the sixth floor, riding freight elevator to first floor and walking from freight elevator to front door: 1 minute 54 seconds

3. Walking from window on sixth floor to freight elevator, calling freight elevator from first floor to sixth floor, riding freight elevator from sixth floor to first floor, and walking from freight elevator to front door: 2 minutes 33 seconds

4. Walking from window on sixth floor to stairway, walking down stairway to fourth floor, walking from stairway to passenger elevator which was on the fourth floor, riding passenger elevator to first floor, and walking to front door: 1 minute 46 seconds

5. Walking from window on sixth floor to stairway, walking down stairway to fourth floor, walking from stairway on fourth floor to passenger elevator, calling passenger elevator from first floor to fourth floor, riding passenger elevator from fourth floor to first floor and walking to front door: 2 minutes 9 seconds

6. Walking from window on sixth floor to stairway, walking down stairway to second floor, walking on second floor from stairway to lunch room, spending 30 seconds in lunch room, and then walking to front stairway and walking downstairs to first floor and then walking to front door: 2 minutes 25 seconds

on 11/29/63   at Dallas, Texas   File #   DL 89-43

by Special Agents BEN S. HARRISON and
                   WILL HAYDEN GRIFFIN:vm   Date dictated   11/30/63

120

281

7. Walking from window on sixth floor to freight elevator which was on sixth floor, riding freight elevator to second floor, walking to lunch room, spending 30 seconds in lunch room, and then walking to front stairway, down stairway to first floor, and then walking to front door: 2 minutes 52 seconds

8. Walking from window on sixth floor to freight elevator, calling freight elevator from first floor to sixth floor, riding freight elevator to second floor, walking to lunch room, spending 30 seconds in lunch room, walking from lunch room to front stairs, down front stairs and walking to front door: 3 minutes 31 seconds

9. Walking from window on sixth floor to stairway, walking down stairway to fourth floor, walking from stairway to passenger elevator which was on fourth floor, riding passenger elevator to second floor, walking from passenger elevator to lunch room, spending 30 seconds in lunch room, walking from lunch room to front stairway, and down stairway, and walking to front door: 3 minutes 26 seconds

10. Walking from window on sixth floor to stairway, down stairway to fourth floor, walking from stairway to passenger elevator, calling passenger elevator from first floor to fourth floor, riding passenger elevator from fourth floor to second floor, walking from passenger elevator to lunch room, spending 30 seconds in lunch room, walking from lunch room to front stairs and down front stairs and walking to front door: 3 minutes 49 seconds

From the interview of witnesses and the position where the gun used in the assassination was located, which was in the general vicinity of the door entrance to the stairway on the sixth floor, it appears that LEE HARVEY OSWALD possibly walked from the window on the

sixth floor to the stairway, walked down the stairway to the second floor, walked to the lunch room where he spent an unknown amount of time, estimated at 30 seconds, then walked from the lunch room to the front stairs, down the front stairs, and then walked to the front door which as set forth above took 2 minutes and 25 seconds.

One is struck first of all by the perfect fit between the numbers in time trial #6 and key numbers in the Warren Commission testimony of:

- Baker-Truly (the farcical $Z313^{94}$ + 90 seconds "minimum" for lunchroom incident)
- Baker (30 seconds for duration of lunchroom incident)

and

- Reid (office area Oswald encounter at $Z313$ + 2 minutes).

Over and above this though is the observation that the above document charts a most curious exercise. The FBI supposedly by this stage already knows full well from Truly, Baker, and Reid that Oswald's only possible escape route was that outlined in time trial #6 above. Yet here they are trying out lots of alternative routes by which the guilty Oswald could have made it down from the Sixth Floor and left the building by the front entrance.

In half of these time trials, the Second Floor lunchroom was not even featured! Perhaps they were conscientiously covering possible escape routes by an alternative shooter or a confederate of Oswald?

Not possible: not a single exit-by-back-door or exit-by-side-door scenario is even time-trialed—proving that ***Oswald's possible movements, <u>and his alone</u>, are being considered.***

The final note in the document does however make clear that the strong frontrunner in terms of Oswald escape routes is #6:

- descent by rear stairway to Second Floor
- lunchroom incident
- through office area
- down front stairs
- out front entrance.

Sean points out how remarkable it is that even now, days after the assassination and long after the lunchroom incident has supposedly become a fixed matter of record thanks to the detailed information given by Truly, the FBI are still hedging their bets by stating that escape route #6 is only "possibly" the route taken by Oswald—and by spreading their bets 50/50 across a range of lunchroom/non-lunchroom scenarios. It's as if they know only too well just how problematic and open to challenge the whole self-corroborating Truly-Reid story-complex is. And just how nervous they are as to whether Marrion Baker is going to play ball with the lunchroom charade.

Speaking of charades, let's see what others have to say about Prayer Man and Sean Murphy at The Popular Forum. Here's a small sample of raw and unedited comments by popular members there:

We can't tell who the guy in the corner is. We can pretty much rule out that it's Oswald though. The guy appears to be much thicker than Oswald was.

"Praying Man" looks like "Praying older heavy woman in a rain coat"

Sorry guys, whoever that is in the Depository entry way, it isn't Oswald.

The guy's shirt appears to be open, yet the white shirt that Oswald had on cannot be seen. If that was Oswald then how in the world did he beat Baker and Truly to the second floor lunch room without being seen by anyone? And why would he charge up there anyway?

You seem to be suggesting that both Baker and Truly lied about encountering Oswald in the second floor lunch room. Am I understanding that right? If so, then what about Mrs. Reid, who saw and spoke to Oswald on the second floor? Was she lying as well?

May be it will wonder you or not, neither I think the man in the circle is Frazier nor I think "Prayer Man" is Ozzie. And as you know, I'm very far to be a Lner.

How can we imagine in the wildest of our dreams a scenario in which the Patsy was in full view of the public at the very time of the shots?

Btw if you think that whoever is in that photo is clear and recognizable then good luck to you!

My initial reaction was that PM is Lovelady. Problem is, I believe he said he'd left the entrance before Baker arrived. Maybe it's Jack Dougherty?

My "feeling" is PM is Joe Molina and BWF can clear this up.

I see one man in a suit. That may be Williams. He was to the left of Molina. "Standing together" is a somewhat relative description. Having read through the witness statements, you'll agree with me I'm sure. PM seems to be gesturing to someone on his left.

Otis Williams—office employee, not warehouse worker: aged 64: said he was standing against the center railing on the east side of the steps area: cannot be Prayer Man. Joe Molina—office employee, not warehouse worker: said Otis was standing right next left of him, which puts Molina himself in the center of the steps area too: cannot be Prayer Man. Billy Lovelady—ask poor Steve, he'll fill you in. Any other bright suggestions, boys?

The silence is golden on this find Sean. Nothing from Steve for a while. Maybe the boys are regrouping.

I'm busy sitting back here watching you guys making a bunch of fools of yourselves over a blurry image that you think is "proof" that Oswald is standing in the doorway.

Don't flatter yourself, Sean.

You have a reading comprehension problem Sean. Read what I said, again. S-L-O-W-L-Y!

Steve, I have already <u>proven</u> that Prayer Man cannot possibly be Lovelady. Even your fellow Lone Nut Theorists realized this days ago and are mortified at the scale of the gaffe you're making. K-E-E-P G-O-I-N-G-!

I'm not into "debating" when it comes to blurry images of people in film. It is non productive. You guys can sit and "debate" over who it is until you are blue in the face, and it's still non productive and a waste of time. That is why I said you are a bunch of fools.

It just does not look like Oswald. The body doesn't match. Oswald was so trim. I can't say that of PM. No! I'm seeing the outline of PM's body, and it is not trim enough to be Oswald.

No, Tim, it looks as if his buttons are buttoned. Nope! Oswald is just too slim to be PM. Sorry, Colin and Sean.

If Otis Williams, Joe Molina and Billy Lovelady (!) is the best you guys have got, then you're in very deep trouble indeed. Those who are not as blinkered and biased as you understand this fact already.
At least Ralph Cinque attempted to link Lovelady and Oswald with his 20+ point checklist, but your even more pathetic attempts are just sad! Btw who says that this guy even worked at the Depository, the public steps were hardly private property!

I can only say, as the 50th approaches you people are getting real desperate! Even partially side on, gorilla man is much bulkier than Oswald.

Anyway, Suck on this, Gorrilla Man has enormous forearms compared to spindly Oswald and his hair is more receded and is parted on the wrong side.

Sean, perhaps this man was not employed by the Depository?

PM looks to be older than Oswald. His shoulders seem to droop to the sides. He appears to be pudgy and out of shape.

John, your montage proofs nothing except that your fantasy is playing tricks with you. This person is not a Gorilla bulkie lookalike. Just a slender build person. In fact, in a fictionary recreation placing the real Oswald in this spot, we would face the same shapes incl. the hairline.

The Nutters have gone awful quiet, haven't they? Probably waiting for emergency relief from Dale or Todd or Jean. Meanwhile, John McAdams over at Nutter Central (aka alt.assassination.jfk), having been brought up short with the realization that this new Oswald-in-Doorway claim is a whole different affair to the Cinque BS, appears to be blocking further posts on the matter. He—and his less moronic fellow propagandists—know Prayer Man is Oswald. And they're praying he goes away.

What an amazing thread. Bunnies in the clouds time. We have a new winner. Sean Murphy is Ralph Cinque in drag. Interesting to see Ralph...er... Sean drag a whole bunch of cts into la la land.

Another LN fail.

LOL! the drag queen speaks...You have a unidentifiable mass of pixels and the worst possible evidence of all...witness testimony. Exactly the same crap your alter ego cinque has. And it leads you nowhere except kooksville. Nope its another Murphy EPIC fail...a fail of Cinque proportions.

Drag queen?

Utter nonsense. That's the summation of the entire thread. I was very clear but let me say it again for the reading impaired. An unidentifiable mass of pixels and the most unreliable evidence of all...witness testimony.

Reality really drives you whack jobs crazy...welcome to la la land. You too are a perfect cinque clone!

If it's illogical then identify positively WHO that unidentifiable mass of pixels is....Oh wait, the pixels are unidentifiable, so you can't identity WHO it is. YOU are illogical...and a whackjob...Reality bi8tes once again.

Worthless...like your theory Sean...

ROFLMAO! And the drag queen illustrates his incompetence...

Sean cinques fantasy continues. How many pages now and he has gotten nowhere

---

That's enough. I think you get the picture. It went on like this for weeks—the name calling and personal attacks. Now there *were* many supportive, thoughtful comments, but a large number of negative, hostile, and insulting comments were made by a vocal few. A different environment exists at The Popular Forum. An environment I don't like.

Some of us at ReopenKennedyCase (ROKC) wondered why Sean Murphy even bothered to post in this forum, and why he wasn't posting at ROKC. Sean had this to say in a post to Greg Parker:

Jesus, Greg, I'd be extremely upset to think that my not posting here might be taken by you or anyone else as some kind of "boycott" on my part of this forum! This is a brilliant forum, and I often check in here to keep up with the conversation. Not only is there no bad blood between you and me but I continue to hold you in the very highest regard. You were on to the lunchroom thing LONG before I was and, to your eternal credit, have never let up on the issue. It's a cause of huge regret to me that you and several other people here are no longer on the Education Forum. Your presence there was an important reason why I went over to the Education Forum in the first place, for goodness' sake! The reason I've been posting there and (to a far lesser extent) on [The Popular Forum] is related more to the fact that my time and energy are not infinite and I must prioritise taking the case precisely to venues where the case really, really needs to be made—i.e. to less than hospitable audiences.

If Prayer Man is Oswald, as I am still confident he is, then I cannot shirk the "away matches." The Lunchroom Faithful, especially the benign ones, need to be challenged head on. And the Lone Nut Faithful need to be flushed out for the nutters and rogues they are.

All best to you (and everyone here),

Sean

"Less than hospitable audiences." Sean certainly found all that and more that at this popular JFK assassination "research" destination.

Chapter Eight Recap

While there's been a great deal of new research presented over the past four weeks, the pace has clearly slowed down. As this chapter drew to a close, Sean Murphy was posting less frequently, largely answering questions and defending his brilliant work. I was surprised at the level of criticism he received, much of it sarcastic and otherwise unconstructive.

- Despite evidence to the contrary, many people think Prayer Man is anyone but Lee Oswald. Some even think Prayer Man is a woman.
- Police initially admitted the Baker-Oswald-Truly encounter happened on the front steps just after the assassination.
- The Shelley-Lovelady timeline was distorted to keep them on the front steps longer so as to explain away Oswald's "out with Bill Shelley in front" comment to mean when Oswald left the building after the fictitious Second Floor lunchroom encounter.
- The Second Floor lunchroom encounter was a series of stories.
- The first account simply has Oswald "in" the lunchroom.
- Then Oswald is "sitting at one of the tables."
- Next, Oswald is "leaning against the counter."
- Finally, the story has Oswald standing at the coke machine sipping a Coca-Cola.

- The reason for this was to provide a reason for Marrion Baker to enter the Second Floor lunchroom—the sound of the coke machine in operation.
- Marrion Baker had problems remembering what he told the Warren Commission concerning the Second Floor lunchroom encounter, slipping back to his earlier affidavits. He had to be coached and corrected.
- Baker doesn't even mention Oswald by name in his September 1964 statement.
- There is much inertia associated with the Second Floor lunchroom encounter, i.e., there's resistance to any ideas that challenge the notion that it ever occurred in the first place.
- It's highly significant that Buell Wesley Frazier was unable to identify Prayer Man as someone other than Lee Oswald when Gary Mack showed him the improved Darnell image.
- Many people are openly hostile to the notion that Lee Oswald is Prayer Man and to the work of Sean Murphy in general.

When I was in England many years ago, I saw some impressive stone lions in front of a building. I saw flocks of birds sitting on them, pooping away. As I gazed on this scene for a while, I realized the birds come and go, but the stone lions remain. They've endured tons of bird poop over the years and will continue to do so.

Sean Murphy's work is impressive. Over the past weeks, I've seen many people "poop" on Sean and his work. Like the birds, the flocks of naysayers and detractors come and go as well. But like the stone lions, Sean's work will remain. It's solid and it will endure.

CHAPTER NINE – CODA

The treadmill always wins.

– Stan Dane

October 26, 2013. It's been a week since Sean has made a post in the "Oswald Leaving TSBD?" thread or the Prayer Man thread over at The Popular Forum. He now returns and resumes:

No words, just the picture. Sean figures it speaks for itself. He is correct.

Member Thomas Graves said if Prayer Man is Oswald, we should be able to see some of his white T-shirt. He realizes that Prayer Man was standing in the shadows, but we should still be able to see something.

Sean replied Prayer Man's shirt appears to be buttoned up fairly high. Fritz's transcription of Bookhout's interrogation notes indicates that Oswald told Fritz he changed shirts back at his rooming house—the shirt he was wearing when arrested was not the shirt he went to work in—that was a "reddish" shirt. A "maroon and grey cotton" shirt was found among Oswald's effects at N. Beckley Ave.

"What I wouldn't give to see a photo of it," said Sean.

Looking at the photos of Lee Oswald above, Richard Hocking said his wide-neck T-shirt is hanging low, below his clavicle. With the shirt buttoned up, it could be that very little, if any of the T-shirt is visible from the angle of the photograph. On another message board, it has been suggested that Prayer Man was buttoning up his shirt. Another possibility for what Prayer Man was doing with his hands.

Sean said everyone is familiar with CE 150, Oswald's brown arrest shirt:

COMMISSION EXHIBIT 150

Less well known is CE 151, which is described in Warren Commission Volume XVI as a light-brown shirt:

150 . . . .
    Man's brown shirt.
151 . . . .
    Man's light-brown cotton long-sleeved sport shirt.

Here it is:

COMMISSION EXHIBIT 151

It is given a strikingly detailed description in a January 1964 FBI list of Oswald's personal effects taken from the Paine residence and from Oswald's N. Beckley rooming house:

```
Q369    Item A16    Men's brown cotton sport shirt with long sleeves,
                     "Briarloom Traditionals by Enro"
```

It is not however included in a November 27, 1963 Secret Service list of Oswald's clean clothes taken from Beckley:

FOLLOWING IS LIST OF CLEAN CLOTHES TAKEN FROM APARTMENT OF LEE HARVEY OSWALD
AFTER THE ARREST:

```
1 - Brown tie
1 - Man's sleeveless, sweater - beige
1 - brown belt - Size 32
1 - pullover bulky sweater - Size small, 36-38
      olive green color, with white & black stripes
1 - short sleeve grey & black pullover knit shirt (small size)
1 - Maroon & grey cotton long sleeve sport shirt (no size shown)
2 - light blue cotton short sleeve sport shirts
      (one small size - 14-14½)
      (one large size 16-16½)

1 - white cotton short sleeve sport shirt.
```

This is hardly surprising: if the photo of the shirt is anything to go by, it is not a freshly laundered shirt, said Sean.

Now according to Captain Will Fritz's transcription of FBI Special Agent James W. Bookhout's interrogation notes, Oswald said he "changed shirts" back at his rooming house:

Both Bookhout and Secret Service Agent Thomas Kelley report that Oswald described the shirt as "reddish" rather than straightforwardly red.

Sean submits that the disheveled looking "light brown" long sleeve shirt itemized by the FBI as Q369/A16 and by the Warren Commission as CE 151 is none other than the shirt Oswald wore to work the day of the assassination. And he submits that it's the very shirt we see Prayer Man wearing:

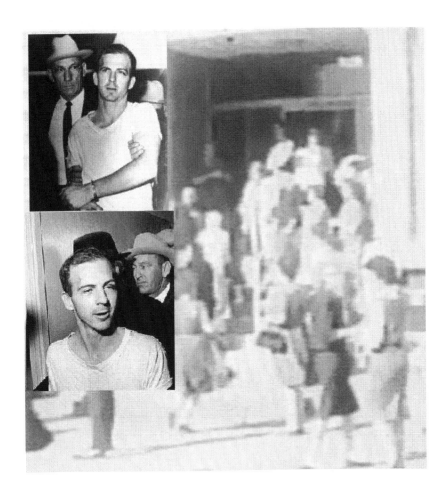

Sean said further confirmation that this button-down shirt...

...was amongst the non-clean clothes found at Oswald's N. Beckley rooming house:

POLICE DEPARTMENT
CITY OF DALLAS

PROPERTY CLERK'S INVOICE OR RECEIPT

Received of _H.M. Moore; W. E. Potts; R. M. Turner; Bill Senkel, Homicide Bureau_ _____the following described articles,

November 26 _____ 19 63

§ recovered stolen property:

Evidence in Offense No. _____ Arrest No. _____ Charge _Murder_

Continued from Inv 11198

QUANTITY	ARTICLE	BIN NO.	DISPOSITION
1	Passport No. 1733242 of the USA in the name of Lee H. Oswald #449	Released	
1	Application for Texas Driver's License #450	"	
9	Photos (6 of Oswald and one of his wife) two scenic shots, a Mexican Airmail Stamp and New Orleans Library card No. NA N8040 in the name of Lee H. Oswald #451	"	
1	Sewing kit with metal (religious) Mexican 20 cent piece, package of needles with thermonitils #452	"	
1	World Atlas; The Catholic Geography Series #453	"	
1	Writing tablet (Fifth Avenue #454	"	
1	Postcard-City-New Orleans; 5 Russian stamps and one 10 cent U. S. postage stamp #455	"	
1	Blue plastic- 2 zipper compartments - type B		
1	Man's tan sportshirt "Briarloom Traditionals by Euro"		
1	Pair man's heavy socks		
1	Pair man's boxed gray shorts (torn & ripped)		
1	Pair man's blue shorts		
1	Pair man's white shorts		
1	White with flower design - light green trim pillow case		
2	Red, white & pink stripe hand towels		
2	Red & white stripe bath towels		
2	White handkerchiefs		
1	2-tone gray with red stripe handkerchief		
1	White cloth - approx 18 x 24"		
3	Yellow & white wash rags		
2	White T-shirts		
1	Shirt undershirt		
4	Pairs socks - brown-white-tan		
1	Pair brown cloth work gloves		
1	Pair man's black low quarter shoes "John Hardy Brand"		
1	Pair man's shoes "Thongs style"		
1	Brown-yellow-gold Russian make portable radio		
1	Unknown electronic device - Brown plastic case - broken		

Arrested: Lee Harvey Oswald w/m/24

Search Warrant dated 11/23/63, 1026 No. Beckley, Dallas, Texas

This inventory was made & invoice typed in FBI Office, Dallas, Texas

H. W. HILL
Property Clerk

Nº 11199 G

If neither evidence nor recovered stolen property, write on face of this form in detail reason for police possession.

Continuation of list of articles picked up at suspect's house:

Page 2 of 2

A letter from Socialist Worker Party, 116 University Place, New York, 3, New York, AL 5-7460, this letter dated November 5, 1962, regarding membership into party.

Miscellaneous photos in small envelope.

U. S. Passport dated June 25, 1963.

Russian passport.

Miscellaneous papers written in Russian.

Birth Certificate - #17034

Parish of Orleans - Carondelet and Lafayette Street, Lee Harvey Oswald, son of Robert E. Lee Oswald, (Dec.) and Marguerite Claverie, born 18th of October, 1939.

Letter dated June 22, 1962, from Johnny Tackett of Fort Worth Press regarding an interview.

Undesirable Discharge from U. S. M. C., 9-13-60.

1 brown shirt with button-down collar.

1 pair grey trousers and other miscellaneous men's clothing.

Sean notes that the last document above relates, as the previous page in the document makes clear, to Oswald's Beckley residence rather than the Paine house.

From Bookhout's Fourth Interrogation Report:[95]

> He stated that after arriving at his apartment, he changed his shirt and trousers because they were dirty. He described his dirty clothes as being *a reddish colored long sleeved, shirt with a button-down collar* and gray colored trousers. He

indicated that he had placed these articles of clothing in the lower drawer of his dresser.

From Thomas J. Kelley's First Interrogation Report:[96]

He said he went home, changed his trousers and shirt, put his shirt in a drawer. This was a red shirt, and he put it with his dirty clothes. *He described the shirt as having a button down collar and of reddish color. The trousers were grey colored.*

CE 151 is surely the "reddish" long-sleeved shirt with button-down collar that Oswald told Fritz he took off at his rooming house.

COMMISSION EXHIBIT 151

Again, Sean submits that...

Commission Exhibit 151

I know he's a researcher, but where does Sean keep coming up with this stuff? Just amazing. I'm glad Prayer Man's skivvies weren't showing, or we might be discussing boxers or briefs too.

In studying the Prayer Man figure, Sean said, it's important to be aware that there is a lady standing just in front of him:

Jesse Curry—the man who let the cat out of the bag to reporters on the evening of the assassination about a cop's encounter with Oswald who was apparently exiting the front entrance right after the shooting—gives serious attention in his 1969 book *The JFK Assassination File* to the possibility that Oswald was the man in the doorway in Altgens 6, said Sean.

The fact that we now know for certain that the man in question was actually Billy Lovelady should not blind us to just how interesting this is. Here we have a law enforcement official at the very heart of the investigation treating as perfectly credible the notion that Oswald was at the front entrance at the time of the shooting. This suggests at the very least that he heard not a syllable from Fritz or from anyone else about Oswald himself having claimed to have been somewhere other than the front entrance at the time.

Less conservatively, one might say that it suggests Curry knew all about Oswald's claim to have been at the front entrance: **hence the unease caused him in subsequent years by the Altgens doorway figure**.

It's a pity he never got to see Prayer Man, said Sean.

Sean said he has just been listening to the May 1978 HSCA interview of Billy Lovelady, as archived by Greg Parker over at ReopenKennedyCase.[97] There are two electrifying exchanges:

1. The FBI contacted Lovelady about the Altgens doorway figure *the very evening of the assassination.*

The wording in the May 1964 Dom Bonafede article is misleading: the "night following the assassination" means the night of November 22:

> Lovelady maintains it is he standing in the door-
> way at the moment of the assassination. "I was stand-
> ing on the first step," he told me when I interviewed
> him two weeks ago in Dallas. "Several people in the
> picture saw me. That lady shading her eyes works here
> on the second floor."
>
> Lovelady said that the night following the assas-
> sination two FBI agents visited his home. "They said
> they had a blown-up picture they wanted me to see.
> Right away I pointed to me and they seemed relieved.
> One had a big smile on his face because it wasn't Os-
> wald. They said they had a big discussion down at
> the FBI and one guy said it just had to be Oswald."

One hears Lovelady sharing with the HSCA interviewer his clear recollection, corroborated by his wife who is present during the interview and who was with him at the time of the visit on November:

At around 6pm on November 22, Lovelady arrived home to his 22 Hume Drive apartment house to find two officials waiting for him on the porch.

They showed him a blowup of the doorway area in Altgens and asked for an identification:

"...I immediately pointed to myself and there was a sigh of relief when I pointed to myself."

A sigh of relief, said Sean. Somehow, within a very few hours of the shooting, the FBI have been given cause to:

a) notice, and
b) get so worried about a tiny figure in the background of a photo that has already gone out on the wires as to make a beeline for Lovelady's home.

We really need to reflect on this circumstance, for it's telltale, Sean said. If Oswald had been telling Fritz, in the presence of FBI agents, that he was (for instance) in the First Floor Domino Room or (for instance) in the Second Floor office area at the time of the assassination, why in heaven's name would the FBI be obsessing over and "actioning" an assassination-time doorway image?

The Altgens doorway figure is of truly explosive significance not because he's Lee Oswald (he isn't) but because the FBI— within hours of the assassination and with full access to Oswald's claims in custody—were thrown into a panic by the possibility that he might be. This panic, and the subsequent "relief," does not make sense unless Oswald himself was claiming to have been at the front entrance.

If Lovelady had failed to identify himself in Altgens that evening, it is doubtful that the phony lunchroom story would have gone on the record that night—or any time after that. The neutralization of the Altgens problem by the visit to Lovelady is what made the audacious switch of the Baker-Oswald-Truly encounter from front entrance to lunchroom a viable option.

2. Lovelady is asked explicitly about a Prayer Man-style scenario.

First, Sean said, the HSCA interviewer asks Lovelady to identify himself in Altgens. Lovelady immediately does so.

Next Lovelady is shown an image he has never seen before: a frame from the John Martin film showing him (Lovelady) standing over by the east side of the entrance some 8-15 minutes post-assassination (a time estimate given by photographic consultant Robert Groden, who is present in the room). Lovelady identifies himself immediately.

Then the interviewer, *out of nowhere*, adopts a very curious line of questioning:

> HSCA: If a movie camera showed you farther in the center of the doorway than that person there [i.e. Lovelady in Altgens, who appears, due to the deceptive angle, to be well over to the left/west of the entrance] would you still identify that person as being yourself?
> LOVELADY: Sure would. I would say the other picture was not taken at the split second as the one to the left is.
> HSCA: Okay, alright. **If it showed two figures in that doorway at the same time, and you could positively**

identify one as yourself, would that have any bearing on your identification of that other figure?
LOVELADY: No, that's still me at the left [of the] doorway.

Whether knowingly (i.e., with knowledge of the Prayer Man figure in Wiegman) or unknowingly (i.e., by pure speculation), the HSCA interviewer has preempted the very discussion we have been having in this thread:
Two Lovelady-resembling men caught on film at the time of the assassination, one over on the west ("left") side of the entrance and the other more towards the center.
Quite, quite extraordinary.

Indeed, indeed.

Richard Hocking replied that this is a startling discovery. "Well done, Sean," he said. Bearing in mind that one of the tasks assigned to the HSCA photo panel was to examine the Altgens photo and develop convincing evidence to identify the man in the doorway who bore a strong resemblance to Lee Oswald, it seems likely they would have studied all available film and photos of the entrance for the time frame just before and just after Altgens snapped his shot. That means the panel should have looked at the Couch film, Wiegman, Darnell, Towner, in addition to Martin. And they would have been looking at originals, or very good copies. (Perhaps someone with more knowledge in this area could pitch in.)

Richard said the questions posed to Lovelady hint strongly that—at the very least—one or more of the panel members were aware of the figure in the upper NW corner of the entrance. It had to be more than idle speculation.

Going back to the question posed to Billy Lovelady:

HSCA: Okay, alright. If it showed two figures in that doorway at the same time, and you could positively identify one as yourself, would that have any bearing on your identification of that other figure?

LOVELADY: No, that's still me at the left [of the] doorway.

Unfortunately, Billy did not answer the question posed concerning the implications of identifying "that other figure." And puzzling that the logical follow-up question was not asked. Richard said he can only guess the mission was carefully defined to identify Lovelady and not open up any larger issues.

Listening to the recordings, Richard said there was another exchange on the first tape that also caught his attention. After establishing Lovelady's position on the entrance steps, some key elements of the following exchange are shown below:

> HSCA: Did you see Lee Oswald on the steps?
> Lovelady: No
> HSCA: "Would it have been possible from where you were sitting ... that he could have been there ...?
> Lovelady: "He could have ..."

Lovelady had the chance, but declined to rule out the possibility that Oswald could have been there at the entrance. This exchange is around 25:25 in the first tape. There are a few indistinct words designated by the ... if someone has better ears than mine, said Richard.

Sean thanked Richard. Yes, he said, it is interesting that Lovelady is categorical that he didn't see Oswald "at any time" on the front steps but refuses to rule out the possibility that he may have been there at some point. Sean said he's listened over and over to his indistinct words following "Could have" but just can't make them out. "Frustrating," he remarked.

It's also interesting that the HSCA interviewer asks Lovelady if he was holding his lunch bag at the actual time of the shooting. Again, one has to wonder is the question prompted by the interviewer's being aware of the Prayer Man figure who is clearly holding something in his hand or hands.

What really makes the interviewer's hypothetical about "two figures in that doorway at the same time" remarkable is that he locates these two figures precisely as per the configuration seen in Wiegman:

1. Lovelady-resembling male standing way over on the left/west side of the entrance area
2. Lovelady-resembling male standing more towards the center of the entrance area.

What are the odds against this being a lucky guess?

Sean mentioned that Robert Groden was in the room, but wondered if he was in the loop on the Prayer Man question.

Worth noting is that Lovelady himself evidently believes—mistakenly—that Altgens is showing him right over on the left/west side of the entrance area. It's an understandable mistake, given not just the tricky perspective of Altgens, but also the fact that, just seconds before Altgens took his photo, Hughes' film caught Lovelady significantly more to the left/west. Lovelady moved a little east to keep the President's car in view as it passed west down Elm Street.

Richard Hocking said, having spent much time using software to tweak the bass, treble, pitch, and playback speed settings, he finally stumbled onto a combination that rendered the indistinct portions of the conversation intelligible. He said this is his latest, and hopefully final, transcription of the exchange discussed above:

> HSCA: Did you see—see Lee Oswald around the steps?
> Lovelady: NO, at any time.
> HSCA: Could he—would it have been possible from where you were sitting eating your lunch, that he could have been there and you didn't see him?
> Lovelady: Could have—
> HSCA (interrupting): OK
> Lovelady (continuing): inside or out.

Richard said Billy Lovelady has confirmed the observation made previously in this thread that Prayer Man could have joined the group on the entrance steps unnoticed by most, as their attention was focused on the limousine with the President and Jackie approaching. Saying he did not see him does not exclude the reality of Prayer Man standing behind the group in the NW upper corner. While most of the group on the lower steps and in front may not have noticed Prayer Man, Richard believes that Frazier, Shelley and possibly one or two others near the top steps did.

Regarding Robert Groden, Richard said the same thought passed through his mind. He may have noticed Prayer Man, but his attention would have been focused primarily on the question of establishing Oswald or Lovelady as Doorman in the Altgens photo. Richard said he scanned through Groden's *Case for Conspiracy* DVD (1988 version) the night before. There is no mention of the figure in the NW corner of the entrance.

Sean cited *three interesting exchanges* between Jesse Curry and reporters in the hall on November 23, 1963:

First

A reporter asks Curry if Oswald has "admitted that he was in the building at the time the shots were fired." Curry says "Yes" but then, *as though thinking twice about this answer,* follows up with a more qualified response:

> CURRY: Well, we know he couldn't deny that, we have witnesses.
> REPORTER: But he did deny it, didn't he?
> CURRY: He denies everything.

Second

> REPORTER: Did you say, Chief, that a policeman had seen him in the building?
> CURRY: Yes.
> REPORTER: After the shot was fired?
> CURRY: Yes.
> REPORTER: Why didn't he arrest him then?
> CURRY: Because the manager of the place told us that he was an employee, that he's alright, he's an employee.
> REPORTER: Did he look suspicious to the policeman at this point?

CURRY: I imagine the policeman was checking everyone he saw *as he went into the building.*

Third

REPORTER: Does he say he was anywhere else at the time this was happening?

Again Curry seems hesitant to commit to a straight answer:

CURRY: *I don't know.* He says he was *at* the building, he says he was there because he worked there.

Sean said it seems to him that Curry's answers are pointing to a front-of-house encounter between Oswald and Baker: a liminal place that is technically "in the building," certainly "at the building"—but not really inside the building. Curry cannot quite say that Oswald is "admitting" to being "in the building." Nor, however, can he quite say that Oswald is denying being "in the building."

If Curry is aware that Oswald has been naming a place like the Domino Room or the Second Floor office area, then Curry's markedly ambiguous answers do not make sense. If, however, Curry is aware that Oswald has been naming the front steps or front entrance or vestibule/lobby area, then Curry's ambiguous answers *do* make sense.

Especially as his words about the policeman "checking everyone he saw as he went into the building" seal the deal: ***Front-of-house.***

Thomas Graves said that since we'll never know for sure everything Oswald told his interrogators, it's a shame he didn't yell out to the reporters in the hallway "I was right outside the front door!" when asked, "Were you inside the building at the time?"

Sean replied, that he thinks it's reasonable to allow for Oswald's having considered that front entrance area as part of the building. It's not as if the front door gave out immediately on to the street: there were steps, and those steps were roofed as well as enclosed on both sides. Very much part of the building. Only when one had stepped down off the last step on to the street pavement could one be said to have properly left the building.

Two further things to bear in mind here, said Sean.

First, Oswald doesn't say "I was in the building" in response to the question, "Where were you at the time of the shooting?" He is instead asked a very different question: "Were you in the building at the time?" And he delivers a sharp rebuttal to the reporter's clear insinuation that his being there was somehow suspicious in itself: "Naturally if I work in that building, yes sir."

Second, intonation is important. The reporter doesn't ask, "Were you IN the building at the time?" He asks, "Were you in the BUILDING at the TIME?" Oswald, who is having questions shouted at him left, right and center, understands the question to relate to his basic LOCATION at the TIME of the shooting. And he confirms that, yes, the TSBD was his location at the time. He wasn't on the sidewalk on Houston Street. He wasn't on the overpass. He wasn't in his rooming house. He wasn't at the movies. He was at his place of work. Hence the exasperated emphases: "NATURALLY, if I WORK in that BUILDING, YES, sir."

Sean pointed to another important archival discovery from ReopenKennedyCase.[98] The text bears close reading, he said:

> March 25, 1964
> MEMORANDUM
> TO: Messrs. Ball, Belin, Craig
> FROM: Norman Redlich
> SUBJECT: The Mystery of the West Elevator
>
> This memorandum results from a discussion between Mr. Belin and myself on March 24, following Roy Truly's testimony.
>
> Roy Truly has testified that when he and Patrolman Baker ran to the rear of the first floor, neither elevator was there. Truly pressed the button for the west elevator and shouted up the shaft asking that the elevator be released. It was necessary to do this since the elevator would not work if the gate was open. Once the gate was closed the elevator would come if the button was pressed. Truly did not try to get the east elevator, because this operates only by hand and can be run only by a person who is in it.
>
> Truly claims that he looked up the shaft and saw that both elevators were together on the same floor.

As part of this picture we should also remember that approximately 15 minutes before the assassination Jarman and Norman took the west elevator up to the fifth floor.

Truly and Baker started climbing the stairs no more than two or three minutes after the assassination. (Mr. Belin timed it at less than two minutes.) At each landing Truly and Baker looked to see whether an elevator was present and they did not see one. They certainly would have noticed the west elevator because this was most directly in line with their vision at each landing.

It was only when they reached the fifth floor that they saw an elevator, but, surprisingly enough, it was the east elevator which they saw. The west elevator was not present on the fifth floor where Truly thought he had seen it from below, and where it could have been expected to be found since Jarman and Norman had taken it there to have their lunch.

Truly testified further that he and Baker took the east elevator to the seventh floor. The west elevator was not on the seventh floor when they reached that floor. He cannot say that the west elevator was not on the sixth floor at this time.

Truly and Baker then looked around the roof and took the east elevator back down from the seventh floor. **On the way down he noticed that the west elevator was on the fifth floor again.**

There are several alternative explanations for the movements of the west elevator.

First, let us assume that Truly was correct in his first observation that the east and west elevators were both on the fifth floors of approximately two minutes after the assassination. This means that by the time Truly and Baker reached the fifth floor, it was gone. We know that someone would have had to close the gate during this period, because Truly was unable to get the elevator by pressing the button when he was on the first floor. This person then might have taken the elevator up the sixth floor while Truly and Baker were running up the stairs. At this moment, however, we have Jarman, Williams and Norman who say that they didn't hear any elevator. Moreover, they have never admitted that anyone else was on the floor.

It is also possible that someone got on the elevator on the fifth floor at this time and headed down while Truly and Baker were running up the stairs. Here again, Jarman, Norman, and Williams didn't hear anyone and it is quite unlikely that Truly and Baker would not have noticed the elevator moving as they reached each landing.

While it is possible, therefore, that a worker moved the west elevator either up or down from the fifth floor during this period, **we**

don't know the name of such a worker and we have the problem of Jarman, Williams and Norman who have to be questioned again as to whether they heard anyone on the floor and whether they heard the elevator move.

The second possible assumption is that the elevator was not on the fifth floor at all, but was on the sixth floor with the gate open at the time that Truly rang for it on the first floor. This would mean that someone on the sixth floor would have had to close the gate and take the elevator down—either directly to **the fifth floor where Truly saw it after he was on the roof**, or to some lower floor and then back up to the fifth floor. In either case, it would mean that someone got on the west elevator on the sixth floor just a very short time after Oswald left the floor via the stairway. **Significantly, none of the investigations appears to have turned up anyone who admits to being on the west elevator at this time.**

Truly thinks that **Dougherty** was working there at this time. I know that Messrs. Ball and Belin plan to question Dougherty, who would have to explain why he was up there working so soon after the shots were fired. A previous memorandum on Dougherty, written by Mr. Eisenberg, raises questions about Dougherty which should be looked into on the next trip to Dallas.

If Oswald was not acting alone, it is very likely that an employee of the TSBD building was his accomplice. It is also possible that an employee of the TSBD might have information and for some reason be afraid to come forward. Through persistent questioning on such matters as the elevator locations we might be able to locate the person or persons who may know more than they are telling.

I have discussed this matter with Mr. Belin and he shares my feeling that this matter will be the subject of questioning when Messrs. Ball and Belin travel to Dallas again.

Sean believes this document confirms that Jack Dougherty took the rear stairs down from the Fifth Floor, not the west elevator.

How was the massive problem of the west elevator's movements, as flagged in this memorandum, solved by the Warren Commission? By getting Dougherty to testify—quite falsely—that he was the person responsible for the movements of the west elevator.

The reality, as Sean's already argued, is that the west elevator was used by Truly and Baker to ascend from the First Floor to the Fifth Floor. They never went up the rear stairway. They never set foot on the east elevator on the Fifth Floor, Sean said. While they were ascending the building in the west elevator, the assassin(s) came down in the east elevator.

Sean asked why the Redlich memo is so revealing.

1. Redlich writes that "it is possible...that a worker moved the west elevator either up or down from the fifth floor" while Baker and Truly were ascending by the stairway.
2. Redlich then notes that "we don't know the name of any such worker" and that "none of the investigations appears to have turned up anyone who admits to being on the west elevator at this time."
3. Yet Roy Truly, just the day before (March 24), has offered the name of just such an employee: Jack Dougherty.
4. Perhaps Redlich is unaware of or has forgotten Truly's mention of Dougherty? No, for Redlich himself writes: "Truly thinks that Dougherty was working there at this time. I know that Messrs. Ball and Belin plan to question Dougherty, who would have to explain why he was up there working so soon after the shots were fired."
5. So why is Redlich ignoring Truly's solution? Why is he still treating the movement of the west elevator as a total riddle? Why isn't he simply recommending that Dougherty, as a matter of priority, be asked to confirm that it was indeed he who used the west elevator?
6. We are surely compelled to conclude that Redlich has knowledge that Dougherty has already ruled himself out as the person who took the west elevator off the fifth floor.

Thomas Graves said that Sean seems to be saying that Redlich knew that Dougherty couldn't have taken the west freight elevator to the First Floor at that time (right after the shots) because Truly said that, although that elevator wasn't on the Fifth Floor when he and Baker were climbing the stairs on their way to the roof, he had seen it on the Fifth Floor again when he and Baker were taking the east elevator down from the roof. Couldn't Dougherty have been riding down in the west freight elevator from the Fifth to the First Floor while Truly and Baker were ascending the stairs, and then couldn't somebody else have taken it from the First Floor back to the Fifth

Floor in time for Truly and Baker to find it there as they were coming down from the roof?

Sean said the point is rather that Truly has only the day before handed the Warren Commission a simple solution to the west elevator problem: Jack Dougherty. Yet Redlich seems to be taking Truly's solution as a non-starter. *Why?*

Sean asked when did Jack Dougherty first identify himself as the person who took the west elevator off the fifth floor just after the shots. *Did he do so at any point prior to his own April 8, 1964 appearance before the Warren Commission?*

Dougherty's November 22 affidavit says nothing about the use of an elevator:

AFFIDAVIT IN ANY FACT

THE STATE OF TEXAS
COUNTY OF DALLAS

BEFORE ME, _____ Patsy Collins _____

a Notary Public in and for said County, State of Texas, on this day personally appeared _Jack E. Dougherty_

w/m/40, 1827 So. Marsalis _WH-6-7170_

Who, after being by me duly sworn, on oath deposes and says: I am employed at the Texas School Book Depository at 411 Elm and have been since 1952. I was working on the sixth floor today. There was six of us working on the floor. The others were Bill Lovelady, William Shelby, Danny Arce, Bonnie Williams, and Carles Givens. I worked until 12:00 noon, and went down on the first floor and ate my lunch and went back to work at 12:45 p.m. I had already gone back to work and I gone down on the fifth to get some stock when I heard a shot. It sounded like it was coming from inside the building, but I couldn't tell from where. I went down on the first floor, and asked a man named Eddie Piper if he had heard anything and he said yes, that he had heard three shots. I then went back on the sixth floor. I didn't see anyone on the floor except the people I named. There was another employee that is named Lee Oswald that I saw on the sixth floor. He works all over the building, but I saw him on the sixth floor shortly before noon. I didn't see Oswald in the building after lunch.XXXXXXXXXXXXXXXXXXXXXXXXX

Jack E Dougherty

SUBSCRIBED AND SWORN TO BEFORE ME THIS 22 DAY OF November A.D. 1963

Patsy Collins
Notary Public, Dallas County, Texas

CPS-OF-410

On December 18, 1963, Dougherty does mention his use of an elevator, but only in relation to his return to the Sixth Floor after the shooting:

FD-302 (Rev. 3-3-59)   FEDERAL BUREAU OF INVESTIGATION   C 0-206

Date _____ 12/19/63

1

      JACK EDWIN DOUGHERTY, 1827 S. Marsalais, employee of Texas School Book Depository, was reinterviewed to clarify information previously furnished by him to FBI on November 22, 1963, in relation to information furnished by him to Dallas Police Department on same date.

      DOUGHERTY advised that he arrived at work at the Texas School Book Depository just prior to 7:00 AM on November 22, 1963.

      DOUGHERTY stated that he saw LEE HARVEY OSWALD, who had been working there for just a few weeks, at approximately 8:00 AM when he, OSWALD, arrived. He stated that he saw OSWALD again at approximately 11:00 AM on the 6th floor but did not see him again after that.

      DOUGHERTY stated that just prior to 12:00 PM he and five other men were working on the 6th floor. He said that the others were WILLIAM SHELLY, DAN ARCE, BONNIE WILLIAMS, BILL LOVELADY, and CHARLES GIVENS.

      DOUGHERTY stated that he worked on the 6th floor until 12:00 PM at which time he went to the 1st floor to eat his lunch. He said he went back to work at approximately 12:45 PM, at which time he returned to the 6th floor. He stated that as soon as he arrived on the 6th floor, he went down to the 5th floor to get some stock.

      DOUGHERTY stated that it was while he was on the 5th floor that he heard a loud noise. He said that it appeared to have come from within the building but could not tell where. He said that he went down to the 1st floor and saw a man, EDDIE PIPER, and asked him if he had heard a loud noise, and PIPER told him that he had heard three loud noises. He also told him that someone had just shot the President.

      DOUGHERTY stated that he then went back to the 6th floor. He said that he used the elevator to go up and when he went back up there, there was no one on the 6th floor. He stated that the five other men whom he had previously mentioned had gone down to the 1st floor to watch the President go by.

11

on ___ 12/18/63 ___ at ___ Dallas, Texas ___ File # ___ DL 100-10461

by Special Agent ___ WILLIAM O. JOHNSON:jj ___ Date dictated ___ 12/19/63

This document contains neither recommendations nor conclusions of the FBI. It is the property of the FBI and is loaned to your agency; it and its contents are not to be distributed outside your agency.

It seems to Sean that Dougherty, prior to his April 8 Warren Commission testimony, has been telling authorities he came down from the Fifth Floor using the stairs. Hence Redlich's implicit dismissal in his March 25 memo of Dougherty as the person who brought the west elevator off the Fifth Floor. And hence, one suspects, the disastrously incoherent (because coached) nature of the "admission" Dougherty is to give before the Warren Commission on April 8: *I took the west elevator down from the Fifth Floor.*

Sean submits that:

- Jack ran down the rear stairs immediately after the shooting
- The assassin(s) took the east elevator down from the Sixth Floor
- Baker and Truly took the west elevator up from the First Floor
- Jack took the east elevator, which had just been brought down by the assassin(s), back up to the Sixth Floor

Sean said it was worth mentioning in the light of the above that Sandra Styles told him in an email that she recalled Vicki Adams telling co-workers that *she had heard the sound of elevator cables moving while she and Sandra were running down the stairs*.

Very, very interesting.

Sean reminds us according to James Bookhout's solo interrogation report, written just after Oswald's demise, Oswald told Fritz "he was on the second floor of said building, having just purchased a Coca-cola from the soft-drink machine, at which time a police officer came into the room with pistol drawn and asked him if he worked there."

Fritz himself, in his Interrogation Report for the Warren Commission, backs up Bookhout's recollection: "I asked Oswald where he was when the police officer stopped him. He said he was on the second floor drinking a coca cola when the officer came in."

319

Both Bookhout and Fritz are clear: Oswald claimed he had already bought the coke by the time the officer came into the room.

It is not generally appreciated just how deeply problematical Oswald's reported words are for the Second Floor lunchroom story. First, they harmonize quite uncannily with a story that will appear in *The Washington Post* on 1 Dec 1963:

> "That's my building!" Truly shouted back. "I work in there."
> . He was quickly joined by a policeman, and they ran up the steps together, the officer with gun drawn. The two men scrambled up the stairs to the second floor. As they made their way to a back stairway, the policeman saw Oswald standing beside a soft drink machine, sipping from a Coke bottle.
> The officer ran toward Oswald and held the revolver at close range. "He's all right. He's one of my employes," assured Truly. The two men then continued on their way. Later, the employer described Oswald's demeanor in this incident as "cool as a cucumber —although he seemed a little bothered by the gun."
> Oswald walked past a girl clerk who exclaimed, "Oh my land! the President has been shot!"

If this is nothing more than unverified hearsay or a reporter's error, asks Sean, then how exactly did Oswald manage to anticipate its content so uncannily in custody?

Argued contrarily: if Oswald never said this in custody, but has had the words put in his mouth by design or accident by Bookhout and Fritz, then how exactly have the words put in Oswald's mouth managed to anticipate so uncannily the Washington Post version of events?

Secondly, said Sean, we have this, Marrion Baker's September 1964 statement:

Same problem, said Sean. *"I saw a man standing in the lunch room drinking a coke"*: How exactly is one to explain the very weird match between these words and the claim reportedly made by Oswald in custody?

No matter how one spins all this, it's a mess for the lunchroom story, he said.

> **SPIN #1: Oswald really did make this claim in custody, but he was lying**.
> **PROBLEM**: How then is it that Oswald's lie manages to reappear with uncanny accuracy in a) a story written by a national news reporter several days later, and b) Marrion Baker's September 1964 statement?

> **SPIN #2: Oswald really did make this claim in custody, and he was telling the truth.**

PROBLEM: If Oswald's claim is true, then Marrion Baker's entire Warren Commission account of how he caught his first glimpse of Oswald is untrue.

SPIN #3: **Oswald never made this claim in custody**.
PROBLEM: How will a claim that Oswald never made in the first place manage to find its way not just into two interrogation reports but also into a story written by a national news reporter and a statement given by Marrion Baker months later?

Sean believes Oswald did indeed tell Fritz that he was standing drinking a coke when the officer came in and asked him if he worked there. But Harry Holmes was right: Oswald didn't put the encounter up in the Second Floor lunchroom.

He put it at the front entrance of the building. And he was telling the truth.

Sean said French *Le Figaro* correspondent Leo Sauvage was puzzled by press references to Oswald's sipping a coke when the officer saw him. So he asked Roy Truly about it in January 1964. Here's what Truly told him: "From where I stood, I couldn't see if Oswald held something in his hand."[99] As we know, Truly will change his tune for the Warren Commission appearance a couple of months later:

> Mr. BELIN: All right. Could you see whether or not Lee Harvey Oswald had anything in either hand?
> Mr. TRULY: I noticed nothing in either hand.
> Mr. BELIN: Did you see both of his hands?

Mr. TRULY: I am sure I did. I could be wrong, but I am almost sure. I did.

Why the change? Because it has become painfully clear to the Warren Commission investigators that an Oswald with a coke already in his hand is an Oswald with even less time to descend from the Sixth Floor, said Sean.

Now it is this aspect of the coke—the timing aspect—that has tended to exercise most researchers over the years. This is unfortunate, said Sean, as the significance of the coke's finding its way into the interrogation reports, the newspapers and Marrion Baker's September 1964 statement goes way beyond a question of mere timing. No, it goes to the heart of the very credibility of the lunchroom story itself.

Here's why:

If Oswald already has a coke when Baker comes into the lunchroom, then Baker's Warren Commission story is dead. Because that story depends upon Oswald's being on his way into the lunchroom. If Oswald is already in the lunchroom, then Baker has absolutely no reason to be diverted from his route up the rear stairway. Remember: Baker has nothing close to a line of sight into the lunchroom from his position on the Second Floor landing, said Sean.

So there is a whole lot more at stake in Oswald's reported claim (per Bookhout and Fritz) to have already bought (and even started drinking) the coke before the officer came in.

Sean said the options facing those who still believe in the lunchroom story are deeply unattractive.

A. If Oswald is telling the truth about the coke, then the following happened:

1. Oswald went into the Second Floor lunchroom and bought a coke from the machine
2. Oswald then left the Second Floor lunchroom
3. Oswald was then seen by Baker through the door window
4. Oswald went back into the lunchroom to—the coke machine.

Utterly absurd.

B. If Oswald is lying about the coke, then the following happened:

> The exact contents of Oswald's lie would be replicated, quite independently, in newspaper reports and in a statement by Marrion Baker.

An incredible coincidence.

C. If Bookhout and Fritz are misreporting or misremembering what Oswald said in custody, then the following happened:

> The exact contents of something Oswald never actually said but was falsely reported to have said would be replicated, quite independently, in newspaper reports and in a statement by Marrion Baker.

Another incredible coincidence.

Again, Sean believes a front entrance encounter between Oswald and Baker was transplanted wholesale up to the Second Floor lunchroom. At first it included the true-but-transplanted detail about Oswald's sipping a coke when seen by Baker. Oswald's true claim in custody about the coke did not make it into Bookhout and Hosty's joint interrogation report. It did however make it into Bookhout's solo interrogation report, written after the lunchroom switcheroo had been decided upon.

In the end, the "sipping coke" detail was eliminated as toxic to the fairy tale, leaving behind just the interrogation report references, the newspaper references, and the September 1964 Baker statement.

But those references are an invaluable resource for us as—fifty years later—we try to reconstruct what really happened.

Either Prayer Man is Lee Oswald or he is a non-TSBD person, said Sean.

The first option makes sense:
Oswald, being a TSBD man, emerges from the vestibule to the front steps just as the President is passing the building. At this time everyone else's attention is riveted on the motorcade, so the presence back in the shadows over on the west side of nondescript "grunt" Oswald goes unremarked.

The second option does not make sense:
A stranger to the building cannot emerge from the First Floor vestibule. They must walk up the front steps in full view of everyone already there and, instead of sticking out like a sore thumb like they might be expected to do, have their presence go completely unnoticed and unremembered.

Now why would a total stranger go up the front steps all by their lonesome amidst all these TSBD people? To get a better view than is obtainable from down on the street?
Well, if that's the reason then isn't it just a teeny weeny bit odd that Prayer Man, as evidenced in Wiegman and Darnell, makes absolutely no effort to keep the Presidential limousine in view as it proceeds down Elm Street?
That Prayer Man is conspicuous *precisely* by the fact that he has by far the poorest line of sight down Elm Street of anyone in the doorway?
Way to secure yourself a better view, *non-Oswaldian* Prayer Man!
I'm sorry, said Sean, but the smart money is still on Prayer Man's being Oswald:

Thomas Graves said it's interesting to note that the light-brown-jacket-wearing guy Baker encountered "on the third or fourth floor" comes suspiciously close to CIA's "marked card" description of Oswald in Russia in late 1959. Oswald was 5 ft. 9 in. but weighed only 131 pounds at his autopsy. His own mother said that he never weighed more than 140 pounds in his life, if he remembers correctly, said Thomas. And didn't Howard Brennan somehow arrive at the conclusion that the shooter he'd seen in the Sixth Floor window was 5 ft. 9 in. and 165 pounds, which description was broadcast to the patrolling policemen right after the assassination?

Sean replied the too-good-to-be-true coincidence of Baker's and Brennan's November 22 descriptions is indeed troubling. Sean believes Baker went back to City Hall that afternoon and told his superiors the truth: he and the building manager went upstairs and saw and found nothing and nobody. This caused consternation, so Baker was given the "Oswald" description, as well as the detail as to "tan jacket," which had come in either from Tippit witnesses or from someone at the Depository imperfectly recalling Oswald's tan shirt (CE151), and instructed to go on the record with a phony story about intercepting an employee who was obviously coming down the stairs.

Just as Baker was giving this affidavit, Oswald was brought in, said Sean.

Baker was shocked when he recognized the suspect in custody as the man he had met at the front entrance.

Up to this point, he had assumed the affidavit was simply a white lie designed to nail a truly guilty man—and a cop-killer to boot.

How did Baker react to this sudden revelation that he was being enlisted to frame an innocent man? He refused to make a positive ID of Oswald. And he clammed up for *several months*.

Sean said the story told by Baker is clear and maximally damning of the "man":

> *As we reached the third or fourth floor I saw a man walking away from the stairway. I called to the man and he turned around and came back toward me.*[100]

1. He and Truly were coming up the stairs together, Baker leading.
2. As they were reaching the third or fourth floor (i.e., both of them just reaching the landing—not Truly way ahead already halfway up to the next floor), Baker (being in front) was the first to spot a man walking away from the stairway up which Baker and Truly were running.
3. The man had clearly been on his way down when he had heard Baker and Truly running up, so he had turned around and started walking away from the stairway.
4. But not quickly enough—Baker saw him walking away.
5. Baker immediately called out to him (i.e., without running 20 feet over to a door, opening the door and hollering).
6. The man came back to Baker's location at the top of the stairway.

The man, we have been given to understand in no uncertain terms, was escaping down the building by the rear stairway. And that's how Fritz will describe the incident to Curry on December 23, 1963: "Baker says that he stopped this man on the third or fourth floor **on the stairway**."

Fritz—fully a month after the assassination—knows nothing about the Second Floor lunchroom incident! This despite the "fact" that, as he will tell the Warren Commission months later, Oswald had personally confirmed the details of said lunchroom incident in custody!

Oswald never confirmed the lunchroom incident. Nor did he confirm a rear stairway incident. Instead he talked about an incident at the front entrance.

And he was telling the truth, said Sean.

Yes, Oswald was telling the truth.

Sean said after several weeks of canvassing hardline Lone Nut Theory believers over at The Popular Forum for credible alternatives to Oswald as Prayer Man, the results are as follows:

They've got nothing.

They've thrown the world and his brother at that doorway, and not a single suggestion has come close to holding up under close inspection. It started with a guy named Steve taking one look at Prayer Man and identifying him confidently as Billy Lovelady. And that about set the standard intellectually for the Warren Commission defenders' subsequent suggestions.

Meanwhile John McAdams[101] has blocked all discussion of Prayer Man—while happily facilitating endless discussion of Ralph Cinque's[102] barmy Altgens-Doorman claims. Prayer Man is evidently too toxic for Professor Factoid.

As of this, the 50th anniversary of President Kennedy's assassination, there remains only one viable candidate for Prayer Man:

Richard Hocking asked if there was any reason given for McAdams blocking the discussion.

Sean replied no, it's as if the topic doesn't exist. On the (very) rare occasions Prayer Man does get a passing mention, it is strictly in the context of a Cinque-focused discussion. The policy is clear: force an association of Prayer Man with Cinque's nonsense, he said. The editors of Pravda circa 1975 would have been proud of McAdams's performance.

And that was it. At the conclusion of this last entry at 5:41 p.m. on November 22, 2013, Sean Murphy abruptly ceased all posting—not only at The Education Forum, but everywhere else as well. As the weeks and months passed by, it became clear to me that Sean planned to make his arguments right up to the 50th anniversary of the assassination of President Kennedy, then rest his case and move on.

Chapter Nine Recap

- The reddish button-down collar shirt (CE 151) was most likely the shirt Oswald wore to work on November 22, 1963, not the brown shirt (CE 150) that he was later arrested in.
- The FBI contacted Lovelady about the Altgens doorway figure the very evening of the assassination.
- The Altgens doorway figure is explosively significant not because he's Lee Oswald (he isn't) but because the FBI, within hours of the assassination and with full access to Oswald's claims in custody, were thrown into a panic by the possibility that it might be him.
- This panic and the subsequent relief do not make sense unless Oswald himself was claiming to have been at the front entrance.
- Lovelady is asked explicitly about a Prayer Man-style scenario.
- Lovelady said he didn't see Oswald at any time on the front steps but refused to rule out the possibility that he may have been there at some point.
- Dallas Police Department Chief Jesse Curry's answers to reporters on November 23, 1963 pointed to a front-of-building encounter between Lee Oswald and Marrion Baker.

- The March 25, 1964 Redlich memo confirms Jack Dougherty took the rear stairs down from the Fifth Floor, not the west elevator.
- Dougherty ran down the rear stairs immediately after the shooting.
- The assassin(s) took the east elevator down from the Sixth Floor.
- Baker and Truly took the west elevator up from the First Floor.
- Dougherty took the east elevator, which had just been brought down by the assassin(s), back up to the Sixth Floor.
- Vicki Adams told co-workers that she had heard the sound of elevator cables moving while she and Sandra Styles were running down the stairs.
- Early accounts of the Second Floor lunchroom encounter have Oswald drinking a coke.
- Later accounts omit the drinking the coke reference because it removes any reason for Baker to enter the Second Floor lunchroom.
- Oswald was drinking a coke, but it was transplanted from the First Floor entrance to the Second Floor lunchroom.
- If Prayer Man was a stranger from the street who climbed the steps to have a better view of the motorcade, he made no effort to keep the Presidential limousine in sight as it went down Elm Street.
- One month after the assassination, Fritz was still talking about Baker stopping this man on the Third or Fourth Floor on the stairway.
- Fritz—fully a month after the assassination—knows nothing about the Second Floor lunchroom incident.
- Oswald never confirmed the lunchroom incident.
- Oswald never confirmed a rear stairway incident.
- Oswald talked about an incident at the front entrance.
- The Darnell images show Oswald was telling the truth.
- Weeks of canvassing others for credible alternatives to Oswald as Prayer Man show they have nothing.

- There remains only one viable candidate for Prayer Man: Lee Harvey Oswald.

Years ago when I was in my prime and very athletic, I had a comprehensive physical at a sports medicine facility that included a treadmill test. After hooking me up for EKG and blood pressure monitoring, the doctor started the exam. Over time the pace picked up but I was handling it like a champ. Brimming with confidence, I said something to the doctor about beating the treadmill. He looked up at me smiling and said slowly "Nobody *ever* beats the treadmill." Breathing heavily, I said "So the treadmill always wins." The doctor nodded.

And it soon did.

No matter how good you are, there comes a time, when—after having done your very best—you realize that you need to step off your "treadmill."

While he definitely could have stayed on longer, Sean Murphy must have realized that he had done all he could do.

He had successfully made his case over and over, so he stepped off on November 22, 2013.

He aced his test.

EPILOGUE – MOVING ON

Long as I can see the light.

– John C. Fogerty

In the weeks and months following Sean Murphy's departure, the "Oswald Leaving TSBD?" thread meandered directionless, like a boat adrift. Within a year scoffers crept in, questioning the value of Sean's research and rejecting his conclusions. Most objections center around the resolution quality of the Darnell images, i.e., they're not clear enough to say with a high degree of certainty that Prayer Man is Lee Oswald. While this is technically true, the cynics miss the larger purpose of Sean's work. This was pointed out by researcher Lee Farley:

> One hundred plus pages of, mostly, real collaborative research that takes every witness statement, every report, every newspaper clipping that we know of, TSBD diagrams, and all of the relevant testimony and builds to a theoretical, but logical, conclusion that the unidentified man in the doorway (standing next to Buell Wesley Frazier), as seen in two separate films, is Lee Harvey Oswald.

The improved Darnell images are icing on the cake. Considered in isolation, they have little significance. Considered in the context of Sean Murphy's entire body of work, they are highly significant, for they support the conclusion that Prayer Man is Lee Oswald.

I find it amazing that most JFK assassination research forums are largely silent on the subject of Prayer Man. It's like the 600 pound gorilla in the room; just ignore the big fella and he may go away. They say Prayer Man cannot be Lee Oswald. Or Prayer Man is a woman. Or Prayer Man in another TSBD employee. Or Prayer Man is somebody who wandered up from the street. Or somebody altered the films and placed Prayer Man there. *Any* explanation but Oswald will do. *Anybody* but Oswald.

There's one place I know of where Prayer Man is welcome and routinely discussed and that's at Greg Parker's ReopenKennedyCase (ROKC) website and forums.[103] Greg and the members there continue to actively research the subject with a focus on having high-resolution, digital scans done on the original or first generation copies of the Darnell film.

Since seeing is believing for many people, a little more clarity in the Darnell images might settle the question of the identity of Prayer Man once and for all. That would be kind of a big thing, no? Even for those who think Oswald squeezed off the shots, wouldn't it be cool if they could show that Prayer Man looked like Gomer Pyle or Little Orphan Annie? One would think so.

Then again, perhaps some people *don't* want to know the answers to certain things.

A ROKC member who goes by the name of Goban Saor proposed that Prayer Man be a *litmus test* for people who are serious about getting answers and not just posturing, endlessly debating, selling books, or otherwise. If Prayer Man doesn't get the juices flowing, it makes me wonder if someone can even fog a mirror. I like it.

There have been some developments since Sean Murphy "retired." Recall that Gary Mack said that Buell Wesley Frazier couldn't identify himself in the improved quality Darnell image, nor could he identify who Prayer Man was. A member of the old ROKC forum[104] attended the Assassination Archives and Research Center (AARC) conference in 2014 and approached Buell Wesley Frazier with the improved Darnell frame and asked Frazier if the man on top at the center rail was him and if he could identify the other figure (pointing to Prayer Man). Frazier said it was "very probably" him in the image, "look at the hairline," he said, but the other figure was not clear enough for certain identification. Frazier said Prayer Man probably wasn't Lovelady because by that time he had taken off with Shelley for the railroad yard.

Let's see: Frazier *wasn't* able to identify himself in the Darnell image in 2013, but he *was* able to do so in 2014. Perhaps in the future, he'll be able to identify Prayer Man? One can only hope.

At ROKC, we created a series of video clips (GIF files) from selected Darnell and Wiegman frames that focus on the movements of Prayer Man and Buell Wesley Frazier to try to discern what they may be doing or holding. A lot of work and testing has been done on the possibility that Prayer Man was holding/using a camera, and how light is reflected in dark areas.

I already mentioned a ROKC project underway to have high-resolution digital scans done on original/early generation copies of the Darnell film. If this project is successful, it could be an enormous breakthrough toward officially exonerating Lee Oswald of the murder of President Kennedy.

There's other groundbreaking research underway as well, such as the great thread "Buell Wesley Frazier: 'Where's your Rider?'"[105] and "Dallas Transit Transfers."[106] And, of course, Greg Parker's *Lee Harvey Oswald's Cold War: Why the Kennedy Assassination Should Be Reinvestigated* trilogy. Volume One[107] was released in 2014; Volume Two[108] was released in August, 2015, and Volume Three will be released sometime in 2016. You won't find this information anywhere else!

The questions, ideas and research never stop at ROKC.

Light reveals beauty and ugliness. Darkness hides both. As long as we can see the light, we can differentiate between good and evil, truth and lies. Sean Murphy's work sheds much light on the identity of Prayer Man. But more work remains to be done. If you'd like to help, please join us at ReopenKennedyCase.

We keep the light on.

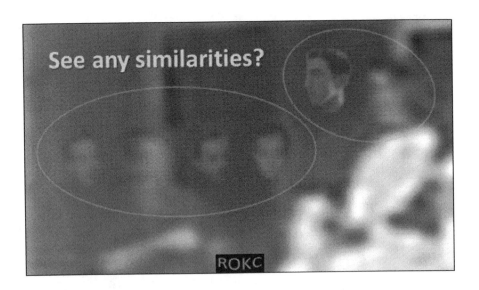

AFTERWORD

In the Darkened Theater, Alone

In a minute or so, while the shock settled in,
I said, "You want a coke or maybe take in a show?"
never questioning how history would view us,
not thinking about being any part of the history then.
Just needing some time alone with someone close to being a friend
never realizing things are never as simple as it seems.

Yes, I've had a history of tight spots and close races
in a variety of locales and other places where reason may seem skewed
though the outcomes we choose from the choices offered
are far more tangible than others on other horizons
when dreams about the future carried more meaning
than the horror witnessed; never as simple as it seems.

I now see more of the players in this Texas tragicomedy
and the veils drawn tight have been rendered transparent, clear,
scenes flicker onscreen, like lightning flashing on the empty seat...
a Greeley remark intrudes, "Go Wes young man" and he has gone
though the direction is unclear, opaque as is most of this case
as we stumble through our lines, never as simple as it seems.

The actors on the screen have it easiest, lines learned and scars of paint
while the rest of us stumble around, searching, seeking
like snow in a war-torn forest or a rose falling lightly
calling slightly back to simpler days of youthful dreams
the cry of a new-born reminding me to remind her that
Baby June needs new shoes...and it's never as simple as it seems.

APPENDIX A – ABBREVIATIONS & ACRONYMS

ARRB – The Assassination Records Review Board.

BWF – Buell Wesley Frazier.

CE – (Warren) Commission Exhibit.

CIA – Central Intelligence Agency.

CT – Conspiracy Theorist. CTs don't believe the Warren Commission account of the assassination.

DPD – Dallas Police Department.

FBI – Federal Bureau of Investigation.

HSCA – House Select Committee on Assassinations.

JFK – John Fitzgerald Kennedy.

LBJ – Lyndon Baines Johnson.

LHO - Lee Harvey Oswald.

LN – Lone nutter. LNs believe the Warren Commission account of the assassination.

SBT – Single Bullet Theory. Also known as the "Magic Bullet."

SN – Sniper's Nest on the Sixth Floor of the TSBD building.

TSBD – Texas School Book Depository.

WC - Warren Commission.

APPENDIX B – WHO'S WHO

Victoria Elizabeth Adams.[109] Worked for Scott, Foresman and Co. on the Fourth Floor of the TSBD. She watched the motorcade from the sixth window from the east end of the building on the Fourth Floor. She was with Sandra Styles, Elsie Dorman, and Dorothy Garner as Dorman filmed the motorcade with her home movie camera as it progressed down Houston Street to Elm. After the shots, Vicki and Sandra Styles ran over to the rear stairway and went down the stairs to the First Floor. They saw or heard no one on the steps as they went. When they got to the First Floor, which Vicki estimates took no longer than one minute, she saw Bill Shelley and Billy Lovelady near the east elevator.

Danny Garcia Arce.[110] Worked as an order filler at TSBD. He stood outside in front of the building toward the west end as the motorcade passed by. He heard three shots. He then returned to the TSBD and went inside.

Carolyn Arnold.[111] Worked as a secretary at the TSBD. She insisted that she spotted Oswald in the Second Floor lunchroom several minutes before the assassination. She said she left her office between 12:00 and 12:15 p.m. to go downstairs and stand in front of the building to view the motorcade.

As she was standing in front of the building, Arnold stated she thought she caught a fleeting glimpse of Oswald standing in the hallway between the front door and the double doors leading to the warehouse, located on the First Floor. She could not be sure that this was Oswald, but said she felt it was and believed the time to be a few minutes before 12:15 p.m. At the time President Kennedy was shot, she said she was standing in front of the building with Ochus Campbell and others.

Marrion L. Baker.[112] Dallas police motorcycle officer. According to the Warren Report, he said he was riding towards the rear of the motorcade on Houston Street when he heard shots. He saw pigeons scattering in the air from the top of the TSBD building.

He raced his motorcycle to the building, dismounted, scanned the area to the west and pushed his way through the spectators toward the entrance. There he encountered Roy Truly, the building superintendent, who offered Baker his help.

They entered the building, and ran toward the two elevators in the rear. Finding that both elevators were on an upper floor, they dashed up the stairs, Truly leading the way. As they came out on the Second Floor, something caught Baker's eye and he went over and into the lunchroom. Pointing his revolver at Oswald, Truly said he worked there and they resumed climbing the stairs.

Again, this is the official version of the story. What actually happened is the subject of this book.

Joseph A. Ball.[113] Assistant counsel for the Warren Commission. Chosen by Chief Justice Earl Warren who had known Ball from California political circles, Ball and David Belin, were assigned to determine the identity of Kennedy's assassin. Ball wrote most of the Warren report, which concluded that Lee Harvey Oswald acted alone in the shooting of the president. He took the report to the Chief Justice. The report was assailed by critics and fueled conspiracy theories that continue to be debated today. Ball rejected them all. He characterized conspiracy theories as "half-baked arguments from dishonest critics" that failed to produce any new evidence.

David W. Belin.[114] Assistant counsel for the Warren Commission. He, along with Joseph Ball, concluded that Lee Harvey Oswald had worked entirely on his own as Kennedy's assassin, which the Commission affirmed in its final report. Belin stood by the findings of the Warren report until his death. He would argue the minutest detail with anyone who challenged him, and he would excoriate Oliver Stone and others who preached of conspiracies. "That issue could make his blood boil."

Hale Boggs. US Congressman and Warren Commission member. Along with John Cooper and Richard Russell, Boggs was said to have reservations about the findings and conclusions of the Warren Commission.

Howard Brennan.[115] A witness to the assassination. He was seated on a concrete retaining wall at the southwest corner of Elm and Houston. Brennan was the only witness the Warren Commission could find who said he saw Oswald on the Sixth Floor at 12:30 p.m. The Warren Report said he made a positive identification of Oswald as being the person at the window. On November 22, Brennan told police the man he saw was in his 30s and weighed between 165 and 175 pounds.

Four months later, he told the Warren Commission the same thing, adding that the man was about 5'10" tall and was wearing light colored clothes, more of a khaki color. Oswald, however, was 24, 5'9" tall, weighed 132 pounds, and he was wearing a dark brown shirt and dark trousers. Brennan also was unable to pick Oswald from a police lineup. He told the Warren Commission that he could not make a positive identification.

Gloria Calvery.[116] Worked for Southwestern Publishing Company on the Second Floor of the TSBD. She said she was standing on the sidewalk on the north side of Elm Street and heard the first shot when the President's limousine was directly in front of her. After the shots she immediately ran back to the TSBD. See encountered Joe Molina and told him Kennedy had been shot.

Ochus Virgil Campbell.[117] Vice-president of the Texas School Book Depository. He was outside watching the motorcade with Roy Truly and Jeraldean Reid. He separated from them after the shots and ran into the TSBD after Marrion Baker. According to the *New York Herald Tribune*, Ochus Campbell was quoted as seeing Oswald in a small storage room on the First Floor near the entrance.

John Sherman Cooper. US Senator and Warren Commission member. He had doubts that Lee Oswald acted alone.

Jesse Edward Curry.[118] Chief of Police, Dallas Police Department. He drove the lead car in the motorcade and provided security for Lyndon Johnson at Parkland Hospital. After hearing the first shot, Curry said his immediate reaction was to order men be sent to the railroad yard area and check it out. After Oswald was in custody, Curry allowed journalists and camera men into the basement area to witness the transfer of Oswald to the county jail. During this transfer, Oswald was shot by Jack Ruby.

Elsie Dorman.[119] Worked as a supervisor for Scott, Foresman and Company on the Fourth Floor of the TSBD. Dorman filmed the motorcade with her home movie camera as it progressed down Houston Street to Elm. This became known as the Dorman film, one of several films of the JFK assassination.

Jack Edwin Dougherty.[120] Worked as a shipping clerk at the TSBD. He said he was on the Fifth Floor about 10 feet from the west elevator when he heard one shot, then he came downstairs. He said when Oswald came to work that morning, he didn't see him carrying anything in his hands.

Allen W. Dulles. Former head of the CIA fired by President Kennedy following the failed Bay of Pigs invasion. Warren Commission member.

Buell Wesley Frazier.[121] Worked as an order filler at the TSBD. He reportedly drove Oswald to work the morning of the assassination. Frazier said Oswald brought a package carrying curtain rods that was about 2 feet long. After arriving at the parking lot, Frazier stayed in his still-running car to charge up his battery. Oswald, who got out and had begun walking toward the TSBD, stopped and waited for him, but when he saw Frazier watching rail cars, he continued walking to work. When Frazier finally got out and walked toward the TSBD building, he was about 50 feet behind Oswald and didn't try to catch up with him.

Frazier watched the presidential motorcade from the top step, a few feet away from Prayer Man. After the assassination, he said he ate his lunch in the basement, which was a departure from his normal practice of eating his lunch in the First Floor Domino Room.

John Will Fritz.[122] Captain, Homicide and Robbery Bureau, Dallas Police Department. He interrogated Lee Oswald after his arrest. Also present were FBI agents, James Hosty and James W. Bookhout and a few others. There were no stenographic or tape recordings of the interrogation sessions. Fritz did not get a confession from Oswald but became convinced of his guilt, telling reporters "This case is cinched." Under the direction of Police Chief Jesse Curry, Fritz helped plan the transfer of Oswald to the county jail and was present when Oswald was shot and killed by Jack Ruby on November 24, 1963.

Dorothy Ann Garner.[123] Office supervisor for Scott, Foresman and Co. on the Fourth Floor of the TSBD. She watched the motorcade with Vicki Adams, Sandra Styles and Elsie Dorman. Immediately after the shots, Garner said Adams and Styles went down the rear stairs. After they went down, she saw Roy Truly and a policeman come up, but she didn't say how they came up (stairs or elevator).

Charles Douglas Givens.[124] Worked as an order filler at the TSBD. He said he was about one block away from the TSBD when the shots occurred.

Geneva L. Hine.[125] Worked in the credit office on the Second Floor of the TSBD. She said she was alone at her desk between 12:25 and 12:35 p.m. while the other office personnel were watching the motorcade. She heard three shots. She saw Jeraldean Reid, Ochus Campbell and several others reenter the Second Floor together after the shots.

Harry D. Holmes.[126] Postal inspector for the US Post Office Department (now the US Postal Service). His office was on the Fifth Floor of the Terminal Annex Building located at the corner of Houston and Commerce Streets, facing the TSBD two blocks away. He watched the motorcade turn onto Houston Street and make its way to Elm. He was looking through binoculars. He heard what sounded like firecrackers.

Holmes joined the final interrogation session of Oswald on November 24 after Fritz invited him to attend. He said there was no formality to the interrogation. Holmes said Oswald was quite composed, flatly denying any knowledge pertaining to the assassination of the President or the shooting of Officer Tippit. Oswald was not particularly obnoxious. He seemed to be intelligent and clear minded with a good memory. Oswald said he went downstairs when all the commotion started, and a police officer stopped him at the front door, and started to ask him questions, and the superintendent stepped up and told the officer that he was one of the employees of the building.

James Earl Jarman.[127] Worked as a checker at the TSBD. James "Junior" Jarman was on the Fifth Floor of the TSBD during the assassination.

Marvin Johnson.[128] Dallas Police Detective. Johnson was one of the officers that initially protected the evidence found in the area of the sniper's nest on the Sixth Floor of the TSBD. Johnson took Marrion Baker's November 22 affidavit.

Carl Edward Jones.[129] Worked as an order filler at the TSBD. Jones said he was sitting on the front steps of the TSBD with Roy Truly, Ochus Campbell, Jeraldean Reid and Billy Lovelady when the motorcade passed by. He said he heard three shots and saw President Kennedy slump in his seat.

Roy Edward Lewis.[130] A worker at the TSBD. Lewis said at approximately 12:25 p.m. he stood by himself on the inside of the front entrance of the TSBD to watch the motorcade. He heard three shots.

Billy Nolan Lovelady.[131] Worked as a stock clerk at the TSBD. At approximately 12:15 p.m., Lovelady said he went to the front entrance of the TSBD to wait for the motorcade. He was standing on the top step to the far right against the wall of the entryway when the President's car passed by. He said William Shelley and Sarah Stanton were standing next to him. As the Presidential limousine travelled down Elm, he heard several loud reports which he thought to be firecrackers. He did not think the shots came from the TSBD. After the shooting, he says he ran toward the spot where President Kennedy's car had stopped. He and William Shelley stayed in that area for approximately five minutes and then re-entered the TSBD by the door located on the west side of the building.

Lovelady can be seen peering around the entrance wall in Altgens 6.[132]

John J. McCloy. Warren Commission member.

Joe R. Molina.[133] Worked as credit manager for the TSBD on the Second Floor. He left his office at approximately 12:20 p.m. and took a position on the top step at the entrance of the TSBD to watch the motorcade. He stood with Otis Williams and Pauline Sanders. He recalls seeing Roy Truly and Ochus Campbell as well. After the President's car passed by and out of view, he heard three shots. He saw Truly come into the building. He remained outside for a few moments and then went back inside the TSBD. As he was standing in the lobby, Gloria Calvery came up with another girl and told Molina the President had been shot. Molina later wrote a letter to the Warren Commission requesting to testify.

Harold Dean Norman.[134] Worked as an order filler at the TSBD. At about 12:10 or 12:20 p.m., he said he was with James Jarman and Bonnie Ray Williams on the Fifth Floor of the TSBD watching the motorcade when he heard three shots fired. Norman believed they came from the floor directly above him.

Ruth Hyde Paine.[135] A woman who was friends with Marina Oswald, Lee Oswald's wife. She met the Oswalds at a party at a friend's home in February 1963. Marina and her baby daughter moved in with Paine when Lee moved from Dallas to New Orleans in April. In May, Paine drove Marina to New Orleans. In September, Paine drove Marina and daughter back to Dallas. Lee returned after this. Paine notified Lee Oswald in October that there was a job opening at the Texas School Book Depository, where her neighbor's brother, Buell Wesley Frazier, worked. Lee was soon hired. After the assassination, much evidence turned up in Paine's garage.

Eddie Piper.[136] Worked as a janitor at the TSBD. He watched the motorcade from a window on the First Floor. He heard three shots and believed that they came from inside the TSBD building.

Martha Reed.[137] Worked as a biller at the TSBD. She was on the sidewalk on the north side of Elm about halfway between Record and Houston Streets at 12:30 p.m. when she heard what she thought were shots. She was alone at this time and did not know where the shots came from.

Mrs. Robert A. (Jeraldean) Reid.[138] Worked as clerical supervisor on the Second Floor at the TSBD. She stood in front of the TSBD toward the street and watched the motorcade as it passed with Ochus Campbell and Roy Truly. She heard three shots. She told Campbell and Truly that she thought the shots from the TSBD because she looked up and saw "three colored boys up there," recognizing James Jarman. Campbell told her the shots came from the grassy area down the street. She then ran into the building, pointing out that she didn't recall seeing anyone in the lobby. Reid then ran up the front stairs to her office. She kept walking and looked up and saw Oswald coming through the back door of the office. She told him the President had been shot but maybe they didn't hit him. He mumbled something and kept walking. She said he had gotten a coke and was holding it in his right hand. The bottle was full. Reid said Oswald was wearing a white T-shirt.

Pauline Sanders.[139] Worked as a clerk at the TSBD. She said she was standing on the top step at the east end of the TSBD entrance. She recalls Sarah Stanton standing next to her. Immediately after the presidential motorcade passed she heard three loud blasts and thought that the shots came from the building above her. Pauline said within a matter of 10 seconds a uniform police officer in a white helmet ran into the building but she did not observe him any further and didn't know where he went in the building.

Herbert Sawyer.[140] Inspector of Police, Dallas Police Department. He was in charge of the crowd detail on a portion of Main Street. After he heard of shots on the police radio and mention of the Texas School Book Depository, he drove to the TSBD and met with some officers there, took the front passenger elevator to the

Fourth Floor, looked around and came back down to ensure the officers were stationed at the building exits to ensure nobody came in or out. After setting up a command post in front of the TSBD to handle witnesses, Sawyer broadcast a description given to him of a wanted person: "a slender white male about 30, 5 feet 10, 165, carrying what looks to be a 30-30 or some type of Winchester." This was between 12:43 p.m. to 12:45 p.m.

William H. Shelley.[141] Manager of the Miscellaneous Department at the TSBD. At 12:15 p.m., he walked just outside the glass doors at front entrance of the building to watch the motorcade. Billy Lovelady was seated on the entrance steps just in front of him, and Wesley Frazier, Sarah Stanton, and Carolyn Arnold were also standing near him at the time President Kennedy was shot. Immediately following the shooting, Shelley and Lovelady accompanied some uniformed police officers to the railroad yards just west of the building and returned through the west side door of the building about ten minutes later. He said he last saw Oswald on the First Floor at 11:50 a.m.

Sarah D. Stanton.[142] Worked as a clerk at the TSBD. When President Kennedy was shot, she was standing on the front steps of the TSBD entrance with William Shelley, Otis Williams, Pauline Sanders and Billy Lovelady. She heard three shots after the President's car passed the front of the building but she couldn't see the President's car at that time. She could not say where the shots came from.

Sandra K. Styles.[143] Worked for Scott, Foresman and Co. on the Fourth Floor of the TSBD. She watched the motorcade from a window in her office on the Fourth Floor with Vicki Adams, Dorothy Garner, and Elsie Dorman. She heard shots that she thought were fireworks. At this time, she left the office with Vicki Adams and went down the back stairs and left the building at the back door. They went around to the side of the building when they saw a policeman who told them to leave that area. She then re-entered the building through the front door and returned to her office.

Roy Sansom Truly.[144] Superintendent of the TSBD. He left his office with Ochus Campbell about 12:10 p.m. for lunch. They saw a large crowd standing along the street, so they decided to wait and watch the motorcade. At the time President Kennedy was shot, he was standing in the street with Campbell just in front of the TSBD entrance. He heard three shots fired and moments later accompanied a uniformed Dallas Police officer to the Second Floor. The officer looked into the lunch room, and just inside the lunchroom door Lee Oswald was standing facing the officer. Then they proceeded to the roof area. After a quick examination, they went back to the First Floor and Truly started to account for the location of each of his employees. He was not able to locate Oswald.

Henry Menasco Wade.[145] District Attorney of Dallas. He participated in two of the most notable US court cases of the 20th century: the prosecution of Jack Ruby for killing Lee Harvey Oswald, and the U.S. Supreme Court's decision legalizing abortion, Roe v. Wade. A cowboy mentality and a culture of "win at all costs" existed under his leadership and he compiled a conviction rate over 90 percent. He retired in 1987 and died in 2001. In recent years, at least 19 of convictions by Wade and his successors have been overturned.

Troy Eugene West.[146] Worked as a wrapper at the TSBD. He was on the First Floor making coffee and was alone at the time. He wasn't aware that President Kennedy had been shot until he walked toward the front of the building and heard about it from people rushing in.

Bonnie Ray Williams.[147] Worked as a checker at the TSBD. He was with Harold Norman and James Jarman on the Fifth Floor watching the motorcade. He heard three shots and thought they came directly above him. Williams, Norman, and Jarman ran over to the west side of the building to get a better view. While they were standing there, a policeman came up on the elevator to the Fifth Floor, looked around and left. He did not see anyone come down from the Sixth Floor via the stairs.

Otis Neville Williams.[148] Supervisor of the Bookkeeping Department at the TSBD. He was standing on the top step against the railing on the east side. He doesn't recall who was standing on either side of him, but he remembers Pauline Sanders being present. After the motorcade passed by and out of sight, he heard three loud blasts. He thought the blasts came from the direction of the viaduct that crosses Elm Street. He remained momentarily on the steps and then went inside the building. After this, he assisted a police detective in making a search of the Second Floor of the building.

NOTES

[1] *Esquire* magazine, November 1973.

[2] *Case Closed*, Gerald Posner, 1993.

[3] *JFK*, film directed by Oliver Stone, 1991.

[4] *The Girl on the Stairs: My Search for a Missing Witness to the Assassination of John F. Kennedy*, Barry Ernest, 2010.

[5] *JFKcountercoup*, William Kelly, http://jfkcountercoup.blogspot.com/

[6] *JFKcountercoup*, "The Doors of Perception - Why Oswald Is Not Guilty," http://jfkcountercoup.blogspot.com/2013/07/the-doors-of-perception-why-oswald-is.html

[7] *Into the Nightmare: My Search for the Killers of President John F. Kennedy and Officer J. D. Tippit*, Joseph McBride, 2013.

[8] *Accessories After The Fact: The Warren Commission, The Authorities & The Report*, Sylvia Meagher, 1967.

[9] *The Plot to Kill Lee Harvey Oswald*, C. Fenway Braxton, 2014.

[10] A cinch in time saves nine.

[11] HSCA Report, Volume XI, The Warren Commission.

[12] Ibid.

[13] *JFK*, film directed by Oliver Stone, 1991.

[14] *The Education Forum*, "Oswald Leaving TSBD?" http://educationforum.ipbhost.com/index.php?showtopic=20354&page=1

[15] James Darnell, reporter and cameraman for WBAP-TV in Dallas-Fort Worth TX, filmed the immediate aftermath of the assassination which included the entrance to the TSBD building.

[16] Dave Wiegman, cameraman for NBC, rode in a press car behind Kennedy and was filming at the time of the assassination, capturing briefly capturing the entrance of the TSBD building in the process.

[17] Robert J. Groden, American researcher who has written several books about conspiracy theories regarding the assassination. He is considered by many to be an expert on the photographic evidence in the JFK case.

[18] Altgens 6 is the famous photo taken by James William "Ike" Altgens, photojournalist and field reporter for the Associated Press, of the presidential motorcade just prior to the fatal head shot that killed President Kennedy. The entrance of the TSBD building is seen in the photo.

[19] *No More Silence,* Larry A. Sneed, 1998, pp. 117-118.

[20] Ibid.

[21] Altgens 6 is the famous photo taken by James William "Ike" Altgens, photojournalist and field reporter for the Associated Press, of the presidential motorcade just prior to the fatal head shot that killed President Kennedy. The entrance of the TSBD building is seen in the photo.

[22] *On Trial: Lee Harvey Oswald,* TV Documentary, 1986. This mock trial featured all of the surviving witnesses with prosecuting attorney Vincent Bugliosi and Gerry Spence, attorney for the defense.

[23] "Lee Harvey Oswald Declares 'I'm Just a Patsy'"
https://app.box.com/shared/5mto6y3w4k

[24] Warren Commission testimony of Buell Wesley Frazier, March 11, 1964.

[25] Robert Hughes captured the presidential motorcade on 8mm color film as it proceeded down Houston Street and turned onto Elm. The entrance to the TSBD building can be seen in many of the frames.

[26] Warren Commission testimony of Harry D. Holmes, April 2, 1964.

[27] Dom Bonafede, "The Picture With a Life of Its Own," *New York Herald Tribune,* May 24, 1964.

[28] *JFKcountercoup*, "The Doors of Perception - Why Oswald Is Not Guilty," http://jfkcountercoup.blogspot.com/2013/07/the-doors-of-perception-why-oswald-is.html

[29] Anthony Summers, journalist and author.

[30] Earl Golz, Texas journalist.

[31] Warren Commission testimony of Danny G. Arce, April 7, 1964.

[32] *JFKcountercoup*, "The Doors of Perception - Why Oswald Is Not Guilty."

[33] Bookhout-Hosty FBI joint interrogation report, 11/22/63.

[34] Ibid.

[35] Bookhout FBI interrogation report, 11/22/63, dictated 11/24/63.

[36] Warren Commission testimony of Geneva L. Hine, April 7, 1964.

[37] Martha Reed.

[38] David Lifton, researcher and author.

[39] Williams-Pinkston FBI report, 11/22/63, dictated 11/22/63.

[40] Ibid.

[41] Pinkston FBI report, 11/24/63, dictated 11/26/63.

[42] Vincent Drain FBI report, 11/29/63, dictated 11/29/63.

[43] Bookhout FBI interrogation report, 11/22/63, dictated 11/24/63.

[44] *No More Silence,* Larry A. Sneed, 1998, p. 151.

[45] Harold Weisberg, researcher and author.

[46] Note from J. W. Fritz to Jesse Curry of December 23, 1963, https://www.maryferrell.org/showDoc.html?docId=29121

[47] Affidavit of M. L. Baker, Patrolman Dallas Police Department, November 22, 1963.

[48] Bookhout FBI interrogation report, 11/22/63, dictated 11/24/63.

[49] Warren Commission testimony of J. W. Fritz, April 22, 1964.

[50] Affidavit of M. L. Baker, Patrolman Dallas Police Department, November 22, 1963.

[51] Warren Commission testimony of Buell Wesley Frazier, March 11, 1964.

[52] Warren Commission testimony of Marrion L. Baker, March 25, 1964.

[53] Report On Officer's Duties, by Marvin Johnson, (date unknown); John F. Kennedy/Dallas Police Department Collection, John F. Kennedy Archive - Box 1: Folder 7, Item 26; http://jfk.ci.dallas.tx.us/box1.htm

[54] Warren Commission testimony of J. W. Fritz, April 22, 1964.

[55] Warren Commission testimony of J. Herbert Sawyer, April 8, 1964.

[56] *No More Silence,* Larry A. Sneed, 1998, pp. 117-118.

[57] Warren Commission testimony of Roy S. Truly, March 24, 1964.

[58] Signed statement of Bonnie Ray Williams, March 19, 1964, Commission Exhibit 1381.

[59] Warren Commission testimony of Bonnie Ray Williams, March 24, 1964.

[60] Ibid.

[61] *The Girl on the Stairs: My Search for a Missing Witness to the Assassination of John F. Kennedy*, Barry Ernest, 2010.

[62] "Another Ignored Witness Found," Barry Ernest, 2011, http://www.whokilledjfk.net/another_witness.htm

[63] Warren Commission testimony of Marrion L. Baker, March 25, 1964.

[64] *On Trial: Lee Harvey Oswald*, TV Documentary, 1986. This mock trial featured all of the surviving witnesses with prosecuting attorney Vincent Bugliosi and Gerry Spence, attorney for the defense.

[65] Ibid.

[66] "FBI Sifts Oswald Data," *New York Herald Tribune*, November 27, 1963.

[67] Odum and Griffin FBI interrogation report, November 23, 1963.

[68] Warren Commission testimony of Marrion L. Baker, March 25, 1964.

[69] *JFK*, film directed by Oliver Stone, 1991.

[70] Bookhout-Hosty FBI joint interrogation report, 11/22/63.

[71] *Assignment: Oswald*, James P. Hosty, Jr., 1996.

[72] Bookhout FBI interrogation report, 11/22/63, dictated 11/24/63.

[73] Robert Oswald, brother of Lee Oswald.

[74] Marina Oswald, wife of Lee Oswald.

[75] Telephone Conversation between the President and J. Edgar Hoover, 29 Nov 1963, 1:40PM, http://www.maryferrell.org/showDoc.html?docId=882&relPageId=5

[76] Warren Commission testimony of William H. Shelley, April 7, 1964.

[77] Warren Commission testimony of Billy Nolan Lovelady, April 7, 1964.

[78] Gloria Calvery.

[79] Dom Bonafede, "The Picture With a Life of Its Own," *New York Herald Tribune*, May 24, 1964.

[80] Robert Hughes captured the presidential motorcade on 8mm color film as it proceeded down Houston Street and turned onto Elm. The entrance to the TSBD building can be seen in many of the frames.

[81] Gary Mack, curator of the Sixth Floor Museum in Dallas, passed away on July 15, 2015.

[82] Bookhout FBI interrogation report, 11/22/63, dictated 11/24/63.

[83] Joe Nick Patoski interview with Pierce Allman, http://www.kenrahn.com/Marsh/Jfk-conspiracy/transcripts_1.html

[84] Albert Sayer FBI Interrogation Report, 11/23/63, dictated 11/23/63.

[85] Warren Commission testimony of Geneva L. Hine, April 7, 1964.

[86] Sean Murphy believes "policemen" here is a stenographer's error and should read "policeman," i.e., James Powell.

[87] http://www.maryferrell.org/mffweb/archive/viewer/showDoc.do?docId=10755&relPageId=4

[88] Warren Commission testimony of Mrs. Robert A. (Jeraldean) Reid, March 25, 1964.

[89] "The Oswald Affair," Leo Sauvage, March 1, 1964.

[90] Len Osanic, host of Black Op Radio.com.

[91] Warren Commission testimony of Marrion L. Baker, March 25, 1964.

[92] Ibid.

[93] Ibid.

[94] Z313 was the number of the frame in the Zapruder film where President Kennedy was shot in the head.

[95] Bookhout FBI interrogation report, 11/23/63, dictated 11/24/63, dated 11/25/63.

[96] First Interview of Lee Harvey Oswald, Inspector Thomas J. Kelley, U.S. Secret Service, 11/23/63.

[97] http://www.reopenkennedycase.net/audio.html

[98] http://reopenkennedycase.forumotion.net/t516-the-mystery-of-the-west-elevator#5134

[99] *The Oswald Affair: An examination of the contradictions and omissions of the Warren report*, Leo Sauvage, 1966, p. 30.

[100] Affidavit of M. L. Baker, Patrolman Dallas Police Department, November 22, 1963.

[101] John C. McAdams, a well-known lone nutter and Warren Commission apologist.

[102] Ralph Cinque, a JFK assassination researcher who clings to and promotes extreme conspiracy theories.

[103] http://www.reopenkennedycase.org/

[104] http://reopenkennedycase.forumotion.net/t388p840-prayer-man-on-the-education-forum#13667

[105]
http://www.reopenkennedycase.org/apps/forums/topics/show/13125405-buell-wesley-frazier-where-s-your-rider

[106]
http://www.reopenkennedycase.org/apps/forums/topics/show/13122617-dallas-transit-transfers-

[107] http://www.amazon.com/Harvey-Oswalds-Cold-Assassination-Reinvestigated-ebook/dp/B00IXOA5ZK

[108] http://www.amazon.com/Harvey-Oswalds-Cold-Assassination-Reinvestigated-ebook/dp/B014KJPNBW/ref=sr_1_2?s=digital-text&ie=UTF8&qid=1440858403&sr=1-2

[109] Warren Commission testimony of Victoria Elizabeth Adams, April 7, 1964. Signed statement of Victoria Elizabeth Adams, March 23, 1964, Commission Exhibit 1381.

[110] Warren Commission testimony of Danny G. Arce, April 7, 1964. Signed statement of Danny G. Arce, March 18, 1964, Commission Exhibit 1381.

[111] Signed statement of Mrs. R. E. (Carolyn) Arnold, March 18, 1964, Commission Exhibit 1381.

[112] Warren Commission testimony of Marrion L. Baker, March 25, 1964.

[113] Elaine Woo, "Attorney Joseph A. Ball Dies; Played Key Warren Commission Role," *Los Angeles Times*, September 23, 2000.

[114] Eric Pace, "David W. Belin, Warren Commission Lawyer, Dies at 70," *The New York Times*, January 18, 1999.

[115] Warren Commission testimony of Howard Leslie Brennan, March 24, 1964.

[116] Signed statement of Mrs. Robert R. [sic] (Gloria) Calvery, March 19, 1964, Commission Exhibit 1381.

[117] Signed statement of Ochus Virgil Campbell, March 19, 1964, Commission Exhibit 1381.

[118] Warren Commission testimony of Jesse Edward Curry, April 22, 1964.

[119] Signed statement of Mrs. John T. (Elsie) Dorman, March 20, 1964, Commission Exhibit 1381.

[120] Warren Commission testimony of Jack Edwin Dougherty, April 8, 1964. Signed statement of Jack Edwin Dougherty, March 18, 1964, Commission Exhibit 1381.

[121] Warren Commission testimony of Buell Wesley Frazier, March 11, 1964. Signed statement of Buell Wesley Frazier, March 18, 1964, Commission Exhibit 1381.

[122] Warren Commission testimony of J. W. Fritz, April 22, 1964.

[123] Signed statement of Dorothy Ann Garner, March 20, 1964, Commission Exhibit 1381.

[124] Warren Commission testimony of Charles Douglas Givens, April 8, 1964. Signed statement of Charles Douglas Givens, March 18, 1964, Commission Exhibit 1381.

[125] Warren Commission testimony of Geneva L. Hine, April 7, 1964. Signed statement of Geneva L. Hine, March 18, 1964, Commission Exhibit 1381.

[126] Warren Commission testimony of Harry D. Holmes, April 2, 1964.

[127] Warren Commission testimony of James Jarman Jr., March 24, 1964. Signed statement of James Earl Jarman, March 18, 1964, Commission Exhibit 1381.

[128] Warren Commission testimony of Marvin Johnson, April 6, 1964.

[129] Signed statement of Carl Edward Jones, March 18, 1964, Commission Exhibit 1381.

[130] Signed statement of Roy Edward Lewis, March 18, 1964, Commission Exhibit 1381.

[131] Warren Commission testimony of Billy Nolan Lovelady, April 7, 1964. Signed statement of Billy Nolan Lovelady, March 19, 1964, Commission Exhibit 1381.

[132] Altgens 6 is the famous photo taken by James William "Ike" Altgens, photojournalist and field reporter for the Associated Press, of the presidential motorcade just prior to the fatal head shot that killed President Kennedy. The entrance of the TSBD building is seen in the photo.

[133] Warren Commission testimony of Joe R. Molina, April 7, 1964. Signed statement of Joe R. Molina, March 25, 1964, Commission Exhibit 1381.

[134] Warren Commission testimony of Harold Norman, March 24, 1964. Signed statement of Harold Norman, March 18, 1964, Commission Exhibit 1381.

[135] Warren Commission testimony of Ruth Hyde Paine, March 18, 1964.

[136] Warren Commission testimony of Eddie Piper, April 8, 1964. Signed statement of Eddie Piper, March 18, 1964, Commission Exhibit 1381.

[137] Signed statement of Martha Reed, March 18, 1964, Commission Exhibit 1381.

[138] Warren Commission testimony of Mrs. Robert A. Reid, March 25, 1964. Signed statement of Mrs. Robert A. Reid, March 18, 1964, Commission Exhibit 1381.

[139] Signed statement of Mrs. Robert E. (Pauline) Sanders, Sr., March 19, 1964, Commission Exhibit 1381.

[140] Warren Commission testimony of J. Herbert Sawyer, April 8, 1964.

[141] Warren Commission testimony of William H. Shelley, April 7, 1964. Signed statement of William H. Shelley, March 18, 1964, Commission Exhibit 1381.

[142] Signed statement of Sarah D. Stanton, March 18, 1964, Commission Exhibit 1381.

[143] Signed statement of Sandra K. Styles, March 19, 1964, Commission Exhibit 1381.

[144] Warren Commission testimony of Roy S. Truly, May 14, 1964. Signed statement of Roy Sansom Truly, March 19, 1964, Commission Exhibit 1381.

[145] Michael Graczyk, "After Dallas DA's death, 19 convictions are undone," *USA Today*, July 29, 2008.

[146] Warren Commission testimony of Troy Eugene West, April 8, 1964. Signed statement of Troy Eugene West, March 18, 1964, Commission Exhibit 1381.

[147] Warren Commission testimony of Bonnie Ray Williams, March 24, 1964. Signed statement of Bonnie Ray Williams, March 19, 1964, Commission Exhibit 1381.

[148] Signed statement of Otis Neville Williams, March 19, 1964, Commission Exhibit 1381.

We hope you have enjoyed this presentation.

Other books on the subject of conspiracy are available from Martian
Publishing (martianpublishing.com):

The Plot to Kill Lee Harvey Oswald by C. Fenway Braxton,
Foibles and Follies by C. Fenway Braxton, and
The Plot to Kill John Wilkes Booth by C. Fenway Braxton.

View our other selections of fiction and
non-fiction at martianpublishing.com

More on the Prayer Man subject can be found at the
2015 November in OZ Symposium, proudly sponsored by:

Made in the USA
San Bernardino, CA
20 October 2015